AGELESS VOICES

AGELESS VOICES

FUN FEARLESS FABULOUS

JOYANN GOLD

DEDICATION

In the spirit of gratitude, we the authors of Ageless Voices, dedicate this book to the past, present, and future generations. To those who have charted the paths before us, whose experiences and stories lay the foundation upon which we stand. To the present generation, courageously navigating their own journeys and finding strength through shared narratives. And to those yet to come, may these stories serve as a compass that guides you, offering wisdom and inspiration as you create your own legacy. We intend this collection of 77 stories to illuminate the timelessness of human experience and celebrate the ageless spirit that unites us all.

CONTENTS

Introduction   xiii

PART ONE
FUN

1. Ageless Voices of Change   3
   Tina Taylor

2. What Soap Bubbles After Midnight Taught Me   5
   Dr. Angelika Christie

3. Don't Miss The Dance   9
   Barbara J. Morris

4. Forever Young At Heart   12
   Barb Laubman

5. When The End Is Really Just The Beginning   15
   Bev Walkner

6. The 1962 Barbie Dream House   22
   Bonnie L. Senftner

7. Empowered Living: Mastering The Art Of Joy   25
   Debbie Prediger

8. Always A Song In My Heart   29
   Denise Yonkers

9. Experience The Life You Were Meant To Live!   31
   Elizabeth Lupacchino Donohue

10. You've Got 40 More Years   35
    JoyAnn Gold

11. Destiny's Subtle Push   38
    Dr. K. Mhina Entrantt

12. Adventures In The Moments   43
    Laura Taylor Cox

13. Real Joyful Life Started at 70   46
    Lucie Rosa-Stagi

14. God Has A Great Sense Of Humor   49
    Moriah Hudson

15. Make Age "Not Count"   51
    Dr. Sally L. Cleland

16. What's In Your Cup?   55
    Shirley Turner

17. Embracing The Joy Of Youthfulness 57
Sunshine Deb

18. Camping With The Sisters 60
Susan Farling

19. My Superhero Moment 66
Susan "SueZee" Finley

20. Lunch, Laughter, And Life Lessons 68
Tina Taylor

21. The Fountain Of Youth 73
Terese Parkin and Sheryl Lynn

22. Never Too Old To Learn 75
Winnie Anderson-Brown

PART TWO

FEARLESS

23. How A Curse In Childhood Led To My Life's Mission 81
Dr. Angelika Christie

24. Climbing For Change 85
Anne Lorimor

25. Nourish Your Soul And Live Abundantly! 92
Carol Koppelman

26. Like A Diamond – The More Pressure The More Beautiful 100
Cheryl McKenzie-Cook

27. What's Love Got To Do With It? 106
Cindy McKee

28. Every Challenge Has A Gift For You In Its Hands 109
Cis Ahearn

29. Fearlessly Embracing Joy: A Tale Of Transformation 112
Debbie Prediger

30. Dancing In The Rain 116
Debi Lynn

31. Embracing The Ageless Spirit: Tale Of Resilience And Fearlessness 119
Debi Lynn

32. Playful Paws Of Comfort—Blessings On The Journey 122
Denise Yonkers

33. Survive And Thrive 125
Diane Berg

34. Finding Purpose At The Art Fair 128
Jo Dibblee

35. A Crystal-Clear Passion 133
Joanne Salvador

36. From The Fire To The Diagnosis 138
JoyAnn Gold

37. Something Must Be Done! 141
Dr. K. Mhina Entrantt

38. Beyond Age Limits: Embracing Life's Later Chapters 145
Katherine Merritt

39. From Fearful To Fearless At Fifty 149
Laura Taylor Cox

40. Mind Matters: A Story Of Resilience, Persistence, And Following Your Dreams 152
Cindy McKee

41. How To Prevent Technology From Ruining Your Happy Day Or Life! 155
Lucie Rosa-Stagi

42. I Am Going To Write My Own Eulogy! 157
Moriah Hudson

43. Embracing Emotional And Physical Wellness: My Journey Of Surrender And Life Lessons 159
Nancy Johnson

44. The Quiet Confidence Of Self-Esteem 163
Dr. Sally L. Cleland

45. How I Escape Ageism 167
Susan Farling

46. High Five Bear 172
Susan "SueZee" Finley

47. Full-Circle Beauty! 176
Terese Parkin

48. Dare To Be Ageless: Embrace New Technologies 179
Winnie Anderson-Brown

49. Dance With Delight 183
Winnie Anderson-Brown

50. The House Flipper Who Flipped Her Heart 184
Bonnie L. Senftner

PART THREE

FABULOUS

51. Magnificent Agelessness   191
    Jana Lee Gattung

52. From Triumph To Despair To Divine Awakening:
    The Cataclysm Of 2020 And The Resurrection Of
    My Soul's Mission   193
    Dr. Angelika Christie

53. Advice From A Nonagenarian   197
    Anne Lorimor

54. Find Your Why   201
    Barbara J. Morris

55. A Spring In My Step   204
    Barb Laubman

56. Paradigm Shift   207
    Bonnie L. Senftner

57. The Circle Of Life: The Echo Of Lorraine's love And
    Legacy   212
    Catherine Schwark

58. Friendships   215
    Cis Ahearn

59. The Spirit Of Listening – Lessons   218
    Debi Lynn

60. Our Ageless, Timeless Love   221
    Denise Yonkers

61. Manifesting A Dream…Mine!   225
    Dolly Kennedy

62. Connie, My Infamous Mother-In-Law   228
    Diane Berg

63. Retiring On My Terms   231
    Elizabeth Lupacchino Donohue

64. Living My 20s In My 50s   233
    Joellyn Wlazlowski Martin

65. Lessons For A Magnificent Life   238
    Jana Lee Gattung

66. The Story Behind My Smile   244
    JoyAnn Gold

67. Noise Was My Chocolate   248
    Jo Dibblee

68. Echoes Of Ageless Wisdom   250
    Katherine Merritt

69. Your Choices…Your Extraordinary Life!   254
    Lucie Rosa-Stagi

70. Who Is Your Earth Angel?   256
Moriah Hudson

71. Unconscious Influence: How Our Mother
Shapes Us   261
Nancy Johnson

72. The Joy of Being is the Joy of Living a Conscious
Life   265
Shirley Turner

73. The Magic Of Finding Love Again   270
Sunshine Deb

74. Dream Weaver   275
Susan "SueZee" Finley

75. Love Knows No Age   280
Tina Taylor

76. The Day That Changed The Direction Of My Life   286
Victoria McRay

77. You Are Not Done Yet! Living A Life You Love At
Any Age And At Any Stage   291
Cindy McKee

Afterword   295
Ageless Stars Bios   298

Thank You   361
Join The Ageless Voices Movement!   363

INTRODUCTION

Ageless Voices is not just a book; it is a call to action. It is an invitation to embrace your own ageless spirit, to break free from societal norms, and to live life on your own terms.

Welcome to *Ageless Voices*, a captivating collection of short stories that will inspire you to embrace the timeless spirit of living agelessly. To create this book, I invited authors whom I call my **Ageless Stars** to share their personal journeys and insights on what it truly means to face numerous life challenges, move beyond them, and live lives that are Fun, Fearless, and Fabulous!

Living agelessly is not about defying the passage of time or clinging to youth. It is a mindset, a philosophy, and a celebration of the boundless possibilities that exist at any stage of life. It is about embracing the richness of experience and wisdom that comes with age.

Within these pages, you will embark on a transformative journey through the diverse perspectives of the authors. Each story is a testament to the power of resilience, self-discovery, and the unwavering spirit that defies societal expectations and limitations. Many *Ageless Stars* have reinvented themselves, pursued new passions, and discovered newfound purpose in their lives beyond 60. Their stories will ignite your imagination, challenge your preconceptions, and remind you that age is merely a number, not a barrier.

Through the laughter, tears, and triumphs shared on these pages, you will witness the extraordinary ways ageless living manifests itself. From embarking on daring adventures to finding love in unexpected places, from starting new businesses to making a difference in their communities, the authors exemplify the limitless potential within each of us.

Prepare to be inspired, uplifted, and transformed. Open your heart and mind to the stories that lie ahead. Let our voices guide you on a path of life with an ageless mindset!

Ageless Voices has been a dream of mine for almost 20 years. I wanted to help change the societal story around aging that's been associated with Fear and Decline. It always saddened me whenever a woman shared her fear of growing older. I never felt that way as the years beyond 60 have been my grandest.

I embrace life with an ageless mindset. That's what I desire for everyone, so the **Ageless Star Project** was created. I also knew that having the perspective of many sharing stories of their life experiences would have far more impact than if I were to simply write my own stories about how I live agelessly. I sent out an invitation for women 60 and beyond to join me in creating this collaborative book. Thirty-six beautiful *Ageless Stars* answered the call.

Each came with the desire to inspire and empower others to embrace their ageless mindset. They recognized the need to amplify our voices and share messages to celebrate our lives at any age. The *Ageless Stars* range in age from 61 to 98 and live in many different countries. I invite you to read the bios at the end of this book to discover our vast collective experiences. Through our stories, we hope to ignite a shift in your mindset and encourage you to embrace life's fullness, pursue new passions and create a positive impact in your community.

This book is divided into three captivating themes: Fun, Fearless, and Fabulous. Each theme explores different aspects of ageless living and offers a unique perspective.

1. **Fun:** In this section, we celebrate life's joyful moments and the importance of connection. We share stories of celebrations, the beauty of friendships, the love of family, and the transformative power of both self-love and romantic love. Our narratives remind you that age is no barrier to experiencing life's sheer joy and happiness.

2. **Fearless:** This section delves into life's adventures and the courage to face challenges head-on. We share stories of turning obstacles, loss, and change into remarkable adventures. We inspire you to believe in yourselves, to overcome fear, and to pursue your dreams with unwavering determination. Our stories remind you that living agelessly is about embracing the unknown, taking risks, and refusing to be stopped by any obstacle.

3. **Fabulous:** This section celebrates the incredible **Ageless Stars** who embody ageless living. We inspire you with stories of embarking on meaningful careers, serving humanity in remarkable ways, creating non-profits, and sharing the wisdom we've gained. May our stories remind you that age is not a limitation but a gateway to a life filled with purpose, impact, and fulfillment.

Through these three themes, *Ageless Voices* paints a vivid picture of what it means to live agelessly. It encourages you to embrace your own ageless mindset, break free from societal expectations, and create a truly extraordinary life. You will be inspired, uplifted, and transformed as you journey through the pages.

May our collective wisdom serve as guiding lights, illuminating the path to a life filled with limitless possibilities. Let our experiences constantly remind you that the years beyond 60 can be the grandest, the most fulfilling, and the most vibrant.

As you close this book, carry with you the belief that age is not a limitation but a catalyst for growth, wisdom, and boundless potential. Embrace your ageless mindset, and let it guide you to a life without boundaries.

Thank you for joining us on this extraordinary journey of ageless living. Your ageless story awaits, and it's time to make it truly magnificent.

JoyAnn Gold, Founder of Ageless Star Project
Age 81

PART ONE
FUN

Life is not measured by the number of breaths we take, but by the moments that take our breath away. ~ **Maya Angelou**

CHAPTER 1

AGELESS VOICES OF CHANGE

TINA TAYLOR

To all the women over sixty, hear this call,
It's time to share our powerful message, let's break down every wall.

With strong, confident voices, let us declare,
Aging's a crown, one we're so proud to wear.

In the game of life, like ageless stars, we'll gleam,
For we've found the secret, YES, it's not a dream!

To be fun, fearless, fabulous, and bold,
No matter our age, we'll never grow old.

So let's keep dancing like nobody's watching, my friend,
And cherish each and every moment, from beginning to end.

As we gaze into the mirror, let's embrace who we see,
Envisioning our limitless dreams and every possibility.

Staying fun, staying fearless, forever fabulous and bold,
These are the keys to ageless living, which we all hold.

As a united team of women, we'll change society's view on age,
By sharing our inspirational stories, page by page.

With a timeless outlook, we'll break every norm,
Our "Ageless Voices" WILL take the world by storm!

Tina Taylor
Age 61

CHAPTER 2

WHAT SOAP BUBBLES AFTER MIDNIGHT TAUGHT ME

DR. ANGELIKA CHRISTIE

That night, the moon and clouds became my most powerful tutors, affecting my life in the most amazing way.

Can Perspective Change Everything?

As Dr. Wayne Dyer said, "When you change how you look at things, the things you look at change."

On a warm summer night, after a successful and fun gathering with friends, my kitchen was a fortress of soiled dishes. Beautifully painted china and delicate crystal glasses lay waiting to be carefully washed, too precious for the dishwasher. Although my weary husband peeked into the kitchen with a "so-sorry-my-love-smile" and a "why don't you leave it for the morning" remark while heading for bed, I've always loved a clean kitchen to enjoy starting my morning routine.

The lingering scent of our delicious meal and the laughter of friends still echoed in my mind. However, juxtaposed against these fond memories was the heavy weight of the chore at hand, pulling my spirits down again. Every dish and every piece of silverware seemed to resonate with my exhaustion, each more mocking in its silent expectation of being carefully cleaned than the last.

Once joyous, the evening's labor of love now felt like an unending saga of labor-heavy aftermath. The beautifully hand-painted dishes and crystal glasses were symbols of the night's success but also witnesses of my solitary situation.

In this cocoon of isolation and weariness, feelings of abandonment gnawed at me. The world, including my husband, had retreated into the warmth and comfort of their beds, leaving behind the chaos of the aftermath in my hands alone. The distant sound of the nocturnal world only added to the depth of my solitude. My heart murmured its grievance loudly, feeling the acute sting of injustice, while my mind spiraled into a pit of despair and resentment.

Seeking a brief respite from the overwhelming task, I wandered onto the balcony, where a cool breeze brushed against my face. I glanced up into the sky to witness a cosmic ballet. The clouds rushed past the moon, creating the illusion of the moon in a fevered sprint across the heavens. This simple yet profound spectacle jolted me out of my downward spiral, and a question arose: What if my current despair was merely a product of how I chose to perceive my circumstances? What if the dishes weren't a chain of drudgery but a tangible remnant of a night filled with joy, love, and companionship?

With the moon and the clouds as my silent tutors, my heart swelled with newfound curiosity. If a mere shift in my external perspective could make it seem like the moon was altering its path, could an intentional shift recalibrate my emotional trajectory? I rushed back into the kitchen, eager to find out.

Embracing this newfound revelation, the dishes began to transform in my eyes. No longer were they mountains of fatigue;

instead, they became canvases of memory. I felt a sense of gratitude as I traced each dish and its beautiful hand-painting with my soapy hands, smiling as I treated each dish with appreciation.

The trick my eyes played on me with the moon and the clouds was no longer just an optical illusion but a metaphoric guidepost, a gentle reminder that the innate power of perspective and its profound influence on me could change everything.

With every dish I cleaned, I relived a moment from the evening— each laugh, each shared story, each toast to good health and happiness.

The previously burdensome task now became an extension of the evening's joy. With renewed vigor and my heart bathed in peace, I approached each item not as a chore but as an act of mindfulness, cherishing its beauty and the memories of the evening it held. The previously dreaded task had become my most potent awareness thanks to the moment on my balcony with the moon and the clouds that warm and starry night.

Since then, I know that I can change my feelings by changing my perspective.

Synopsis

At the end of a very long night with friends enjoying my home-cooked meal, I resented the aftermath of cleaning up my kitchen. Why is it always me who is left alone to labor in the kitchen with the aftermath of a fun evening while my husband throws a kiss and a "good night, Sweetheart?"

As I embarked on this daunting task, resentment built up; I felt abandoned, reminiscing about the long hours of preparation and the short time it took to consume the meals. Suddenly, fatigue took over, and the world seemed overwhelmingly unfair and punishing. Eager to get away, I stepped onto the balcony for respite.

The sight of the moon seemingly racing across the sky made me laugh momentarily because it was such a powerful optical illusion. This led to an epiphany. What if our experiences and reactions were all about perceptions?

What if changing how I viewed a situation could alter my feelings toward it?

And it did—big time, and not just for that daunting task but for everything I encountered afterward and changed by changing my perspective.

That night, the moon and clouds became my most powerful tutors, affecting my life in the most amazing way.

Dr. Angelika Christie
Age 78

CHAPTER 3

DON'T MISS THE DANCE

BARBARA J. MORRIS

**Have you heard the metaphor of the Mason Jar?
It holds an important lesson for all of us. And I have seen it
demonstrated!**

You start with an empty Mason Jar and then fill it with rocks. These rocks represent the big things in your life: your family, your spouse, your health, your hopes, and your dreams. Ask yourself, is the jar full? It seems to be because you can't fit any more rocks in it. The next step is to fill it with pebbles. They fall between the rocks into the empty spaces. These pebbles are the things that give life meaning: friendships, work, hobbies, etc. Now, is the jar full? Again, you can't put any more pebbles in, so it appears full. But we aren't done yet!

Take some sand and pour it into the jar; watch what happens. The sand fills in all the empty spaces between the rocks and the pebbles. Now it looks like it is truly full, right? Nope! There is one more step. Pour water into the jar. This time, it is full!

The sand and water represent the small stuff that fills the rest of your time. Let's talk about the sand. All those tiny grains of sand represent each little moment of your life. They are what really make up your life. All the little moments! Do you know that each moment, one at a time, is all we have? The old adage that says, "The past is history, the future is a mystery, but right now is a gift, and that is why it's called the Present."

This is a universal truth in my book! Life is right now, in this very moment, with no history to bog us down and no mystery to give us worries. This present moment is where we can find joy. That's what I want to talk to you about—all those little grains of sand that make up our lives and are the building blocks upon which our lives unfold. Do you let those big rocks rule your life?

I'm not saying they shouldn't take precedence; they are the big, important things that propel us forward. But when you really get it—that it's each little moment that adds up to your lifetime—you realize that it IS time to stop and smell the roses, as the saying goes. Or for some, it may be, stop and smell the coffee!

I'd love to share with you about being present in the moment and what it can do for your life. I'm not talking about sitting and meditating, although that can certainly help you to be more present. It's more about really allowing yourself to experience each moment. When you can do that, it opens you up to gratitude and joy. And a life filled with gratitude and joy is a life that feels fulfilled. In each moment that you are truly present, your world will open to much more than you have ever imagined it could! Inspiration will visit you. Acting on those inspired thoughts is what moves you through your life with a smile on your face and in your heart. As I am sitting here writing this, I am present in each moment, letting my pen flow across the paper as I am divinely guided, and it feels so good!

So, live each moment, from the time you first open your eyes to right before you close them in sleep. Let each moment give you more discernment, more allowing, and more joy! That is what we live for! That is why we are here—to see and feel everything and everyone around us. Don't hide from life, even when it brings pain and sorrow, for each moment is a lesson. Even at my age, I'm still learning those lessons, and I am grateful for each one, even the ones I thought might break me. They all contributed to who I am right now. And, as the Garth Brooks song goes, "I could have missed the pain, but I'd have to miss the dance."

So, I invite you to DANCE, to live each moment of your life that fills those spaces between the rocks and pebbles.

Barbara J. Morris
Age 77

CHAPTER 4

FOREVER YOUNG AT HEART

BARB LAUBMAN

Age is merely a reflection of the experiences we've collected, the love we've given and received, and the memories etched into the tapestry of our souls.

I grew up surrounded by the extraordinary women in my life—my beloved grandmother and mother, who had a unique perspective on aging and the boundless nature of the human spirit.

As a child, I was often puzzled by my grandmother Florence's enchanting words. She looked in the mirror and claimed to see a sixteen-year-old girl staring back at her. To my young mind, it seemed almost surreal; how could my grandmother see herself as a teenager when she was, in my eyes, the epitome of a wise and graceful lady?

A funny story is that I was out shopping with my grandmother when a man opened the door for us. My grandmother remarked, "He did that for me." She owned it!

My mother, Laurene, shared a similar enigmatic quality. She is still vibrant and lively, possessing a contagious laughter that fills our home with warmth and joy. Laurene has an uncanny ability to keep her age hidden, playfully guarding it as a secret treasure. She believed that sharing her birth year would somehow limit the perception of her everlasting youthfulness.

Even as Laurene moved to a retirement home, her spirit remained untamed. I admired her ability to embrace the company of her peers, finding solace in shared memories and hearty laughter. With her radiant red hair, she became an alluring mystery, often teasing that her color was purely natural, much to everyone's amusement.

As I matured into a young woman, I began to understand the wisdom behind their perspectives. Both my grandmother and mother lived their lives to the fullest, regardless of the number of years that passed.

They embodied the notion that age is just a number and that the spirit, the essence of who we are, knows no boundaries.

Their legacy instilled in me a genuine passion for life. I carried their enduring belief that one's age does not define one's worth or capabilities. I vowed to live with the same unwavering enthusiasm, daring to savor every moment and cherish the connections I formed with others.

Throughout my own adventures, I encountered people who were drawn to my exuberant spirit. They marveled at my infectious laughter and the way I embraced life with an open heart. I found joy in sharing the stories of my grandmother and mother, illuminating their timeless secrets of staying young at heart.

As the years gracefully advanced, my grandmother's physical presence transformed into cherished memories. Yet the love and wisdom she imparted remained ever-present within me, shaping the person I became.

With gratitude in my heart, I embraced the knowledge that we are as young as we feel within. Age is merely a reflection of the experiences we've collected, the love we've given and received, and the memories etched into the tapestry of our souls.

Barb Laubman
Age 70

CHAPTER 5

WHEN THE END IS REALLY JUST THE BEGINNING

BEV WALKNER

"Let go of something old that no longer serves you in order to make room for something new."
~ Roy T. Bennett

"To my shock, I realized that I knew very little about myself."
~ Bev Walkner

As I sat on the balcony of our new condo, I couldn't help but smile. Life has a way of surprising us and bringing us to the most unexpected places. At that moment, I knew that I was exactly where I was meant to be, with the person I was meant to spend the rest of my life with.

The sun was deliciously warm on my face as I relaxed in the stillness of the morning. It was late August in Alberta, and we had just moved into our new condo in a new city. It was our "new beginning". My heart was full.

I took a deep, slow breath and inhaled the calming aroma of my first cup of coffee. I sank into the quiet. I was truly at peace for the first time in over two years—actually, when I really thought about it, maybe for the first time in my life.

My fiancé was asleep inside. I could hear her gentle puffs of air through the nearby window as she softly exhaled, and I smiled. We joked about those puffs - it was one of the many things we joked about. One of the many things I loved about her.

Yes! A new condo. A new city. A new love. A new life. She was 63, and I was 68.

We were living a dream come true - a dream we had separately manifested. It was a new day, a new beginning, and I was ready to embrace it with all the love, self-acceptance, and hope that had brought me to this beautiful moment. And as I savored my coffee and sank into the memories, I journeyed back to where this all began, where we began.

On a rainy morning in September 2021, at the age of 67, I made a decision that changed my life forever. I finally found the courage to end my 47-year marriage. Leaving my husband was the most challenging and painful decision I had ever made—not only for me but for my children and grandchildren, the center of my world. My decision impacted them, and I grappled daily with the guilt that accompanied it. However, it was a necessary decision for my health, my well-being, and even my life.

I had thought about leaving so many times before but never had the strength to follow through. I always convinced myself that somehow things would get better; I could fix him and fix us. I told myself it really wasn't *that* bad—at least he didn't hit me anymore. I could still find a way to save us.

This was the story I kept telling myself over and over until that morning when I woke up and stopped telling it. I stopped lying to myself.

This was the end.

"The most terrifying thing is to accept oneself completely."
~C.G. Jung

What came next was fascinating and unexpected. I began to question who I really was. Now that I was no longer someone's wife, who was I? *To my shock, I realized that I knew very little about myself.* I knew I had the capacity to love deeply, that I was kind and compassionate, and that I drew people to me. I craved connections with like-minded souls. **But who was I? What lit my soul on fire? What did I want from life? What is my purpose now?**

Around the same time, some younger, single friends suggested I try something entirely new. They encouraged me to join a dating site. My initial reaction was, "Are you serious at my age?" I thought they were crazy. I had already made up my mind that I never wanted to be involved with another man. I was so done.

But they had something else in mind. They saw something in me that I hadn't seen or admitted to myself in my 67 years. I had been raised in a time when women had very specific roles, and the expectation was to get married and have children. I wasn't even aware that there were other options for me. *I had followed the script handed down from generation to generation.* But my friends suggested that maybe it wasn't men I should be considering, but women.

While I had never really been attracted to men, I had always felt that something was broken or missing in me. I had never thought of women in that way, either. But there was a tiny part of me that began to wonder, *"What if I am gay?"* It was a shocking thought, but my friends explained that joining a dating site for women could also be a way to make new friends and meet women with shared interests without necessarily being romantic. That idea appealed to me, so I decided to give it a try, thinking, *"What do I have to lose?"*

First, I developed my profile. Trying to describe myself was tricky, given my realization that there were many things about myself I didn't know. But I worked with what I did know and thought about the kind of person I wanted to meet.

I asked myself: What did I value in someone else? What would an ideal relationship look like? Here, I leaned on teachings from my life coach.

She said, "When dreams or desires match what you believe is possible along with your way of being, those dreams or desires will come true." It was a potent statement. The catch was that you had to *truly* believe it was possible—not just think it *might* be, but believe with complete certainty.

So, I made a list of everything I desired in *my ideal* partner. I followed my coach's advice and refused to settle or compromise. No more mediocrity, no more half-measures. I wanted it ALL, the whole enchilada. I wanted someone who would love me completely and unconditionally forever: body, mind, soul, and spirit. ***Dream big or go home, baby!**" was my new mantra! So, I dreamt **BIG**.

After making my list, the next step was to envision what having someone like this in my life would look and feel like. I allowed myself to imagine the emotions it would bring and how it would change my life. The joy, peace, harmony, ecstasy and beauty, the smoothing out of life's ups and downs, the fun and laughter—all of it felt truly like Heaven on Earth. I saw it all, and **I believed it**!

"Sign me up!" I said to myself. It's hard to explain, but it was like I had an inner **knowing** that it would happen. Anything was now possible. The when, the how, and the who of it were not known, but that it *would* happen was absolutely crystal clear. With this clarity and my newfound belief, I began entering my profile.

When I was done and before I posted it, sheer panic set in. I was about to do something I had never done before, and it terrified me. But then, I thought about what I had to lose vs what I had to gain, and I found the courage to post it.

And then I waited.

I didn't have to wait long. Two days later, I had a match. I was beyond surprised. She was everything I had envisioned. Without hesitating, I "liked" her. Then I saw it—she had "liked" me back! After that, we wasted no time. We chatted online the next day. Everything about her spoke to me. I couldn't wait to talk to her; I couldn't get enough of her. She was amazing, beautiful, loving, and compassionate, and I was smitten.

We both fell hard for each other. Until then, I never really believed in "love at first sight." It was the thing of romance novels and fairy tales. However, meeting her changed all of that. Now, I knew what love could be. What is love supposed to be? The astonishing thing was that she felt the same way.

I found out later that just days before seeing my profile, she, too, had been invited by her therapist to think about what her ideal partner might look like. At first, she resisted. She wasn't sure she was ready for a relationship. She was close to finishing her Master's Thesis and didn't think she could afford the distraction. However, she decided to take her therapist's advice and list the qualities she desired in a future partner.

Two days later, from a dating site she hadn't been on for months, she received a notification that someone had liked her profile. It was me. And as impossible as it seemed, when she looked at my profile, she was drawn to me. She recognized something different in me, in my words, that touched her heart.

She was shocked, surprised, and scared all at the same time. *"Now what? Was she ready? What would this mean for her degree?* After much soul searching, she held her breath and hit the "like" button.

Consider the pure magic and miracle of our journey to find each other! What are the chances that complete strangers living hundreds of miles apart—both having left decades-long, unhealthy marriages, both going through a similar exercise of envisioning their ideal partner, both recognizing those qualities in the other—both discover each other within a couple of days on a dating site? Not only that, but what are the odds that we would both fall so instantly and effortlessly in love? Coincidence? Synchronicity? Or was it Divine Intervention? Whatever you call it, it's the miracle that is possible when we choose to be true to ourselves and to believe we deserve it.

We were both willing to make the effort to see where this connection could lead. We planned our first meeting two weeks later, meeting at a quiet, rustic cabin nestled in the beautiful Rocky Mountains. The day of our meeting arrived, and I felt a mixture of excitement and nervousness. It was like going on a first date all over again, but this time, it was different. This time, I was meeting someone who saw me for who I truly was—someone who accepted me without judgment, someone who shared my dreams and values.

As I drove to the cabin, my heart raced with anticipation. I couldn't wait to see her, to look into her eyes, and to feel that connection in person. When we finally met, it was like a scene from a romantic movie. We embraced, and it felt like coming home. The time we spent together was incredibly magical. Neither one of us had ever had a relationship with a woman before. Neither of us had ever experienced such connection, compassion, deep love, tenderness, and intimacy. Our time together was filled with love, laughter, adventure, and deep conversations.

Oh, I just heard something. She is stirring inside, and I know she is waking up. The sound brings me out of my reverie. My joy and happiness are overflowing.

My journey had taken me from the pain of an abusive marriage to the freedom of self-discovery and self-love. It led me to a love that was beyond anything I had ever imagined, a love that was worth waiting for, a love that had the power to heal and transform.

Now I have evidence that dreams really do come true, love is real, *and life* has no age limit. It can bloom and flourish at any stage of life, bringing joy, fulfillment, and a sense of purpose. I learned that it was never too late to pursue your dreams, to rediscover yourself, and to find the love you deserve.

And this is just the beginning.

Bev Walkner
Age 68

CHAPTER 6

THE 1962 BARBIE DREAM HOUSE

BONNIE L. SENFTNER

When my brother Gary and I were young, we created a world of "little people." Our world had little houses with fenced-in yards dotted with trees and tiny potted plants. It had small cars and trucks, miniature dolls, and tiny plastic animals. We would play in the bedroom for hours, immersed in our make-believe world. This world impacted us so deeply that when Gary became a musician (a self-taught guitarist and harmonica player), he named his first band "Make Believe World."

My love of playing continued into adulthood. One Thanksgiving, my husband Michael and I celebrated the holiday with our adult sons, Luke and Tyler. We played a game designed to generate closeness among players. The game involved cards that asked questions, prompting respondents to reflect on and share important moments in their lives. During one of my turns, the question about a disappointing Christmas came up. I recounted a story from Christmas 1962.

I was nine years old, and all the little girls at school wanted the 1962 Barbie Dream House. The house would have fit perfectly into my world of little people. A few days before vacation, our teacher asked us what we wanted for Christmas. Almost every girl, including myself, wanted the Barbie Dream House. There was such hope and anticipation among us that our dream would come true.

On Christmas Day, I excitedly ran to the tree. After all the gifts were revealed, I realized there was no dream house for me. I was a good-natured child and appreciated the other gifts I received. Initially, I didn't feel it was a disappointing Christmas—until school resumed and the post-Christmas gift questions were asked. That's when the feelings of letdown set in. Why hadn't Santa brought me the Dream House?

All these years later, as my family and I sat around the Thanksgiving table, we chuckled at the memory and then reflected on the lesson learned from the experience: You can't always get what you want. This is one of life's most important lessons and part of our spiritual growth. The understanding that our expectations often create unhappiness in our lives helps us learn the importance of expecting nothing and finding gratitude for what we have.

My Christmas gift that year from our son Tyler was very unexpected. He reminded me of my younger brother Joel when we were very young. Joel was always so excited to give our mom his Christmas present that he would always tell her what it was before she opened it. Tyler displayed the same excitement and looked like he would burst, but he held on to this secret. As I tore off the paper, not having a clue what he had purchased for me, I suddenly broke down and started to sob. Others looked concerned, as they could not understand what moved me to such tears. When the wrapping paper came off, there before me was an original 1962 Barbie Dream House. The greatest gift was not the material house itself but realizing that, as parents, we had instilled such empathy and compassion in our son.

I almost immediately set up the Barbie Dream House in our grandson's playroom, where I can admire it when he visits and reflect upon my childhood memories as he creates his own happy memories.

With age and wisdom, I know that even though life is filled with ups and downs, successes and failures, joys and sadness, sometimes dreams do come true, even if it takes sixty years.

Bonnie L. Senftner
Age 72

CHAPTER 7
EMPOWERED LIVING: MASTERING THE ART OF JOY

DEBBIE PREDIGER

It wasn't just about doing what brought joy—it was a battle against old patterns of safety in anonymity, blending in, and avoiding attention.

Years dedicated to others, I lost touch with joy. No horseback rides, no woodland adventures, no playful moments by the water. Joy, once a constant companion, became a distant memory. Endless nights of worry and restless sleep became routine, with past and future entangled in a downward spiral.

Helping others brought purpose but left me hollow, seeking validation outside myself—a quick fix that left me emptier.

Realization struck when I stopped evading emotions and asked, "What would I like to feel?" Emotions, I discovered, are frequencies. We can choose and elevate them. I became the creator of my life, knowing that emotions don't define me. This sparked a profound journey of self-discovery.

Who am I? What ignites my soul? How do I stay at the frequency of love or above instead of drowning in turmoil? Understanding my state and consciously choosing where I wanted to be, I reclaimed my power, unveiling the silenced version of me.

This marked the beginning of my quest for joy. It wasn't just about doing what brought joy—it was a battle against old patterns of safety in anonymity, blending in, and avoiding attention. No wonder I felt numb. With relentless awareness, I asked every hour, "Am I in JOY?" If not, how do I get there? It was uncomfortable at first, but commitment made it easier. Recognizing my emotions, deciding if I wanted to feel them, or choosing again if I didn't became my practice. There was freedom, responsibility, and choice in this action.

Finding joy amidst chaos seemed impossible until I shifted my perspective. "This is not happening to you; it's happening for you." Slowly, I began to see the gifts in the chaos. I became the master of my creations, not from blame or guilt, but from empowerment. One choice stood out: to choose Joy.

Joy became my North Star. A destination I sometimes fully embraced and, at other times, moved towards. I changed routines, habits, and thinking to always align with joy. Emotions were no longer kept in a box but were honored and cherished. I started to live in love, or above frequency, celebrating each choice and allowing this to be my new way of BEING.

To this day, I check in several times, asking, "Am I in JOY?"

I often speak of 'Love or Above,' a way of measuring where I am on the emotional scale. Choosing love, peace, or joy as my foundational emotional home. It's a conscious choice, a deeper awareness of what I am choosing in each moment. From a place of people-pleasing and emotional numbness, I transformed into someone who not only embodies joy but empowers others to do the same. Choosing joy has been a pivotal decision in my life, a commitment made through awareness and followed by aligned action. It's the path to living a life I cherish.

In my coaching and mentorship, I pinpoint the 'Joy Gap' in people's lives, where there's room for more alignment and congruence. Work-life balance isn't my focus; instead, it's about consciously choosing a life we love. Sometimes, that choice or line in the sand moment arises from fear and pain, other times from empowerment. I guide my clients in recognizing misalignment and extending an invitation to embrace a life they'd truly adore. It's about identifying what brings them joy, ignites their hearts, and infuses their days with vitality, then weaving these into new habits and patterns. The magic truly begins when these choices take root. Witnessing this transformation daily fills me with profound joy.

I'd love for you to consider what other words evoke joy for you. Perhaps it's play, magic, creativity, or simply fun. Do they carry the same frequency and vibration as "joy" does for you?

Now, reflect on what joy means personally. To me, it signifies a higher frequency, a vibration of freedom and choice. It means finding joy in every endeavor, wearing a beaming smile, and having an open heart. It leads to connections with like-hearted souls drawn to this magnetic force of joy. It's about embodying joy, love, and peace. It's the knowing that deep within, I can choose these emotions regardless of circumstance, place, or company. And that, my friends, brings me boundless joy.

I highly suggest adding a reminder to your phone or using an app to check in if you are emotionally embodying joy. I personally use the app called "I Am," which resonates with my belief that "I am possible." I love it when I am reminded in various ways how powerful I am and that I am the creator of my own reality. It serves as a potent reminder that I am not subject to my circumstances; rather, I am the author of my own life. This is why my community is called *"Empowering You."* It's not about me; it's about what you would love! What makes you feel fulfilled, cherished, and unconditionally loved?

What brings you JOY? I really do want to know...

Debbie Prediger
Age 61

CHAPTER 8

ALWAYS A SONG IN MY HEART

DENISE YONKERS

Aging is a symphony of memories, each note resonating with the melody of life's timeless song.

After my husband passed away and I retired from my regular career, I decided to pursue something that I had always been interested in. Singing in the choir! I have always loved music and singing. I enjoy many different types of music and always keep a song in my heart. Participating in the choir is a wonderful journey for me, especially around the holidays. It helps me beat the holiday blues, stay active, practice, and it brings immense joy to my soul!

I became part of a close-knit community of people who share a common passion for music and singing. Regular choir rehearsals and performances allow me to refine my vocal techniques and overall singing abilities. The choir provides me with a supportive environment in which to grow. Choir singing promotes teamwork and cooperation. Our members must work together to create a unified sound that fosters a powerful sense of collaboration and mutual respect.

Singing in the choir gives me a platform to express myself creatively through music. I can convey emotions, tell stories, and share messages through the power of voice. Engaging in music, including singing, has been shown to reduce stress and promote relaxation. The act of singing can release endorphins, which can lead to a positive emotional state.

Regular performances with the choir have helped to boost my confidence and stage presence. Over time, I feel more comfortable performing in front of an audience. In a choir, I learned to listen attentively to others, which is crucial for blending voices and staying in harmony. This skill can also translate to better communication in daily life.

Being part of a choir often involves learning music theory, understanding different vocal parts, and reading sheet music. This knowledge can enhance overall musical proficiency. Some choirs have the chance to travel and perform in various venues, which can be a thrilling and memorable experience.

Singing has positive effects on both my physical and mental health. It improves my lung capacity, posture, and overall well-being. Mastering challenging pieces and performing successfully brings a profound sense of accomplishment. Singing in a choir has led to the formation of strong, lasting friendships with fellow choir members.

The joy and benefits of being part of a collective musical experience are truly remarkable. It is an opportunity to connect with others, share my voice, and be part of something beautiful and meaningful.

Denise Yonkers
Age 69

CHAPTER 9

EXPERIENCE THE LIFE YOU WERE MEANT TO LIVE!

ELIZABETH LUPACCHINO DONOHUE

"Raise your voice in truth, love, and compassion, and experience the life you were meant to live."
~ Elizabeth Lupacchino Donohue

I now pronounce you Husband, Wife, and Bonus Mom. The priest did not actually say those exact words, and yet that is what happened. Yes, at 66, I became a wife and an instant Bonus Mom, which was the answer to a lifelong wish and prayer. I prefer the term "Bonus Mom" instead of "stepmom." I feel like I became a bonus mom to my wonderful stepdaughter, whose mother passed away, and she became a bonus daughter for me.

When I was in my 30's I did meet someone who said they also wanted children. I felt so lucky that it appeared as though my wish would come true; until we got married and that is when the verbal abuse started. After two years and the fear that it would escalate to physical abuse, I got the courage and support from family and friends to get a divorce and start my life over in a different State, literally, physically, mentally and spiritually. It was the best decision I made as it prepared me for the wonderful life I have today.

As the years and decades flew by and I saw my 30s, 40s, and 50s, I knew I would not hear the pitter-patter of little feet. I tried not to dwell on it. Although I often thought about adopting or fostering a child, I didn't feel that, as a single mom, I could provide what was needed. Somehow, I kept up the hope that I would be a mom someday. I didn't know how or when, but I felt that this would happen. So, for the time being, I buried myself in my job and my hobbies and let it go. Of course, I had pets that were spoiled beyond measure, but they were a poor substitute for children.

I have enjoyed singing for many years and have been part of great choirs and concerts. To keep my voice in shape, I take lessons. I was in the process of changing teachers, and a friend of mine recommended a very well-known and excellent teacher. He is an incredible writer, director, composer, and singer himself. I felt insecure and lacked the confidence to approach him. After several months of dragging my feet, I finally got up enough courage and auditioned. He was so kind, reassuring, and encouraging. We agreed that I would start lessons the following week.

As the weeks and months went by, I began to feel a tug at my heart unlike anything I had ever felt before—a kind of knowing. It was as if God was speaking directly to me. My heart would jump with excitement every time I saw him. I always did my best, practiced a lot, and hoped that he would notice. We worked hard during my lessons, but we also had fun and laughed. Then, one day, I told him how I felt about him, and he was shocked. He did not expect that at all and told me that he was a widow with a mentally and physically challenged adult daughter living with him, which takes up most of his time.

After a few months, we finally decided to go on a date. It was a big step for me. I was so nervous. What if it didn't work out? Will we end up not liking each other? Will I have to find a new vocal instructor? So many "what ifs" kept crossing my mind.

It was after one of his concerts, and we went to this cute little Italian restaurant not too far from his house. It was a little awkward at first, as he was well-known by the owners. But gradually, we started getting more comfortable with each other, and it was as if we had known each other for years. Well, two years later, he asked me to marry him, and we got engaged. We celebrated our engagement at "our little place," and we continue to celebrate every milestone and every anniversary there as well.

We got married in 2020, during the height of the COVID-19 pandemic. We were lucky enough to get married in the church shortly after the restrictions were lifted. Although the ceremony was not what we hoped—there could be only ten people there, including us—it was wonderful, private, and filled with love from all who could attend. I will always remember it. After all, it isn't about the ceremony but rather about the life that two people who are in love are building together. Restaurants were not allowing people to eat indoors yet, so we celebrated our wedding at home by ourselves.

It was a very cozy, romantic, and wonderful day, just the two of us. And shortly after, my wonderful Bonus Daughter came home, and that was the start of my dream come true.

You see, 66 is not too old to become a mother for the first time. It didn't happen the way I thought it would, but God had other plans. He knew that I would be needed, and He put me here to help love and take care of this wonderful "little girl." When you ask God for something, He answers you in His time and in His way—not always the time when you think it should be. He answers in the way that is best for you. Sometimes, we may not think this is the case, but it is. So don't give up if your dream is to be a mom and it hasn't happened yet; keep listening, and one day, you may hear those precious words: "I love you, Mommy."

Elizabeth Lupacchino Donohue
Age 70

CHAPTER 10

YOU'VE GOT 40 MORE YEARS

JOYANN GOLD

"It's Your Mindset, Not Your Genes That Determine Your Age"
~JoyAnn Gold

It's a well-accepted societal story that women, age 60 and older, do not have dreams, goals, or visions for a grander life. It's my honor, passion, and mission to challenge that narrative. I intend to shout from the rooftops that age is no barrier! The world needs to know the profound wisdom and positive impact women over 60 can bring to our communities, our country, and our world!

Shortly after my 72nd birthday, I attended a wellness retreat focused on mind, body, and spirit. One of the first exercises was to create a 25-year Life Plan! That took me to 97, but I extended it to 100! What a powerful exercise that turned out to be, for until then, I just visualized the next 5-10 years.

The more I dreamed about my future years, the more passionate I became about all the possibilities I could still experience. I saw myself traveling with my soulmate, creating my mission of a book and documentary film to combat ageism, and truly living my grandest years of life! As I continued to visualize, my excitement and joy for life took a giant leap! And the only thing that changed was my mindset, as I had developed an ageless attitude for my life!

The notion of "I'm growing old" vanished with each passing year, replaced by an exciting anticipation of what life had in store for me!

As my 75th birthday approached, memories of childhood birthday celebrations flooded my mind, particularly the joyous trips to the zoo. I decided, why not step back in time and relive the magic of a fun-filled zoo day at 75? On my birthday morning, as I embarked on my journey to the zoo, where I met my daughter, I could hardly contain the bubbling excitement within me! I let my inner child come out and play as we danced, skipped, and exclaimed to many other zoo visitors, "I'm 75 today!" I felt the pure joy of my child-like spirit as I embraced the freedom to be carefree and truly celebrate my age. I actually felt very young!

Nearing my 80th birthday, my twin sister, Joyce and I were in an office setting up an appointment. Being identical twins, we are often stopped by the question, "Are you twins?" This time was no exception.

As we were about to leave, a man approached us, exclaiming loudly, "You've got to be twins!" We paused in agreement, and a conversation began about the joy of twinship. Then, out of the blue, he asked, "How old are you?" My immediate reply was, "Almost 80," to which his joyful and passionate response was, "YOU'VE GOT 40 MORE YEARS!"

We laughed and parted ways, but as we walked towards the car, Joyce and I had the feeling we'd just met an ANGEL with a huge message for us! We were both so very touched by the experience! What a blessing to have been gifted with the idea of living another 40 years!

My Life Plan has now expanded to 120 years! That means at 81, I am just beginning the Third Act of my life! My AGELESS MINDSET has taken another giant leap!

JoyAnn Gold
Age 81

CHAPTER 11

DESTINY'S SUBTLE PUSH
DR. K. MHINA ENTRANTT

"Destiny will slip in between the edges and push you forward!"
~ Dr. K. Mhina Entrantt

When I moved to North Carolina in 2016, I had no idea how much my life and purpose would evolve. I thought I would settle into a quiet life with my family as the matriarch, having Sunday dinners and enjoying connections with my grandchildren. One day, while online, I saw a request from an Art Project for Spanish teachers for their summer program. I am fluent in Spanish and have taught classes for years. I thought it would be a short summer stint that would put a few bucks in my pocket and help young people learn a new language. I applied and got the job. I was allowed to set up the class and meeting time. The Art Project had already acquired the space. Everything was running smoothly, so I thought.

In the third week of class, the Art Project, without warning, closed the program! As I made the parents aware of the program's closing, one of the parents made it clear she wanted her daughter to continue with my classes. She asked me if there was anything I could do. In my mind, I'm thinking of all the obvious reasons why this is not possible. At best, I thought maybe I could plan a class for next summer. I had been in town for less than 2 months. I did not know anyone that I could call to get donated space, and I did not have the money to rent a space for classes.

I let the parent know that I did not have access to free space for a class and presumed it would take a while to do the research and make connections. In turn, she began to make suggestions about where I could find free spaces in the area. She went on to say her daughter was doing so well in my classes, and she did not want her to miss out on this summer opportunity.

When I saw how enthusiastic the parent was for her daughter to continue with my Spanish classes, I said yes, I would do it. I asked her to give me two weeks to get everything together. She left happy that she had advocated for her daughter. I left wondering how in the world I could get it done in 2 weeks. Yet it felt right!

"It is not your job to see how everything will work out; before you get started, your job is to continually step forward with your YES."
~ Dr. K. Mhina Entrantt

Now, I can admit I like a bit of a mental challenge, and this was definitely that, and I had given my word! So now I have a mission and a target date. In 2 weeks, I found available free space at a local library centrally located, created a curriculum, a name for the business, and advertised brochures for the weekly "Conversational Spanish Classes." I emailed the parent the information, and she passed it on to other parents in her social circles.

On the day of class, I had a full room of students ages 4-12. This was the birth of Conversational Spanish Academy, a business I had no idea I would have or desired. Yet, there I was at the library, with a room full of students teaching Conversational Spanish.

Each class was a building block for the previous class, and the students loved learning short mini-conversations to practice with one another. In no time at all, they could introduce themselves, say how many people were in their family and their relatives, and describe their clothing and color.

The children were eager learners, and I began to realize I had a natural knack for figuring out each student's learning style. This allowed me to introduce a new language to students on a one-on-one basis in a way that was easy for them to grasp. I created songs, games, clapping phrases, and so much more to keep the students engaged and moving forward.

I made success easy for students, and we celebrated every forward step together.

When their parents arrived to pick them up, I showed the parents how well their child was doing in class and gave them short practice homework that the parents could join in. I, too, was overjoyed; I was in my element!

A friend of one of the parents contacted me to inquire if her 3-year-old son was too young to attend. She really wanted her child to start learning a new language. I decided to give the child a try to see if he was ready for the class. I created an individualized plan for him, where he would attend the class for the first 30 minutes. Seven years later, he is my best student and can effortlessly have conversations in Spanish and use over 1,000 words at will. Our class is a safe, inviting place for children to learn, practice, and socially engage with peers.

The student that I started the classes for is now a thriving college student.

Unexpectedly, creating this business connected me to the community, allowed me to mentor students, and gave parents educational feedback when requested. It became a soft place to land as children experienced challenges such as close family deaths, severe parental health problems, divorce, changes of schools, and the like. Conversational Spanish became a haven and a predictable constant during challenging life moments.

My new business has given me "unsolicited" yet necessary Pivoting Moments. I often had to be willing to move with the status presented to me. Whenever the parents' schedules, work, or circumstances changed, I had to create new ways of providing classes, like shifting from a physical building to Zoom. I was not familiar with it, but I had classes to do, so I had to figure it out. What I thought would be a temporary or one-year process became very convenient for the parents. I saw the benefits of putting all my Conversational Spanish classes online.

Parents loved the flexibility to run errands and still be able to have their children attend classes on a device in the car. Adult students also enjoyed the flexibility of having classes online. That was an interesting journey, to say the least. I was not tech-savvy—I knew enough to get by, but the world of Zoom had a lot of moving parts. I was intimidated and sometimes frustrated, but I kept going until I could do whatever was needed to get on, stay on, and correct glitches. I was proud of myself and relieved! By the time we were going through the pandemic, my classes had been on Zoom for over a year, which was already the norm for my students and their parents.

Another pivotal move was to create Conversational Spanish classes for adults, groups, and entrepreneurs—family members, friends, co-workers, and business employees can all learn Conversational Spanish together. I make classes fun and engaging for adults. Many of the adults had previously had Spanish classes in a school setting and were frustrated that they could not have a conversation in Spanish. I created an adult curriculum that helps adults immediately have conversations in Spanish. County and state agencies began to hire me to train their staff on how to engage with non-native English speakers to conduct business, fill out forms, etc.

Once I said yes to that first parent, my life and purpose expanded. **I am grateful to say that I change lives by responding to Destiny's Subtle Moves**. May you, too, have the courage and will to say Yes to your own Subtle Destiny Nudges.

Dr. K. Mhina Entrantt
Age 66

CHAPTER 12

ADVENTURES IN THE MOMENTS

LAURA TAYLOR COX

"The past is gone, the future is to come, I can enjoy right now!"

I have learned to enjoy the moments of life as much as I can. One day, I found myself worried and bothered about something that was coming up. At that same moment, I realized that right then, where I was, everything was fine. In fact, everything was great, except that I was worried about the other thing that was going to happen. The thing I was worried about robbed me of the enjoyment of the moment I was in! I decided to enjoy the moments of my life. I decided to turn it into a challenge and an adventure.

How many moments can I consciously consider in a day, and how much of an adventure can a moment be?

I grew up reading Nancy Drew mysteries and dreaming of adventures. I lived in small-town America, and I learned that for me to have adventures, I needed to create them for myself. I found opportunities for grand adventures all around me. Whether it was in the pages of a book, playing in the empty lot across the street, exploring the creek while walking to town, or riding my bike to the library to get more books, I found adventures around every corner.

Oh! My adventures weren't anything like Nancy Drew's, but they were mine! I enjoyed smelling newly bloomed daffodils and eating fresh Concord grapes that hung on our side of our neighbor's fence. Sometimes, I would see license plates from other states and wonder how they found their way to our small town. I wondered what adventures I would go on when I could leave my small town.

Many adventures did occur. There was lots of travel and fun during which I met my husband, and we began our own adventures together. Soon, we began having children, and travel became very expensive. I began to realize that adventures were not limited to far-off lands. My children reminded me of my childhood adventures, and we began exploring the mundane of everyday life to find the adventures hidden there. Even going to the grocery store became an adventure!

However, I was always thinking about the next thing to come in the day. Yes, we may have been having an adventure at the grocery, but in my mind, I was thinking about unloading the bags and putting the food away. Or making dinner. Or getting to Tae Kwon Do class. The adventures cascaded upon one another, but I was not really enjoying them. My mind was involved in the next thing we needed to do because God forbid that I would get my kids late to any endeavor.

Until I mentioned this at the outset of this story, that moment changed my thinking.

As much as I can, I now bask in the adventure of the moment I am enjoying right now.

I have relearned that for me to have adventures, I need to create them for myself. As a child, I naturally enjoyed my moments. Much of my adult life was full of worry and stress. These stole the ability to enjoy many precious moments of my life. I cannot get those moments back, but I can make sure that I enjoy the adventures in the moments of the rest of my life.

I am every day.
Ordinary—
But with a twist.
I am unique.
The only one—
Like a snowflake.
I am redeemed.
Image Bearer—
Child of God
In my every day.
Ordinary—
I am victorious!

Laura Taylor Cox
Age 67

CHAPTER 13

REAL JOYFUL LIFE STARTED AT 70

LUCIE ROSA-STAGI

Don't let anyone ever tell you that you are too old to start a new life!

I started my online business. I started a traveling business class. I took three spiritual pilgrimages with my mentor, who helped me get over the devastation of being single after my 10-year relationship, which took me to Egypt in 2020, Israel in 2022, and Bali in 2023.

My turning 70 might have looked dim initially, as my partner left me after our 10-year relationship. Reservations for October 2015 were already made for Paris and Greece. My partner and I were going to celebrate our 70th and 75th birthdays. My sister and brother-in-law were to join us, as we were all good friends and loved spending our time together.

August 1st came, and I heard the devastating news. I know it takes 'two to tango,' but at 70, you always think that you can work any differences out. My dreams were shattered when I heard those harsh words from my partner: "I've reconnected with someone from my past, and we want to be together again. I want a divorce."

I went to Europe for my sister and brother-in-law's sake. I cried a 'river' for six months. I felt sorry for myself until I realized why I would want to be with someone who didn't want to be with me. I got into a few self-development programs because I knew that staying positive was my life-saving factor.

What was I going to do with the rest of my precious life? Then I realized no one was coming to save me!

I had to create a new plan for the life that I wanted to live. I wanted to travel more, and not only that, but I also wanted to travel only first-class; now reduced to one income, I had to think of what I could do with what I had to make more income. Also, I wanted to help my family members, leave a legacy, and live a more fulfilled life. I knew in my 40s that meant 'serving others.'

I had retired twice from my job. I was going to be an entrepreneur! And I would start an online business. All I knew how to do was answer emails, copy, and paste. But I would learn, and boy, did I learn as I went along. I learned that if you needed help online, you couldn't pick up the phone and talk to someone. Many businesses have this system, where you fill out a form, and someone gets back to you in 24/48 hours. By then, I had forgotten what it was I needed help with.

I paid for courses that didn't serve me; I paid for coaches who didn't want to really get to know me or what I needed but just wanted to teach me what they learned. After a year and a half of not giving up, I finally created my Shopify store and was ready to launch when I had this epiphany: OMG, I want to work with people, not products.

The Universe answered my call when I received an email from Tony Robbins and Dean Graziosi inviting me to join their new legacy: Self-Education as the new norm. While on a pilgrimage to Israel in February 2020, I returned to find that I had made $5,000 in just three weeks while I was away. All I did was share what I was doing with people. From that moment on, everything changed. Now, I work with a dedicated team, serving as the bridge that assists individuals in launching their own businesses organically on Social Media. We guide them to avoid the mistakes and unnecessary expenses that we once made while learning. Our work has a profound impact on people's lives, and I am grateful for the opportunity to witness the power of manifesting dreams into reality!

Don't let anyone ever tell you that you are too old to start a new life!

Lucie Rosa-Stagi
Age 78

CHAPTER 14

GOD HAS A GREAT SENSE OF HUMOR

MORIAH HUDSON

What Is Your Funny God Story?

I've always experienced God as having a great sense of humor! Especially in my life. I've always said that He has never failed me yet, but He sure likes to come close sometimes. It seems like in the really difficult times in my life, when I feel like I am free falling, He waits till the very last moment before I crash to the ground to reach out his hand, and He catches me. I am always yelling at Him, "You don't have to wait so long." His answers are always the same. "You knew I would be there."

Many times, His answers seem to come out of left field. It reminds me of the time that Kelly and I separated after eight years together. I was so lonely. I cried all the time, and the loneliness almost consumed me. I prayed to God, "Please send me someone that I can spend time with. Please send me someone so I won't be alone."

Then, there was a knock at the door. When I opened the door, there was my 6-foot, blonde-haired, blue-eyed baby brother in yellow swim trunks and a cowboy hat. He said, "I've come to stay with you for a while." Really God? You know, God, that's not exactly what I had in mind. Always the jokester.

The stars don't shine without darkness.

Moriah Hudson
Age 74

CHAPTER 15

MAKE AGE "NOT COUNT"

DR. SALLY L. CLELAND

Perceived weaknesses, innate liabilities, or limiting labels can all be diminished or eliminated.

I have been dealing with ageism my entire adult life! As a new graduate, I was minimized and marginalized as being "too young and inexperienced." Nearing my retirement, I was dismissed as being "too old and out-of-date." I was never the "right age!"

The suffix **"ism"** describes a system, principle, or ideological movement. A system is a set of things working together as an interconnected network; a principle is a fundamental truth or proposition serving as the foundation for a system of beliefs or behaviors; and an ideological movement is a philosophic or political movement based on particular ideas or beliefs.

"Ageism" exists; I do not support that any set of ideas or beliefs working together to form a chain of reasoning proves those ideas and beliefs are valid. Because of such beliefs and ideas associated with ageism, we are told obliquely and often outrightly that we are no longer valuable, employable, or worthwhile—that we have little to contribute, have lost our usefulness, and have lost our beauty and attractiveness. As a result of individuals believing and acting on such ideas, women express feelings of being invisible, dismissed, pushed aside, stepped on, and ignored. Women can become overwhelmed with feelings of emptiness and meaninglessness—having no purpose to their ongoing existence.

Commonly, we use specific parameters to select or filter out others as potential friends, partners, or lovers. Such customary parameters include age, background, upbringing, values, career choices, education, and physical appearance. But what if we eliminated such parameters? More specifically, what if age and physical appearance were not factors? Narrowing it down further, what if a man had no idea what age you were? How would he react to your inner self and to who you are as a person? Without seeing or hearing you, what would he make of your inner personality and character, and what makes you attractive such that he would want to engage with you? What is possible? Love, respect, connection, intimacy?

By accident, downloading an app for a medieval war game, I stepped way outside of my technological, knowledge, and experiential comfort zones. The game did not suit my character or personality or fulfill any of my creative or recreational needs. However, there was a global social opportunity in this game, which piqued my interest. Here I was, a 70+-year-old woman in a virtual game where the primary demographic was men 21 to 45. I discovered in cyberspace that age and appearance need not matter.

Consider the chronicle of Maxim.

Maxim expressed his frustration about being betrayed in the game—and worse, betrayed by a friend. This is a simple statement for all game players to read. No one responded publicly, but I responded privately in the chat. I did not know this player except as a fierce warrior whom most feared or spewed anger against— and that he had attacked my castle in the past. He was considering leaving the game. His emotional words about betrayal captured my attention.

Most appreciate that emotional responses to betrayal may vary. Still, they are more intense with our higher level of trust, faith, and loyalty with the one who betrays us. Betrayal is painful and can even be harmful. I shared these thoughts with Maxim and suggested he should not leave the game because of betrayal. He replied with gratitude and said he would never attack my castle again! I had pulled a thorn out of the lion's paw without intention! With sincerity, I inquired about his views on war and peace. He began earnestly, stating that the game is like real life—kill or be killed; the strong attack and conquer the weak. That's the way it is.

He was a 21-year-old professional athlete from an Eastern European country that had known its share of war. I posed: "When can the strong become the defender and protector of the weak?"

"Interesting," he responded. A single-word reply.

I shared this story: Merle, a boy 10, sat crying on the playground dirt. In front of him were several hand-dug holes in the ground used to play "pots" (a marble game). Alex, a boy 2 years older, approached the sobbing lad, asking him what the problem was. Merle said, "I was winning against Berger, and he stole all my marbles!" Moments later, there was a loud scuffle in front of the principal's office window. Opening the window, Mr. Whitehead hollered, "Alex, what's going on?" Alex replied, "Berger stole Merle's marbles; he would not return them, so I hit him." Pausing only briefly, Mr. Whitehead said, "Hit him again, Alex!" Berger was the school bully. That was my Uncle Alex, who started no fights and looked for no fights, but he finished it if there was a fight to be had. He always stepped up to defend and protect the weaker against bullies. In those days, most playground disputes were resolved by the fist. While not acceptable today, it was the norm at one time, and rarely did adults need to intervene.

Maxim said when I finished: "How old are you? I know many girls my age, and they do not talk like you! You sound wise."

Glad to no longer sound like a 21-year-old, I accepted his compliment. Maxim moves his castle next to mine when he plays the game. He is my defender and protector. When I commented on these movements being near me, he said, "Because I like you!"

Reaching out to Maxim as a human being and sharing a common experience with compassion and empathy, even though we were game opponents, connected us. Maxim never inquired again about my age; age was not an issue—being a human being was.

One story, experience, and lesson—unexpected, unplanned, unrehearsed. A person of unknown age and appearance engages with others in a virtual war game—ageism defeated.

Challenge the stereotypes associated with age by speaking up and engaging with life. Reveal yourself and do the unexpected. Stand up and stand out.

At this stage, we can step out of our comfort zones and make our age not count. Do you think you are too old and out-of-date? I do not!

Let's start **our ideological movement with our beliefs, ideas, and truths** and communicate **our chain of reasoning,** thereby shifting public perceptions of us, our capabilities, skills, wisdom, and values. The human connection is indeed ageless! I am, and always have been, the "right age!" As are you!

Dr. Sally L. Cleland
Age 74

CHAPTER 16

WHAT'S IN YOUR CUP?

SHIRLEY TURNER

You are holding a cup of coffee when someone comes along and bumps into you or shakes your arm, making you spill your coffee everywhere.

Why did you spill the coffee?

"Because someone bumped into me."

Wrong answer.

You spilled the coffee because there was coffee in your cup.

Had there been tea in the cup, you would have spilled tea.

Whatever is inside the cup is what will spill out.

When life comes along and shakes you (which WILL happen), whatever is inside you will come out. It's easy to fake it until you get rattled.

"So, we must ask ourselves: 'What's in my cup?'

When life gets tough, what spills over?

Joy, gratitude, peace, and humility? OR

Anger, bitterness, harsh words, and reactions?

Life provides the cup. You choose." Thich Nhat Hanh

Today, let's work towards filling our cups with gratitude, forgiveness, joy, words of affirmation, kindness, gentleness, and love for others.

I love this story, as it speaks volumes about so many aspects of life. Firstly, it highlights the importance of being aware of what we are carrying around and redistributing, which can cause harm to ourselves and others, often unintentionally. Secondly, it underscores the value of living a mindful life, being consciously aware of how we are feeling, thinking, and behaving. This awareness gives us the ability to respond thoughtfully rather than react impulsively.

As we embark on the timeless journey of ageless living, let us embrace each moment with a heart overflowing with love, kindness, laughter, and beauty. May our footsteps leave behind a bountiful trail of joy, compassion, and wisdom, inspiring others to live their lives to the fullest. May our story be a testament to the power of embracing life's challenges with grace and finding the eternal fountain of youth within our hearts. With every passing day, let us radiate the essence of ageless living, reminding the world that true vitality lies not in our years but in the depth of our love, the warmth of our smiles, and the richness of our souls.

Let us consciously choose what we allow to spill over into our lives.

Shirley Turner
Age 64

CHAPTER 17

EMBRACING THE JOY OF YOUTHFULNESS

SUNSHINE DEB

"You're never too old to be a kid again." – Sunshine Deb
"I challenge each of you to rediscover what brings you joy and to make time for it in your life." – Sunshine Deb

I want to share a thought that has always stayed close to my heart: the importance of staying young at heart. In the hustle and bustle of adult life, it's easy to forget the simple joy of being a child—of playing, laughing, and embracing life with unbridled enthusiasm. Yet, I firmly believe that nurturing our inner child is essential for our overall well-being and maintaining a joyful spirit.

I vividly remember the carefree days of my childhood, filled with games, laughter, and boundless energy. However, as we grow older and take on more responsibilities, we often relegate playtime to the past, thinking it's irresponsible or that we're simply too old for such activities. But age is just a number; it's how we feel inside that truly matters. I'm reminded of a phrase I often share with my loved ones: "You're never too old to be a kid again." It's a mantra that has kept me young at heart.

Recreation and play are not mere pastimes; they are essential for our overall health and well-being. They have the power to lift our spirits, infuse us with childlike joy, and breathe life into our hearts and souls. In fact, if you break down the word "recreation," you'll find it's all about re-creating your energy. It's up to each one of us to rediscover that inner child, to seek out the activities that bring us joy and passion, and to incorporate them into our lives.

For me, it's the great outdoors, yard games, creative cooking, nature, photography, and inspiring others to tap into their own energy source. I'm often called "Sunshine Deb," inspired by a passion for life, nature, and a love for sunrises. I wake up to the Beatles' song, "Here Comes the Sun," which motivates me to greet each sunrise with enthusiasm. Each sunrise is a unique, fresh start, a symbol of new beginnings, and an opportunity to meet the day with a new mindset.

I've also found immense joy in reviving old-fashioned games and traditions with my family and friends. Family Fun Day, filled with games like Spud, Dodgeball, and Kickball, has not only lifted my spirits but rekindled the childlike wonder in me and my nieces and nephews. Movie Nights, reminiscent of the drive-in theaters from my childhood, have become cherished occasions to bond with loved ones. We've added modern twists, like a giant outdoor movie screen and homemade wood-fired oven pizzas, making these nights memorable. During Christmas Eve celebrations, I have prioritized good food and quality fun time together over material presents, preserving the true essence of the holiday season and recognizing that the presence of each other's company is the true gift.

Lastly, my heart holds a special place for the Jersey Shore, where my parents used to rent a house in Seaside Heights. The sights, sounds, and smells of that place transport me back to my carefree youth, and I've found a similar haven in Ocean City, Maryland, which we visit on special occasions. As we navigate the complexities of adulthood, let us not forget the simple joys of our youth. I challenge each of you to rediscover what brings you joy and to make time for it in your life.

Nurture your inner child, embrace the boundless energy within you, and keep the spirit of play alive. Allow yourself time for recreation and re-create your soulful energy. Rekindle the kid inside of you, for you are never too old to allow the kid to come out and play.

May your days be filled with laughter, your heart with joy, and your soul forever young.

Sunshine Deb
Age 62

CHAPTER 18

CAMPING WITH THE SISTERS

SUSAN FARLING

These ladies know how to "Let Be"—no one is expected to participate in everything; everyone is invited, yet personal space and time are held as sacred and inviolable. A very special experience, not easy to come by, and one of my fondest and foundational experiences.

It's June 21, 2015.

I'm sitting on a lichen-covered rock on the edge of a small gulf island off the coast of Vancouver Island. There's a stiff breeze coming off the water. It's early and chilly.

Today is my seventieth birthday.

Behind me, just back up from the rock ledge, is the low murmur of morning greetings, a semicircle of small tents, and the smell of the first coffee of the day. I'm here with five wise, accomplished, and rambunctious aging women. We've been friends for decades. We camp together at least a couple of times a summer, reveling in each other's company.

Our conversations are revealing and immensely satisfying, carrying over from one day to the next.

Our meals are feasts prepared with familiar rhythms. We read and paint, walk alone or in twos and threes, roar with laughter, and sometimes weep. We treasure this time on the land—the smells, textures, glorious sunsets, the trees, and the raven calls.

This seventieth birthday feels like a Big Deal, a demanding transformation. This is a good place for me to contemplate what might be happening.

Maybe this inner imperative I feel to grow, to step forward, to be seen, step up, speak up, own who I am, and share what I know is part of a developmental thrust.

The old woman, the crone emerging, is shaking off ancient fears like a dog shakes free of water after a swim.

> I'll burn.
> They won't like me.
> I'll be ostracized.
> Off they fly.
> And so here I sit, late blooming.
> Transitioning. Transforming...

Eight eventful years later, another camping trip, this time on the windswept Pacific West Coast, behind a tangle of massive logs, evidence of pounding winter storms.

> And another birthday!
> How's the crone doing?

Turns out I've written and published a legacy book and given public talks on subjects I feel passionate about, like challenging ageist myths. I've shifted my professional focus from a general psychotherapy practice to supporting women and men to thrive and live vibrant, full, satisfying, and joyful lives in the third phase of their lives. My Full Circle Friends community is closer than ever, having supported beloved members of our group in their dying and death journeys.

And best of all, I became a grandmother right in the middle of a global pandemic. I was able to 'bubble up' with my beloved family and enjoy Lil's first years as a hands-on gran-gran.

The tents are up. I needed help to set up in the wind—and there's time now for a walk on the beach before supper.

What follows shares what CUPS camping has meant to the Sisters, in their words:

Margaret, 72

Our women's camping collective, the CUPS ('Camping Urban Peasant Sisters'), has been a crucial source of joy, inspiration, support, and affirmation for me for years. Our sisterly friendships have deepened, along with many happy hours frolicking in the sun, sea, and forest.

We have learned to accept and celebrate each other's contributions and uniqueness. We are learning to speak our truths and to listen. We all care passionately for our natural environment, and camping together is a kind of sacramental experience imbued with many pleasures: paddling, walking, reading, talking, yoga, cooking, and eating.

Diane, 65

Camping with 'the ladies' was a sacred space for me—apart from the sacredness, spaciousness, and beauty of the land—it was a space and time just for me, within that especially nurturing vessel of women friends. These ladies know how to "Let Be"—no one is expected to participate in everything; everyone is invited, yet personal space and time are held as sacred and inviolable. A very special experience, not easy to come by, and one of my fondest and foundational experiences.

Anke, 70

The spacious natural settings in which we are privileged to put up our little tents have allowed us the rhythm to come together and drift apart throughout the day in a flow that is genuine and nurturing for each of us. Over the decades of camping together, my chosen sisters and I have become a close-knit group of trusted friends. As a person who lives alone, being in close quarters with others while camping, where I get to experience others' habits and values up close, provides opportunities and challenges that, when I engage with them, can expand my tolerance and compassion and make me into a whole person. It can be rare and precious to find folks with whom you can work through the hard stuff. It takes time... and we take that time for and with each other.

Tysh, 70

Circles within Circles

Circling the skies, seeking connection and belonging

Circles of childhood friends, friends of friends, lessons learned friends, special friends

Moving between circles, overlapping on the edges

Circle of life

Concentric circles, ever-evolving, rotating, moving, building

Chosen or swept by capricious winds

Towards a safe place of acceptance, support, and nonjudgment

Friends of my heart

Wandering the conjoined circles

Touching down finally

Surrounded by a bubble of old friends

An invisible circle of strength that holds me true

Allows me to flutter and fly

Encourages seeking and soaring

To circle the skies always

Until death do us part

Christine, 72

Deep Connection
Magic
Sharing
Laughter
Songs
Gratitude
Support
Awe & wonder of the natural world around us

Yvonne, 69

It's a tight net we spin as we sit under the firs and the arbutus trees, bathed in the golden light and the relational ease of the early summer evening. These women, decades together, know each other's camping rhythms so well. Once, it was the children who offered the reason for our relational weave, but now, it is our love of being together outdoors that binds us. We are sisters, bound by years together under the trees, co-investigating textures of living and loving. Time loses the illusion of linearity when camping sisters converge; the magic of sea-sun-shells-sandstone-shade stretches ways of knowing and being. In our familiarity, we help each other unfold the less familiar, the less known, touching into the old ways. We camp to remember how grace, honoring, and ritual sustain life.

Susan Farling
Age 79

CHAPTER 19
MY SUPERHERO MOMENT
SUSAN "SUEZEE" FINLEY

Ever had a superhero moment?

I had mine a few moments ago.

Today, I helped 3 boys after a horrible plane crash! Yes, that's right, little ol' me!

I was walking my dog, Taji, in the park, when suddenly a small plane crashed right in front of my eyes!

A crowd of young boys started running towards the scene, 3 at first, then 5, "Oh noo… Oh nooo… Nooo…." the crowd screamed in unison… Everyone was shaking their heads in sheer horror and disbelief…

Then 2 more ran over screaming what happened???… What happened?????

More and more came running towards the ghastly scene. In the middle of the crowd, a small boy cried out, "M-m-m-my plane crashed… My plane crashed… It…It…

It… Sob… It… crashed into a big pile of dog poop!!!!"

"I ain't touching it!" shouted another little boy

Ewww…."

Everyone started backing up …

I knew I had to act fast, mass hysteria was about to ensue.

I whipped out my dog Taji's poopie bags and her doggie wipes.

I bravely put the doggie poopie bag over my hand and with one swift swoop, flung the poop right off the plane, into the field, just past the crowd.

I then cleaned and buffed the wings with some doggie wipes, and brought the small radio-controlled plane to a beautiful shine!

Poopsaster averted! The crowd rejoiced!!!!

It was epic!!!

Susan "SueZee" Finley
Age 61

CHAPTER 20

LUNCH, LAUGHTER, AND LIFE LESSONS

TINA TAYLOR

"Oh, how I would give anything for just one more lunch date with Gram. The complaints, the critiques, the imperfections... they all fade away in the light of the love we shared."

When I hear the phrase, "Let's do lunch," I immediately think about so much more than the food itself.

As a young child and teenager, I always looked forward to my weekly Saturday lunch dates with my Gram, but it was never just a routine or typical lunch. I often felt as though I was part of a traveling comedy duo, and our dates usually ended with a very valuable life lesson, even though I didn't realize it at the time.

Looking back on it now, I wonder if my Gram was the one who coined the phrase,

"The Customer is ALWAYS right!"

Gram refused to be put on the back burner as she aged and always demonstrated the importance of maintaining a strong backbone! The older Gram got, the more she felt she earned the right to speak her mind, change her mind, and use her voice. As she became older, her voice became LOUDER… and somehow, she always got her way.

Here's what a typical Saturday lunch date at Marc's Big Boy restaurant in Milwaukee, Wisconsin, looked like…

Gram would successfully park her car after seven or eight attempts to get into a space that always seemed to be way too small, but she INSISTED that "she could do it!" Even at a young age, I began to realize the importance of Gram keeping her independence for as long as she could—so I held my tongue.

As we approached the front door of the restaurant, we passed a large glass window. When the staff of waitresses (who all knew us from our routine Saturday visits) saw us coming, it appeared as though they began "drawing straws" to see which one of them would have the "absolute pleasure" of waiting on us. And, yes, I am being sarcastic!

The waitress who drew the shortest straw already knew that she would need to reseat us at least three times, either because the location of the original table or booth was too hot or too cold ("Miss, there's something blowing on me…") or the view was not up to par. I don't know what Gram expected from a low-budget, family-friendly restaurant, so it always made me laugh when she asked for a table that had a more scenic view than the parking lot. What was it that she was expecting exactly? Waterfalls and mountains?

After we were finally seated, it was time to begin the cringe-worthy ordering process—I remember it like it was yesterday!

First came the beverage order, which always started with Gram's request for a HOT and FRESH cup of coffee. The line she used was always delivered with such perfection and feeling, just like a part of a play that Gram had rehearsed for many years. "It better be fresh—I don't want anything that's been standing too long because I get a TERRIBLE HEARTBURN," Gram would say as she clutched her throat and put her hand on her chest to put emphasis on her words.

Then came the Coke request for me. It was ordered "with no ice" so that I would get more Coke that wasn't watered down. This was back in the day when free refills were not common. (There is nothing that I enjoyed more than a warm glass of Coke on a 90-degree day!)

Sometimes, during the warm summer months, Gram would be in the mood for a glass of cold lemonade. Gram's philosophy was that when life doesn't give you lemons, be bold enough to ask for them…and LOTS of them, along with extra ice, extra water, and lots of sugar packets! Why order and PAY for lemonade when you can make your own for free at your restaurant table? I'm surprised that Gram didn't make a homemade sign on the back of her paper menu that said, "Lemonade for Sale," to see if she could make some extra "pin money."

Like clockwork, after the beverage order was placed, Gram would then ask the waitress for lots of extra napkins. Why? So, she could have one or two to spare in case of a spill and then have additional napkins to put in her purse that she could use at home later. Another cringe-worthy and embarrassing moment for me at the time.

Then came the actual food order. Gram would order my cheeseburger "pink" and make it crystal clear to the waitress that it would not be acceptable for her granddaughter (me) to eat "shoe leather" for lunch.

Because Gram took it upon herself to order for me during our weekly Big Boy lunches, I think the waitresses who were familiar with us actually thought I might be deaf. Why do I believe this to be true? I think it became more than obvious after one of our regular waitresses was so excited to let Gram know that she was learning sign language and that she would soon be able to help me place my own order. Huh?

I also loved Gram's responses when she wasn't pleased with her meal. When the waitress asked her how her meal was, and Gram thought it was only mediocre, she would respond by saying, "It's nothing to write home about" or "It wasn't my cup of tea."

If Gram thought our waitress was being rude or disrespectful to her, she would say in a very sarcastic tone of voice, "You're a real sweet girl, aren't you? Your mother would be so proud. Make sure that you look hard for your tip today!" At that point, I wanted to crawl under the table.

All I could do was look at the poor waitress and mouth the words, "I'm sorry," while Gram wasn't looking.

As I became an adult and Gram continued aging, she never mellowed. Her backbone was as strong as ever, and she still always got what she wanted, even if it was becoming more difficult to please her.

I will NEVER forget one particularly hot summer Sunday evening when my dad (Gram's son) wanted to take my Gram out for a family dinner, but she couldn't decide where she wanted to go. All she said was that she wanted a "good, hot meal." My dad passed many places and offered many suggestions, but Gram stuck her nose up at everything. Her responses were, "I wouldn't give you a nickel for it," "The write-up in the paper was horrible," "I'm not in the mood for that," or a very loud and dramatic "PEW!"

It was close to 100 degrees that evening. Everyone was beyond starving, and we were probably riding on fumes at this point because it seemed like Dad had driven more than 50 miles to find a place to please Gram. She was just in the mood for a "good, hot meal," and nothing else would satisfy her.

After more than an hour of trying to find the perfect place for a "good, hot meal," we finally found a restaurant that was worthy of Gram's approval. By the time we were finally seated at our table, we were all exhausted, hot, and famished. Gram looked at the menu with a smile on her face and decided on THE PERFECT meal. When the waitress asked Gram what sounded good to her, she simply replied, "I'll have a cold turkey sandwich with potato salad and a side of fresh fruit."

We drove MORE THAN ONE HOUR to find Gram the "good, hot meal" that would make her happy, and she ordered a COLD sandwich with COLD side dishes. You can imagine the look of disgust and pure disbelief on everyone's face as Gram placed her order. But that was Gram! *She earned the right to use her voice, to speak her mind, and to change her mind without asking anyone's permission. She was bold, she was beautifully authentic, and she refused to be told what she could or couldn't do.*

Looking back at those memories, I am no longer embarrassed. I feel empowered by the example Gram set for me without even knowing it. As a kid, you never really see yourself as being your grandmother's age someday, and you don't realize how often seniors are made to feel like they no longer matter the older they get.

Gram recently celebrated her 122nd heavenly birthday. I would give anything to have just one more lunch date with her. I miss the love, the laughter, and the life lessons. I miss the sarcastic wit, the looks of disgust, and the relentless determination that she used to get what she wanted and what she paid for… or, in Gram's case, maybe even what she didn't pay for.

I'm now 61 years old, and I want to be just like Gram when I grow up.

Tina Taylor
Age 61

CHAPTER 21

THE FOUNTAIN OF YOUTH

TERESE PARKIN AND SHERYL LYNN

While many fear the whispers of age,
You embrace each chapter and every new page.
Losing the judgment, shedding the dread,
With joy in your heart and dreams in your head.
For age is but numbers and wrinkles just tales,
Of laughter, of tears, of storms and of gales.
With every day lived in joy and delight,
You redefine beauty, shining so bright.
Through life's challenges, through thick and thin,
You are the one who inspires others to win.
Living your life without fear but with fun,
Never stop your quest for all that is fabulously done.
The mirror might show a new line or two,
But your ageless spirit remains ever true.
For the fountain of youth isn't found in a cream,
But in loving oneself, in living your dream.
Your beauty is timeless in every way,
Because of your mind, youth will forever stay.
So, here's to all who choose love, awesome and grand,
Teaching us all to joyfully stand.

Embracing our age, whatever it be,
For the true fountain of youth is to live joyfully.

"The Fountain of Youth is in your mind" - Sophia Loren.

Terese Parkin and Sheryl Lynn
Age 66

CHAPTER 22

NEVER TOO OLD TO LEARN

WINNIE ANDERSON-BROWN

We grow neurons at any age. If we don't use them, we lose them.

It was the year 1993. I had enrolled in a computer course because it was clear to me that the days of using a typewriter to get my work done were almost over. As a lecturer in the Language Arts department at a teacher training institution, I could not afford to be left behind, so I invested in learning how to use "WordPerfect," "Lotus 1-2-3," and Excel. It was time to get into new technologies. I did not want to be left behind; therefore, I made the sacrifice to attend classes in the evenings after work.

I looked forward to my classes. I had fun learning how to use the computer keyboard, and the words magically appeared on the monitor. This evening started out differently from the others. Our class began late, so maximizing every moment to complete the evening's task was important.

I was really getting ahead with learning "WordPerfect." Then everything disappeared from the screen. I sat and stared at the blank screen. I felt exasperated and helpless. I had just completed typing some sentences. I watched other students continue their work while I sat and waited for the instructor to assist me. After several attempts to solve the problem failed, I was directed to move to another computer and start all over again.

That evening, I resolved to learn how to fix a computer.

Not many weeks had passed since I saw an advertisement for a computer technology diploma course. This was my opportunity. But there was a problem. I had a Bachelor of Arts Degree, but physics was a requirement. My degree is in the Arts. "What do I do?" I asked myself.

Sure enough, I got the answer to my question. I submitted my qualifications along with the following note: "I am a mature woman who knows what she wants."

I was accepted to do the diploma in computer technology. I was the only female in my class and the only educator. My classmates were working in businesses and were sent by their companies, or they were business owners themselves. Since then, I have never looked back. This experience has prepared me for the current realities. How fortuitous that I was at the right place at the right time when the World Wide Web was made available to the public. I went from an intranet with a server and workstations in a room to the Internet, where we can communicate across continents. From analog to digital computers, and when we are trying to keep up with advances in Artificial Intelligence, there is talk of quantum computers.

One of the joys of being older is that we have the opportunity to learn from past experiences and make wise decisions that benefit not only us but also all those who are willing to learn from us.

When Open AI released ChatGPT 3.5 to the public in November 2022, there were over one hundred million subscribers worldwide by January 2023. This was my cue to act and grasp the available opportunities rather than focus on the threats, real or imagined.

I used the experience gained from being around when the World Wide Web was made available to the public to decide to learn as much as I could, as quickly as I could, to put me in a position to train and guide others in the use of Generative Artificial Intelligence and more.

I am paying close attention to quantum computing developments so I can be ready to make the quantum leap when the time is right. We can never be too old to learn anything we want. We grow neurons at any age. If we don't use them, we lose them. What new can you learn today? Learn it now!

Winnie Anderson-Brown
Age 71

PART TWO
FEARLESS

Life is either a daring adventure or Nothing at all. ~ **Helen Keller**

CHAPTER 23

HOW A CURSE IN CHILDHOOD LED TO MY LIFE'S MISSION

DR. ANGELIKA CHRISTIE

After decades of not knowing my true power due to subconscious coding that I received at age eleven, I broke the curse and became a warrior for my and other women's rights to be seen, heard, and understood.

At eleven years old, I found myself in the Motherhouse of the Ursuline Nuns in Germany, a boarding school with thick stone walls that stood 40 feet tall.

Our uniform was a stern blend of navy and gray, complimented by white blouses and black patent shoes. We were allowed one bath per week without removing the singlet and bloomer to shield our view of what made us females, which could trigger sinful thoughts.

Confession was indoctrinated, as we were obliged to attend chapel twice daily.

Then came this fateful day that I will never forget: On that day, an outing led us through the nearby village. Under Sister Mary's command, we marched, avoiding glances at passersby as we were warned not to look up and especially NEVER to glance at boys.

We must've resembled penguins, moving on the cobblestones as the eyes of curious villagers followed our parade.

A distant merry jingle filled my ears, and my heartbeat jumped up in excitement – scents of cotton candy and roasted almonds hinted at a Carnival, a Village Fair. And then, amidst the allure, I spotted the bumper cars! My favorite! A body in a fiery red car beckoned, waving his arms with glee. I couldn't resist- my feet started to walk faster and faster straight into the red bumper car. I jumped in, and off we went, crashing into other bumper cars. Moments later, I was laughing joyfully and excitedly, feeling the wind in my face as we bumped and jostled.

It was a fleeting joy when I realized that I must rejoin the girl's line again—about one minute had passed when I caught up with the girls. Relief calmed my heart as Sister May didn't seem to have noticed my little excursion. I was mistaken!

Back in boarding school, the chilling moment came, "Angelika von Canal, report to Mother Superior's office immediately!" The sound of those words blasted through the Speaker System for all to hear.

Nobody was ever summoned to Mother Superior's office unless something catastrophic or very serious had happened. Panic filled my heart and stomach. Had something happened to my parents?

Rushing up three flights of stairs to Mother Superior's office, I timidly knocked on the massive mahogany door. Moments later, it swung open to reveal her imposing figure in her black habit and stiffly starched white top, out of which a withered pale face stared furiously at me. I shrieked back, and in an instant, she grabbed my ponytail and pulled me in while her icy, cold, bony fingers dug into my shoulder, unyieldingly forcing me to kneel before her as my knees hit the cold stone floor.

I trembled beneath her furious gaze. She raged, "Angelika, you've marred your future; you ruined your honor! You will NEVER have an honorable life! You may as well be a Whore!!!"

I was only eleven, yet her words ignited an unknown terror that consumed me.

Begging God for relief, darkness stopped all agony as my body gave way to meet the stone floor.

I awoke in the infirmary, only to be told of my expulsion.

Confusion rushed through my body, wiping out my innocence and coding me with self-doubt and shame.

What was my cardinal sin? A mere minute of fun in a bumper car with a boy my age.

"It might seem paradoxical that we are the most likely to find inner light when we willingly enter into the darkness of our deepest pain."

The weight of her condemnation and curse shaped my life for decades.

Trauma has a way of embedding itself deeply, affecting our lives without notice.

Yet decades later, not until I was in my forties did I rise, pledging what became my 'One True Sentence' that I now live by: **"I Break Rules for Justice, Freedom, Love, and to Stay True to Myself."**

The moral of my story:

Your past trauma does not define your future. Rise and grow into your unapologetic, magnificent Self.

Outline:

As an innocent young girl in a strict catholic boarding, my free-spirited, joyful, and fun-loving nature got hit with rules and demands that broke my spirit.

Only after decades of wondering why I blushed when men looked at me and why I was having such a hard time feeling worthy of loving fully and being fully loved did I discover where my wounding stemmed from.

A fateful day in a catholic boarding school where I was condemned to have lost my honor because I disobeyed the nuns and consequently lost every chance to live an honorable and beautiful life.

After decades of not knowing my true power due to subconscious coding that I received at age eleven, I broke the curse and became a warrior for my and other women's rights to be seen, heard, and understood. I became aware of my strengths by knowing myself for who I am: a unique, powerful, loving, and magnificent woman who stands tall in her self-confidence.

My true ONE Sentence emerged: *"I Break Rules for Justice, Freedom, Love, and to stay True to Myself."*

Dr. Angelika Christie
Age 78

CHAPTER 24

CLIMBING FOR CHANGE

ANNE LORIMOR

It's fair to say that determination and persistence are two of my strong points. Being awarded the Guinness World Record title for the Oldest Person to Climb Mount Kilimanjaro made the whole struggle and all the effort worthwhile.

I'm Anne, I'm 94, and I'm not done yet!

With only a change in number, these words have opened and closed my speeches for many years.

From the time I was a little girl, I had a vivid imagination and strong creativity. When I had an errand to run, and the way was long over difficult terrain, I saw myself flying through the air and being there instantly, with no arduous journey in between. In those days, we had no radio, television, or video games. Our family did not have the accounts for the games that did exist.

Therefore, I invented the game Wolf, where the evil wolf dragged us off to his den. This morphed into Joseph being thrown into prison on the Sabbath. Another massive game was Nickeltown, with all the roles of a small town, spread out over our lots and the adjoining lots owned by our pastor. We had a built-up agricultural section from which our baby goats were stolen one sad night.

I turned a circle of scrub oaks into a summer playhouse in New Mexico. When I saw our House Car sitting against our house, I envisioned a sturdy playhouse with only two more walls and a roof. With the abilities of my brother Ivan, this was built. Father let us use old lumber for the walls, and we were allowed to use good, new lumber for the roof if we did it without nails. I had the ideas; Ivan carried them out. My sister, Frances, said that she worked with him. I didn't know; I was off reading or looking at art books.

I was not very kind to Frances. I felt that she cramped my style and meddled with my precious possessions. I told her that she could live in the summer playhouse while Ivan and I would share the built playhouse and that we could visit each other. Fortunately for her, I spent a lot of time by myself reading, writing, and thinking, and during those times, she had Ivan to play with to her heart's content.

When I wanted to reign, we put a handsome highchair on the table in the orphanage's living room, and I sat in it in solitary splendor as the Empress of the World. Ivan was King of Half the World, and Frances was our servant. Aunt May, the matron of the orphanage and a keen amateur photographer, attempted to take our picture, but it was too dark, and the pictures didn't turn out.

As a sophomore in high school, I was asked to draw a plan for a house for our family. I really got into this and drew a house with a spacious floor plan with plenty of bedrooms, a living room, kitchen, dining room, sewing room, playroom, and a gracious verandah. I don't remember whether I included a library. Still, I probably did since that would be the most important room in the house for me, and my grandfather's house did have a library. I was happy and proud of my work, but my teacher commented, "It's far too big." *I'm happy to say that*

I finally live in a house that suits me, despite naysayers and people without my vision.

As for my talents, I have always had a flair for words. I wrote short poems, stories, and descriptions starting at about 6 and longer ones in the 5th and 6th grades. Alas, my efforts were often doomed. I showed some poems to a dearly loved teacher, and she never returned them. (Now, I keep copies of everything.)

I worked very hard on some real-life stories. Another very influential teacher saw them on my desk, and she wrote "Very good" on them. They perished when the building collapsed. I wrote several professional articles and some books while in graduate school and as a teacher. I have also written a couple of children's books, poems, and short stories, which I still hope to have published.

I am articulate verbally and have always done well in language courses. I have some Spanish, can read reasonably well in French and speak a little, and have smatterings of Greek, Italian, German, and Serbo-Croatian. I also studied and enjoyed ancient Greek and Latin and have found that that knowledge helps understand the derivation of English words.

Even as a little girl, I was quite a storyteller, and this has continued throughout my life. This was helpful when I worked as a babysitter or nanny or cared for my brothers and sisters. It has also helped me with my writing and speechmaking. I have always used a lot of gestures, and a staff member at one of my schools wondered if I could talk at all if my hands were restrained! Many people find me very inspiring as a speaker.

I have never learned to draw, but I love art. I have visited many museums worldwide and seen many paintings and sculptures in churches, parks, and other buildings. Photography is a passion of mine, and I have a good sense of design and take very good pictures.

My father's family was musical, in performance and building instruments. I don't have that talent, but I play the piano well enough to give myself pleasure. A very musical young friend said I have a good relative pitch (as contrasted with her perfect pitch). My favorite music teacher said I could learn to play well enough to be an accompanist.

Perhaps my family's talents gave me my great love of music. Opera is my favorite, and I have seen performances and concerts in many famous houses and venues worldwide. I also love other classical music, folk, hymns, golden oldies, and jazz, among other genres.

I have enjoyed many things in my life and have had some success. My innate or learned characteristics and core values have strongly influenced me. My love of adventure leads me to travel widely and enjoy trying new foods and activities. My curiosity has led to a love of continued learning and striving for new experiences, both throughout my life and even at an age when many people feel resignedly that their life is over.

My caring has led me to do volunteer work, strive to give less fortunate people a hand up, and even start a foundation to empower underserved children and youth. My visualization skills let me see incredible possibilities for my organization. My integrity inspires contributions from other people who want to give but not be taken advantage of.

My creativity helps me to see solutions to problems that others may overlook.

My girlfriend still talks about how my idea of hiring someone to be responsible for one meal to relieve her overwhelm was so very helpful. She hired her daughter to shop, prepare, cook, and serve the evening meal. Not only was my friend relieved, but her daughter developed skills that have served her well, and she was happy about having more money for herself. My high energy, often noted by people who know me, permits me to accomplish many things.

The characteristic mentioned again and again by successful people as a requirement for accomplishment is **persistence**, which I possess in spades. Once I have set a goal, I might be slowed, but I never stop. An example is the formal education I acquired from good universities, working my way through with the help of assistantships, scholarships, and occasional gifts from friends.

A more recent example is my climb of Mt. Kilimanjaro. Both climbs supported my cause of creating exciting futures for underserved children and youth. My first climb was scheduled with an experienced climber, the oldest to have climbed all the Seven Summits, the highest mountain on each of the seven continents. I registered, paid for my trip, and began to train. The day after I printed my brochures promoting the climb and the cause, I was told that the trip had been postponed for a year.

Nevertheless, I stayed with it and climbed daily with my little dog, my beloved hiking companion. I climbed and did some hiking in Colorado and northern Arizona to help my acclimatization. The date change allowed me to climb for the title of oldest woman to summit Kilimanjaro. Our group numbered 15 people, and 10 of us made the summit.

I was now the oldest woman to have climbed that legendary mountain!

About four months later, a Russian woman a little older than I climbed Kilimanjaro before we even got through the intricacies of obtaining the official title. I was deeply disappointed. I decided to make another climb three years later for the title of oldest person. At my age, one can't afford to get out of shape, so I hiked and climbed every day and swam most days, as well. Kevan, my cherished canine hiking companion, hiked with me most of the time, but he didn't care for swimming!

A little more than a year before my scheduled climb, I read that a man was planning the climb that year, and he would be a bit more than a year older than I would be when I made my climb. I immediately decided to postpone my climb for a year from its scheduled date to be the oldest person. I also decided to make that my final postponement and settle for the oldest woman if an older man made the climb in between. The man summited in July 2017 and said it wasn't hard, although he used oxygen during the final ascent.

In my opinion, this man had a marked advantage because he lived at 8,150 feet with mountains of more than 14,000 feet all around him. This compares with my 1,342 feet with the mountain on which I do most of my training, which is less than 1,000 feet higher.

Therefore, I trained very hard for the next two years, and I also had a personal trainer for the last eight months. I felt as prepared as possible even though there wasn't the opportunity for as much high mountain climbing as before.

Eight people and about 30 guides, porters, and cooks were in my group for the climb. During the climb, I was in pain from a fall on wet outdoor steps at a tent camp where we stayed during the safari we went on just before the climb. At one point, it became so severe that it interfered with my breathing.

However, I passed the oxygen level test. I was determined to make the climb since it was for my cause, and I didn't want to let down all the people who were rooting for me and my cause.

I managed to make the summit without helping hands or oxygen, as the media put it, "all on her own."

The dramatic part of the story is that when I went to see my doctor after I got home, I found that I had climbed with <u>three</u> broken ribs!

It's fair to say that determination and persistence are two of my strong points. Being awarded the Guinness World Record title for the Oldest Person to Climb Mount Kilimanjaro made the whole struggle and all the effort worthwhile.

I am an ordinary person with some extraordinary characteristics and valuable talents.

My motto is, "When you have found your focus, never quit, but pivot when necessary."

Anne Lorimor
Age 94

CHAPTER 25

NOURISH YOUR SOUL AND LIVE ABUNDANTLY!

CAROL KOPPELMAN

Life, I think, is much like a garden. And if you don't nourish it, feed it, and wait for it, it stagnates.

I've lived on both coasts and traveled all over the country and the world, always ready for a new adventure and a new thrill. Much like my parents, I'm curious about life and am always learning and growing.

My late father loved gardening; it was in his blood. His grandfather was a peasant farmer in southern Italy. Dad would spend hours in the garden, tenderly ensuring that all the vegetables in the garden lived together in peace. He'd nourish the soil—composting in climates where the soil was rich but just needed an extra boost—and amend the soil where it was more acidic and harsher. He had a green thumb; he was always successful in his efforts.

He raised us much the same way. He'd nourish our minds; our conversations at the dinner table ranged from art to politics to science. Both of my parents were well-read and well-informed and encouraged us to have a diverse worldview. We were reading at higher levels well before we entered first grade. We lived in many states; my dad was an editor and writer for technical publications, and with each move, there was a promotion. They'd take us on adventures to national parks and historical locations, which augmented our formal education, which, I might add, prepared me well for life.

As my husband says, "You eat what you grow," which I infer means you get what you put into life. That's always been my philosophy, whether by nature or nurture - and I've lived my life that way.

Sure, there have been difficult times when it felt like my life was falling apart. Twenty years ago, I was in an emotionally abusive marriage to an alcoholic. I was living under a dark cloud, which, in retrospect, I continued to enable—until one day, I woke up and got myself out of it. It took years to recover from the abuse, but thankfully, I met many new friends who encouraged my growth, augmented my soil, and nourished me while I got used to a new normal.

When I finally learned to love myself again and focus on becoming the best me, I found love again and got married once more at the age of 61. We did the whole thing—white dress, 100 guests (including my stepdaughters and step-grandsons), and I got to dance with my dad during the father/daughter dance. A precious snapshot in time that I will forever remember.

Soon after that, we both decided to retire. We'd both been in the corporate grind for decades, striving, striving, striving under cultish corporate overlords. While my husband transitioned easily into retirement—like a light switch turned off—I struggled with turning off my light switch. For months, my head was still spinning like a hamster on its wheel. What was I to do? What was my purpose?

Then COVID hit, and the world changed. Like billions of other people in the world, I was forced to slow down. I learned to cook (something I'd put off for decades as I was always working or partying). I loved it, and I was good at it. I sewed again, something I hadn't done in years.

And I wrote.

You see, I'd been a corporate and technical writer for several decades and had not really focused on anything creative during that period. I didn't have the energy. Now, I have the time for creative pursuits.

And I liked it.

So, I wrote a book about my adventures—traveling to India, traveling across the United States, my lovers, and other life experiences—good and bad. Not an autobiography but more of a lessons-learned manual—something I thought might help other women going through challenges and transitions.

I became a published author at the age of 64!

After that, I continued to contribute to other books. I loved it.

But there was still something missing. A real purpose.

I've always loved babies. Although I'm unable to bear children myself, I'm a natural nurturer. I'd always wanted to hold babies in the NICU. And luckily, after COVID, I was able to do just that. It's the best feeling in the world—like spending several hours in heaven.

About the same time, my parents moved to an independent living facility in Arizona, about four miles from us. We welcomed them with open arms as they'd lived in Colorado for many years, and we'd only been able to see them once a year.

I have many friends in Arizona, but it was nice to finally have some family living here.

And I realized that the time with my parents was precious—they were both in their 90s. Very sharp mentally but starting to have some mobility challenges.

There were many adjustments along the way—my mother could hardly walk, making my dad the primary caregiver. My dad, who had had the foresight to realize it was time for independent living, had a very hard adjustment to this new environment. Apparently, many men of that generation do, as they were used to taking care of everything, and suddenly, people are taking care of them. It's a hit on the male ego.

This was a bit hard on me as I'd never encountered them in such a vulnerable state, and as many people do when they are vulnerable, they'd lash out at those nearest and dearest to them—me.

We had some very frank conversations, which led to what I'd consider a rich adult friendship, although my mother will sometimes still talk to me like I'm 8 instead of 67. I'm sure this is not a unique dynamic.

Luckily, my dad got some counseling and decided to focus his energies on starting an art club and becoming a very active member of the garden club. He participated in an art show there. He knew everyone in the 100-resident facility. It gave him some time away from his caretaking duties.

When I visited, I was in caretaker mode or medical appointment transport for my mom's doctor visits, as my dad, a vet, would have VA transport.

My dad was always sensitive to the fact that I had a life outside of them and didn't want me to wear myself out. I was concerned that he was wearing himself out and many times insisted that he investigate caregiving services. He tried, but his heart didn't seem to be in it. Although worn out, he was devoted to my mother and concerned that she wouldn't do well with someone else.

A few months ago, while caring for my mom, worrying about my dad, and caring for my husband and another family member from afar, I nearly fell apart, both physically and emotionally. Somehow, I'd forgotten that I wasn't supposed to be in strive mode anymore, post-corporate life, and I'd been striving. I was trying to control everything in my sphere by helping, but I was controlling nothing and certainly not helping myself.

I had to create some healthy boundaries for everyone, including my parents, and I did see a change in the dynamic.

I'd forgotten to nourish my own soil. Perhaps my soil had gone fallow again, and I needed to augment and nourish it with self-care and self-love—and, in doing so, be able to love others unconditionally.

Many of us ageless stars are finding ourselves in the sandwich generation, meaning you have kids on one side and older parents on the other. And you are still serving the needs of both, sometimes at your own physical and mental peril. In the past, the sandwich generation was usually in their 40s, but with people living longer, this has changed.

I'm in pretty good condition for my age—no big health issues and fit—but I don't have the energy I had at 40. I certainly have better focus than I did, especially when I'm passionate about something, and much more refined coping mechanisms to maneuver through difficult situations. But I can wear myself out, too.

I'd urge anyone else in my situation to reach out to other caregivers and friends who are in that sandwich generation—create a coalition of sorts—a support system—so that you can learn techniques to navigate this challenging season.

I did, and it's kept me sane.

We'd finally achieved a peaceful level of stasis—the family member my husband and I had been helping was moving forward with life, and my parents had become more comfortable in their surroundings, making many friends and having many visitors near and far. I visited them at least once a week.

Then, I got the call that I knew I'd get one day. I just didn't expect to get it so soon. My mother called me and told me that my father had gone to sleep and did not wake up.

He had passed away.

I didn't believe it. Although 93, he was a fit and healthy 93. My husband and I rushed to their facility, and the manager met us at the door.

It was true.

I immediately went into emergency mode—how is my mother doing, what happened, and how can I hold her up emotionally?

The funeral home transport covered him with a beautiful American flag, as they do for all veterans, and we said our goodbyes before they transported him off-site.

I made the most difficult calls I've ever made to my siblings, all of them breaking down in tears over the phone.

I was still in emergency mode. I could not cry. Yes, I felt grief, but I had to be strong, although I felt like all my nerves were coming out of my body.

My siblings flew in within a few days, and we worked collaboratively to make this an easier transition for my mom. You see, she and Dad had been married for 70 years. At 94, she'd have to start a new life.

My dad was always the creative type—a real Renaissance man— an artist, writer, and scientist, intrigued by everything. You know, when we cleaned his room, it was like an archaeological site—a history of him—his pursuits, his interests, his ever-evolving philosophy of life. We noticed something very interesting—

although strewn with painting brushes, journals, and experiments, his living space revealed a very simple existence—as though he'd been preparing for his Almighty reward.

While we were, and still are, sifting through and finalizing the governmental and financial details that all families deal with after a loved one dies, he's in heaven, and his spirit has left this Earth completely unencumbered.

He is free.

I miss him every single day. The pain is raw.

And I envy him. I told my mother, "That lucky SOB, he's in heaven."

And she understood. My dad would have laughed out loud at my exclamation.

You see, he was an earthy sort. He lived his life to the fullest every single day. He tilled his soil, composted, or augmented it when necessary. He learned from his mistakes, and he reset.

I know that many women idolize their fathers. I never did. I loved him and liked him as a person, and I was in awe of his personal evolution over the 67 years I was lucky enough to have him.

For most of my life, I've continued to evolve, but I will now strive to do it his way—with aplomb, with love, and with generosity.

I think that's the key to vibrant living.

My mom had kind of given up for a few decades when she developed diabetes, had a heart attack, and her joints started hurting.

But she's getting back to herself. And she's doing a great job.

And I know that my dad is up there looking after and encouraging her from beyond the thin veil.

Carol Koppelman
Age 68

CHAPTER 26

LIKE A DIAMOND – THE MORE PRESSURE THE MORE BEAUTIFUL

CHERYL MCKENZIE-COOK

"You're going to be happy," said Life, "but first, I'm going to make you strong." Project Happiness
"It is not about waiting for the storm to pass... but learning to dance in the rain." Vivian Greene

"Hmmm..." said my doctor in that particular tone.

Oh crap! I thought. Not again! My stomach sank. He didn't have to tell me. I knew it in my gut. I went home and grieved. Then, I pulled myself together and made plans.

And so I began my second cancer adventure—stage 3 breast cancer, a second mastectomy, a second set of chemo and radiation. This time, I was much more prepared than seven years before. The first time, the Warrior Queen decided to fight. **Nothing** the Universe threw at me would get the better of me!

This time, the Warrior Queen had shifted perspective. I was mellowing a little, learning to be open and trust the Universe. But still... I gathered up my weapons.

The first weapon is **Indomitable Will**. I decided I would be fine. So, when the biopsy results came back, the doctor prescribed surgery as soon as possible, and he asked: Any questions?

I said: Yes. 1) When can I travel, and 2) When can I return to work?

He sat there, stunned.

I explained that I needed to attend a Christian Pankhurst Heart Intelligence retreat in three weeks. I felt strongly that it would be part of my healing and described why.

Three weeks later, after my mastectomy, wearing a surgical vest and in a wheelchair, I was on a plane en route to North Carolina. And yes, that retreat was life-changing.

At that retreat, I acquired the second weapon in my quiver— **Surrender / Letting Go**. This was very hard for me because the Warrior Queen had been trained to never surrender. Christian taught me that surrender didn't necessarily mean giving up. It meant letting go of trying to control the outcome. I was determined to learn, and as I continue along my journey, I am getting better and better at letting go of control and trusting the Universe to guide me. This is sometimes still hard for me.

The third and fourth weapons I already had and knew how to use were **Generating Positive Energy and Envisioning Positive Outcomes**. Along the way, I was formally trained in the Emotional Freedom Technique (EFT), Stress Management, and Heart Intelligence. I used Brain Wave Entrainment and Hypnosis as part of my daily practice. Recently, I have done the Silva Ultramind method, Unlocking Transcendence, Donna Eden's Energy Medicine, and first-level Reiki. I use all these to keep my energy vibrations high and to remain positive when things seem dark.

And then there was the **Fun, Laughter, and Music** bundle of weapons. Those are absolutely key! Of my many passions, music and dancing are at the top of the list! I also practice Laughter Yoga. My uproarious laugh is one of my trademarks!

But the greatest weapon of all was **Gratitude**. Every morning, as I opened my eyes and realized I was alive, I whispered: **Thank You!**

The outcome of all of that was that I went through my second cancer adventure with ease—seriously!

And I went along happily for another five years until the Universe decided I obviously had more to learn. So yes, it's a third cancer adventure. But by this time, the Warrior Queen had become softer, humbler, and wiser. She was nearer to the Wise Old Woman.

Over and over, I was told that this was a dangerous and delicate surgery and that the possible adverse outcomes included nerve and muscle damage.

Ha!! I now have twelve years of experience with the effect of a positive attitude on healing, backed up by endless scientific research. So, I announced to the doctors that I would be fine! They rolled their eyes... I dug deep and worked on myself. The outcome? No nerve or muscle damage; no pain. I was able to leave the hospital the day after surgery.

The lessons from this one were:

- Letting go of control; **really believing** that the Universe will support and nurture me.

- Asking for help.

- Gathering support.

- Advanced Positive Envisioning.

You're seeing a pattern here, right? But no fighting—just ease and joy!

Now, the Universe and I have an exciting relationship. The Universe knows that I learn best when forced to stop and learn. (I'm a slow learner, OK.) So, BAMM! Two years later, another clout upside my head. The Universe smiled and said, Let's see how much you have learned about **Letting Go!** So, on to my heart failure adventure...

I had known for the past 14 years that my heart was damaged as a result of one of the chemo drugs I was given in my first cancer adventure, but it wasn't bothering me. I had my Life to live, right? I was on a roll.... Happiness workshops, retreats, and private coaching.

Now, somehow, I had developed a virus in my already damaged heart.

I was rushed to the Emergency Room, barely breathing but protesting that I didn't want to go to the hospital. My sons ignored me and took me anyway. The result was that I spent the next year or so in a wheelchair, learning to walk and move around independently. At first, I could do very little for myself—not even stand or dress myself. My younger son came, stayed, and looked after me for two years.

So, here's what I had to let go:

- Independence. I have been fiercely independent since I've known myself. I have lived alone for many years. Now, I could not help myself.

- Dignity. I couldn't even bathe or dress myself. My younger son did all that for me. I didn't want anyone else around me.

- All the plans for expanding my business and going international. I have not worked for the past four years, so I have no income.

- Allowing myself to show vulnerability. Always the Warrior Queen and Superwoman, right? Not anymore.

- Going to live music shows, going on long adventures in the countryside, dancing—until I could regain my balance.

Here's what I did to keep smiling:

- Deepened my gratitude practice. I became even more acutely aware of all the support I had, of all the things I still had (food, clothes, a roof over my head), of my breath, and of my heartbeat—and so much more. My gratitude list grew longer and longer, and I smiled from my soul.

Among the things that I am so grateful for are my phone and the Internet! I could connect with friends here and worldwide via video, watch movies, and stream music concerts! So, when COVID came along, I was more prepared than most! No problem!

On my 75th birthday, I couldn't have the big bash I had planned, so my friend organized a Zoom birthday party for me with friends from all over the world. This turned into the most heartwarming appreciation I have ever had. I cried with Gratitude. And I danced in my room!

But the Universe is not done with me. At all. Two years ago, I was diagnosed with an autoimmune disease. Pftt!! After I cussed, I relaxed, smiled at the Universe, and said- OK, what's the lesson from this one? You know I am now a diamond, right down to my core. Indestructible.

That's just my health adventures. I have so many more.

- Tragedy and resulting PTSD at age 20.

- 2 failed marriages.

- 2 armed robberies.

- Financial collapse.

But that's for another day if you're interested.

Meanwhile, I am back on track—dancing, going to live music, and restarting my business soon! People ask me all the time why I'm so happy. I smile from my soul and say: Happiness is an Inside Job!

Cheryl McKenzie-Cook
Age 78

CHAPTER 27

WHAT'S LOVE GOT TO DO WITH IT?

CINDY MCKEE

The Experience of Choosing and Creating Love in Your Life

"We have to resist isolation." Cindy McKee

"We are all meant to have love in our lives, whether it's with a partner, friends, or family members. We are designed for connection and support rather than isolation and mere survival."
~ Cindy McKee

This story talks about the importance of having love in your life. It talks about how we are all designed for love and connection and how love is a choice in all its beautiful forms. It shares my love journey, from tragedy to triumph, and how I keep love going and growing daily.

I didn't anticipate becoming a widow at 46 with a three-and-a-half-year-old daughter. Who would be? Emma's dad and my husband, Howard, was a terrific man who touched and served many lives. He was a quiet but powerful force in our own lives. He passed just six months after his diagnosis. And so, the new journey began. Many waves of grief would arrive over the months and years but the journey was also touched by poignancy and so much gratitude for having known him.

Over the next eight years, I was responsible for raising Emma by myself. It wasn't an easy journey, but we had each other, and our relationship deepened. I dated and even entered into a significant relationship that wasn't right for the long haul but was suitable for us then. When I moved back into singlehood, I had this inner knowing that it wouldn't be forever. The right guy for both Emma and me was out there. Somehow, I just knew. And with that knowledge, I wasn't anxiously looking.

I met Bob at a personal development seminar we both attended and we became friends. I even helped him create his online dating profile as he was ready to get out into the dating world after his divorce. He lived in another state, and I initially didn't know he was "the one." Until I did. It just occurred to me, "Oh. I like this guy!" (He knew way before I did and was patiently waiting.) We were the same age, and we both had our kids later in life. We both knew this was it. We met in February and got married in September at the age of 54.

My 85-year-old mother walked me down the "aisle" to our beloved Willow Tree that Howard and I had married under at our farm. It was a beautiful full circle. I felt truly blessed to have found love again and for Emma to have a warm father figure in her life. But this is more than a fairy tale of love. We've had our ups and downs, like most relationships. Still, because of our work in personal development, utilizing the best practices of psychology and neuroscience, we've developed a deeper understanding of how we might get tripped up at times, how our dialed-in mindsets and old patterns might be getting in the way. And we continually get ourselves back to equilibrium. At this writing, we are now 17 meaningful years in.

We embrace the hypothesis that "love is a choice." We both know how easy it is to become stagnant in relationships, relying on our weaknesses and sticking to our comfortable routines. We subconsciously accept all that seems good enough; why rock the boat? But what about the passion, excitement, and laughter that came so quickly before? What we've learned, to our delight, is that it is all still in there. The embers are still burning. And we must choose to love intentionally. Even when, perhaps especially, you are not feeling it. We are all meant to have love in our lives, whether it's with a partner, friends, or family members.

We are designed for connection and support rather than isolation and mere survival. Studies show that people live longer with close friendships and relationships. But we must choose these connections with intention, whether that is rekindling relationships gone stale or pursuing new ones. We must resist isolation. Bob and I regularly reach out to friends and family. We get on the road and visit as often as we can. Despite any frustrations, we choose how we want to be with each other daily and try to make it fun, new, and growing. We pause, make regular time for each other, and turn those ordinary moments into special ones. We choose love.

Cindy McKee
Age 71

CHAPTER 28

EVERY CHALLENGE HAS A GIFT FOR YOU IN ITS HANDS

CIS AHEARN

*We learn and share so that other women can bloom and grow.
I learned that there comes a day when we are ready to process the
events of our lives safely and lovingly. We all have this gift
within us.*

As Ageless women, we become who we are through the events of our lives—the good, the not-so-good, and even the tragic. You do not get to be ageless, fearless, and fabulous with your head in the sand. It comes through experiences where we loved, lost, were betrayed, felt shame, blamed, and yet survived to become stronger and more understanding of the frailties of life. We learn and share so that other women can bloom and grow so that they may feel safe in our presence. I want to share a story about life, secret gifts, and the grace of living agelessly.

Most people I know don't know about the plane accident. Why would they? I didn't even remember most of what happened until I was forty.

I decided to go back to school because the hospital where I worked offered to pay tuition if we wanted to pursue a bachelor's degree. I thought, why not? I had almost all my credits; I just needed a few more.

As a young student, I always loved taking one elective per semester just to keep it fun. So, when I went back, I took a Creative Writing class. Our last assignment was to write a story about a "trauma" we'd experienced. The word trauma was not as popular back then.

So, I went home and thought, "Why not write about that?" The plane crashed. I had very little recall of the event up until then. We had not had a "debriefing" of it at all. We never really spoke of it. In fact, the next day, my mother contacted my dad (they were divorced, and he was an airline pilot), and we were immediately put on a plane back to Miami, where he picked us up. He took us on another small plane to visit family in Tennessee. I never feared flying with him, yet it took me a long time to fly comfortably in a small plane with my stepdad again. Years later, I realized that my stepdad saved our lives with his choices that day.

At first, I started with very little recall. Yet, it seemed that this fantastic mind we all possess opened the floodgates, and suddenly, every little detail came flowing back: the sounds, the terror, the words "MAYDAY, MAYDAY," the sense of urgency, the planes overhead, the Coast Guard helicopter, and so much more. I had not remembered any of that.

As the details flowed in from wherever they had been stored, I wrote and wept. I felt fear, shame, confusion, anger, misunderstanding, and release. I could see all the very tiny details: how the beach seemed so far away, my cat's basket floating nearby, the raft and my parents (both with broken, bleeding noses) leaning into the raft to keep the blood out of the water, my little brother hanging on like it was an adventure. It all flowed onto the paper.

After I finished and slept, I woke to this very clear information. My brain, soul, spirit—whatever you want to call it—had done something unique that day by shutting me down throughout that whole event. It had protected me. It had put my mind to sleep. I did everything I was told: "Unlock your seatbelt, climb into the raft, hold the cat," and more. But, until that evening in Denver, I had not remembered.

Sometimes, I hear people beating themselves up because they cannot do more, yet there are times when checking out is better for us. It is a secret defense mechanism—the gift—to save us from traumatic events until we can see them through clearer eyes.

I had no idea that the events of that day were still stored in my body and mind.

Yet, as I released it onto paper, I felt peace and gratitude to my most profound mind for protecting me and doing whatever it took to help me survive. I learned to appreciate significantly how this incredible mind and body have taken care of me and continue to do so.

I learned that there comes a day when we are ready to process the events of our lives safely and lovingly. We all have this gift within us. We just need to trust it and feel safe sharing it.

That inner strength comes from living—genuinely living—your life on your terms through your experiences. The good and the not-so-good. It's about learning. It is the power that we develop as we grow as *Ageless Women*. We are *Sages* of forgiveness and understanding. And we are here for you. Just ask!

Cis Ahearn
Age 70

CHAPTER 29

FEARLESSLY EMBRACING JOY: A TALE OF TRANSFORMATION

DEBBIE PREDIGER

A potent determination to forge a different path coursed through her. She resolved to resurrect her joyful, playful self and to breathe life into once-deemed-impossible dreams. These dreams rekindled their luminance, fueled by her unwavering resolve.

In her world, impossibility surrendered. Dreams whispered, and together they proclaimed: "I am possible."

In a world that once knew no limits, a spirited little girl embarked on a journey, her heart echoing with the beat of endless potential. "I can't" never found a home in her vocabulary. Instead, "Yes, I can" became her anthem, carried by the breeze. Her life became a dance of adventure, a rhythm of excitement, and a chorus of playfulness.

Imagine this: a slender girl with a cascade of freckles, hair tied in mischievous pigtails, perched barefoot on the back of a majestic horse named Red. They weaved stories with every ride through the enchanted woods. Red was more than a horse; he was her confidant, privy to her deepest secrets and audacious dreams. Beside a tranquil stream, they'd pause, sharing hours of conversation or drifting into a peaceful midday slumber. An unspoken connection erased the weight of being unseen.

However, school painted a different picture. She became a master of blending in, watching those who effortlessly balanced mischief and admiration. Beneath her shyness lay a sea of fear—fear of standing out, being "too much," and drawing attention. Her path was to blend, to shrink into the background.

Her curious eyes observed her classmates, who seemed to find a delicate balance between mischief and admiration. She watched their boldness in her quietude and admired their ability to shine without hesitation.

Beneath her shyness lay a storm of unspoken desires and hopes that yearned to escape the confines of her heart.

But fear gripped her—the fear of standing out too much, drawing unwelcome attention, and inviting unnecessary scrutiny. So, she chose a path of subtle presence, navigating bustling hallways and classrooms with the quiet grace of a breeze.

Outside the structured walls of the school, amidst the embrace of the woods and the companionship of Red, she found solace in being her genuine self. ***The world around her transformed into a canvas of endless possibilities, and her imagination painted vibrant scenes across the landscapes of her mind.*** Together, they reveled in the unspoken understanding they shared, their dreams extending far beyond the borders of the forest's embrace.

As she matured, society's expectations settled upon her shoulders like a weighty veil, causing her dreams to be carefully tucked away like precious heirlooms too delicate for the "real world."

Gradually, her perspective shifted, and she began to perceive herself through a lens shaded by what she believed were limitations.

The years marched on, leaving behind the echoes of her unfulfilled dreams. Until one pivotal day, the resonance of motherhood echoed, casting a tender and luminous glow upon the dormant embers of her forsaken aspirations. With her children as willing partners, she rekindled the magic of imagination, infusing life into dreams once tucked away. The canvas of her childhood dreams gained renewed purpose, now adorned with shades of elation and awe.

As her children's universe enveloped her in sheer delight, a gentle wish took root within. Contemplating the moments she had let slip by and the dreams she had stowed away under societal expectations, a transformation stirred within her.

A potent determination to forge a different path coursed through her. She resolved to resurrect her joyful, playful self and to breathe life into once-deemed-impossible dreams. These dreams rekindled their luminance, fueled by her unwavering resolve.

And so, a remarkable transformation unfurled. No longer content with the role of an observer, she stepped onto the stage of her life as a dream-weaver. *Empowerment became her armor, and her steps were guided by a powerful vision that saw the improbable as attainable. Miracles flourished in her wake as ordinary moments underwent a metamorphosis, emerging as extraordinary occurrences. Her world began to thrive on the promise of hope, which she generously shared with those fortunate to walk beside her.*

Embracing her playful side, she found the secret to unleashing endless imagination. Laughter transformed into a guide, like a compass leading her through life's adventures. Play became more than a notion; it was now the beating heart of her creative path. With mindfulness as her trusted friend, she discovered a rhythm that matched her deepest wishes.

Dreams that once seemed distant were now woven into her everyday existence, shining like stars to light her way.

Yet regrets lingered, whispers of missed moments lost in the shadows of conformity. Determination ignited, pledging to infuse life with boundless joy, releasing the playful spirit imprisoned within. Dreams resurfaced, expanded, and turned tangible. The impossible murmured its challenge, met with a resolute reply: "I am possible."

A spark of joy ignited a blaze of desire, pulling dreams closer with irresistible force.

Her creed shimmered in the stars: thoughts shape the world, and the universe conspires in our favor. Tools emerged from these beliefs, guiding her through life's tapestry.

Once carefree, she set aside her dreams for practicality. Yet, her rediscovered spirit lit a guiding light for others. She called them to play, create, and lead, weaving souls into a fearless tapestry. Big dreams, once daunting, found a home in this symphony of possibility.

In her world, impossibility surrendered. Dreams whispered, and together they proclaimed: "I am possible."

"I am possible" became her powerful belief woven into her life. It announced her unwavering faith in making dreams real, a light that banished doubt. She lit the way for others, urging them from doubt to dazzling potential. She encouraged them to dream, find joy in play, and boldly lead. Together, their courage broke the chains of limitations.

Debbie Prediger
Age 61

CHAPTER 30

DANCING IN THE RAIN

DEBI LYNN

"One rainy afternoon, as Debi and Shauna watched the raindrops dance on the windowpane, they realized that life was much like the rain. Sometimes, it poured relentlessly, and the storm seemed never-ending. But eventually, the rain would subside, and the sun would shine again."

It was a gorgeous afternoon in Independence, KS, a tiny town where Debi and Dan resided with their two adorable children, Shauna and Robert. Their hearts were filled with joy as they watched their children grow, cherishing every moment of their young lives.

Robert, who was 2 ½ months old and in good health, was adored by his parents and his sister Shauna, who was two years old. Their home was filled with their family's love and laughter, making it cozy and joyful. They delighted in the simple joys and looked forward to new adventures with the kids.

But catastrophe struck unpredictably one terrible day. Robert fell ill unexpectedly, and despite all efforts, he died. The unbearable loss left Debi and Dan overcome with sorrow and anguish. They felt as if their world had collapsed, and the pain of losing their precious baby boy was too much to bear.

Throughout the storm of emotions, Shauna remained the beacon of light. Although she was too young to understand the loss, her innocent laughter brought moments of joy amidst the pain.

As months passed, Shauna grew, her sparkling eyes reflecting the love and innocence that surrounded her. She became more than a sibling; she was a healer, mending the hearts of her grieving parents. They soon found solace in watching her milestones, knowing that her journey was a testament to life's continuity.

The grieving process was not linear but filled with ups and downs. Debi and Dan felt hopeful some days, remembering the joy Robert had brought to their lives. On other days, they were overwhelmed by sadness, feeling an emptiness that seemed impossible to fill.

Through it all, Shauna became their beacon of hope. Her innocence and boundless love reminded them of the beautiful family they still had. The love for Shauna did not diminish their love for Robert; it expanded it. Debi and Dan found solace in sharing stories about their baby boy with Shauna, keeping his memory alive in their hearts.

Shauna, too young to fully understand the loss, brought her own unique brand of healing. Her laughter became a balm for their pain, and her hugs were a reminder that life still held moments of happiness.

Slowly, they learned to live with their grief, acknowledging that it would always be a part of their lives. They allowed themselves to feel the pain when it surfaced, not suppressing it but allowing it to wash over them like waves. And as they faced their grief head-on, they began to see moments of joy emerge once more.

One rainy afternoon, as Debi and Shauna watched the raindrops dance on the windowpane, they realized that life was much like the rain. Sometimes, it poured relentlessly, and the storm seemed never-ending. But eventually, the rain would subside, and the sun would shine again.

As Shauna grew older, the pain of losing Robert never vanished, but it no longer held them captive. They allowed themselves to be happy, knowing that happiness didn't diminish their love for Robert or grief. Life moved forward, and though Robert's physical presence was gone, his memory lived on in every step Shauna took and every smile she shared. His tiny footprints left an indelible mark on their hearts, guiding them toward hope, healing, and love.

They danced in the rain, knowing that even amidst the pain, life was still beautiful. With every new day, they learned to cherish the gift of life for themselves and Robert.

Debi and Dan had learned a valuable lesson: life could be bittersweet, but their love for their children and the memories they created would be cherished forever. In the delicate balance of grief and joy, they found a way to move forward, with Shauna's bright smile leading the way.

Debi Lynn
Age 67

CHAPTER 31

EMBRACING THE AGELESS SPIRIT: TALE OF RESILIENCE AND FEARLESSNESS

DEBI LYNN

One day, realizing things had to change, she hopped on a bus with the two kids and embarked on a journey of self-discovery and renewal. She packed her baggage, gathered her kids, and embarked on a daring adventure, moving from area to area, searching for opportunities to construct a brighter future.

Debi's existence commenced at a young age when she was with her hero father. She moved from country to country, dwelling on air force bases with enclosed fences regarded as prisons with many regulations. The family moved each year as the child of an Air Force B52 Tailgunner, proud to serve his country.

Debi endured more hardships as a child than many people her age may want to fathom. Life had tested her with losses, struggles, and pain; however, Debi refused to permit those instances to define her every day. She reminded herself that life was a gift and determined to make the most of it.

Debi's journey changed with the loss of her beloved child. The pain was unbearable, and the void in her heart seemed endless. But amid her grief, Debi discovered energy. She channeled her love for her child into a driving force to create a better existence for her remaining two kids, Shauna and Matthew.

Debi faced numerous challenges. She struggled to make ends meet, endured abusive relationships, and suffered many losses along the way. The most challenging loss was her beloved father. Yet she never allowed these tragedies to interrupt her spirit. Instead, she used every setback as a stepping stone toward her dreams.

One day, realizing things had to change, she hopped on a bus with the two kids and embarked on a journey of self-discovery and renewal. She packed her baggage, gathered her kids, and embarked on a daring adventure, moving from area to area, searching for opportunities to construct a brighter future. Despite facing uncertainties and doubts, Debi held her head high, teaching her children the value of perseverance.

The road was rocky, and Debi faced many closed doors when seeking work. However, her determination was unshakable. She decided to take matters into her own hands and embrace entrepreneurship. With a renewed sense of purpose, she discovered her passion for graphic design and art.

Debi poured her emotions into developing beautiful and meaningful artwork. Art became her safe haven, a canvas on which she expressed her pain, resilience, and hope for a better tomorrow. Her graphics business became a testament to the power of perseverance, creativity, and the invincible human spirit.

Despite her success, Debi always remained humble, remembering life's lessons. She gave back to the community, helping those struggling and offering them a glimmer of hope, just as she had received in her darkest days.

Amid the challenges of raising two children alone, Debi always remembered the importance of cherishing each day as a precious gift.

She taught Shauna and Matthew to see beauty in the simplest things, to be grateful for every sunrise, and to find strength in the face of adversity.

As the years passed, Debi's story touched the hearts of countless women across the nation. She became an inspiration, a symbol of resilience and fearlessness, reminding everyone that age was just a number and life was worth living to the fullest, no matter the circumstances.

Debi secured a bright future for her own family. However, her greatest accomplishment was the impact she had on the lives of others. *Women from all walks of life found power in her story, and her message of living each day as a gift resonated deeply.*

Debi's legacy lives on in the hearts of those she touched. Her tale is a beacon of hope for women everywhere, reminding them that they can embrace an ageless spirit and fearlessly conquer life's hurdles irrespective of their struggles.

Today, Debi's journey is about surviving and thriving despite the odds. It is about finding splendor in life's imperfections and celebrating each day with gratitude. Her story serves as a reminder that each day truly is a gift, waiting to be unwrapped with the boundless enthusiasm of an ageless soul.

Through the power of her experience, Debi's goal is to open a non-profit organization to empower women facing similar hardships. She will provide them with resources, mentorship, and a support network, helping them rise above their challenges and discover the ageless strength within themselves.

Debi Lynn
Age 67

CHAPTER 32

PLAYFUL PAWS OF COMFORT—BLESSINGS ON THE JOURNEY

DENISE YONKERS

With every sunrise, we embrace the gift of another day, for time is a precious treasure bestowed upon us with grace.

My husband John and I lived in a quaint little neighborhood in a northwest suburb of Chicago. We were a couple who shared a deep bond and a love for each other and our three cats, Binky, Sharky, and Buddy. We married a bit older and decided not to have children but would adopt pets. As the years passed, they became pets and beloved family members.

John and I had always been there for each other through thick and thin. One day, John fell seriously ill with fourth-stage lung, bone, and spine cancer. It was a difficult time for both of us, but we faced it with unwavering love and support.

Throughout John's illness, Binky, Sharky, and Buddy seemed to understand something was amiss. Buddy, a feral cat released from a shelter in Chicago, had found his way to our door just months before the diagnosis! He came a long way to find us! It was as if he sensed that someone needed him! Buddy would stay close to John, snuggling up to him. He would lay right on the left side of John's chest where the cancer had begun, purring softly as if trying to comfort John in his own unique way. Altogether, our angel kitties brought John such a sense of peace and solace during those trying days. His face would light up when Buddy snuggled next to him, and he would forget about his pain for a while.

John often remarked that the cats played a significant role in his last days, especially Buddy, who showed up at our front door! He would say, "It's as if Buddy knew exactly when to find me and the exact time that I needed him." Buddy was the feral cat that just showed up at our door one Saturday night. We welcomed him into our home and adopted him. The affection and warmth of all three of our pets made all the difference.

John and I cherished every moment with each other and our feline companions. Their playful antics and affectionate gestures added joy to daily routines and always brought a smile to our faces.

However, the day did arrive. One evening, John passed away peacefully in his sleep at his daughter's home, where we had all gathered. I was devastated, and when I returned to our home, totally exhausted, the house felt emptier than ever. Grief weighed heavily on my heart, and I struggled to find comfort in the familiar surroundings that were now filled with memories of my beloved husband.

But amid my sorrow, Binky, Sharky, and Buddy became my pillars of strength. They would curl up beside me, sensing my sadness, and their soothing presence offered me solace. I found myself pouring my heart out to them. In return, they showered me with unconditional love, the kind that only animals seem to possess.

The routine of caring for them gave me a sense of purpose and responsibility. They were my family, my constant companions at home. Loyal and understanding, they never failed to bring a smile to my face and love to my heart.

With the continued love and companionship of my four-legged family, I found the strength to move forward while cherishing the beautiful memories of my life with John. Though he was gone, I knew our love would forever reside in my heart.

Our love story was not just about our affection for each other; it was also a tale of our deep bond with our furry family members. Binky, Sharky, and Buddy taught us the true meaning of unconditional love.

I was blessed that our home remained filled with the spirit of love, the legacy of a beautiful love story that transcended time and the boundaries between humans and animals.

Denise Yonkers
Age 69

CHAPTER 33

SURVIVE AND THRIVE
DIANE BERG

For my 65th birthday, I was served divorce papers. After 35 years of what I thought was a happy marriage, my husband chose to have an affair with our neighbor and friend (well, ex-friend now). Despite my earnest efforts to salvage our marriage, it became painfully clear that our union was irreparably damaged. I must now embrace the reality of being a newly single woman. Though the circumstances are far from ideal, I am resolved to approach this new chapter of my life with strength and determination. While the pain is undeniable, I am committed to seeking joy and personal fulfillment moving forward.

However, I am no stranger to pain and healing. In the past, I have endured great heartache, having lost my only child after a long and arduous battle with cancer when he was just 32 years old. Through that experience, I learned how to navigate through anguish, finding strength and resilience within myself.

Recognizing that I possess the power to overcome adversity once again, albeit under different circumstances, I embarked on a journey of healing. Seeking professional guidance, I hired a life coach to assist me in navigating through this difficult period. Additionally, I recognized the importance of nurturing my physical and mental well-being, so I enlisted the help of a personal trainer to shape my body as well as strengthen my mind. I also joined a yoga class and started practicing tapping, a technique that helped me release emotional burdens and rediscover my inner strength. I began writing in my journal again, a safe place to express my emotions, fears, and hopes. When I look back at what I wrote during this painful time, I hardly recognize that person.

As part of my personal growth, I constructed a vision board, a visual representation of my aspirations and dreams. This tool not only provided motivation but also acted as a constant reminder of the life I envisioned for myself. Despite the betrayal and pain that marked the end of my marriage, I dared to dream of finding a new partner, someone who would embody loyalty, love, and a shared joy for our retirement years. I set new goals for what I wanted to achieve over the next 12 months, both personally and in my career. Through these various methods, I gradually rebuilt my life, piece by piece.

With perseverance and patience, I eventually crossed paths with the man of my dreams, the man I had described on my vision board. On my 72nd birthday, he surprised me by proposing. As I stand on the precipice of this beautiful chapter in my life, I am filled with optimism for our future together.

Through the highs and lows, the trials and triumphs, I have grown stronger and wiser. Life is a tapestry woven with both pain and joy, and it is up to us to embrace the journey and create our own destiny.

Maya Angelou said, You cannot really know where you are going until you know where you have been.

Buddha says, "Pain is inevitable, suffering is optional."

I chose not to suffer but rather to build an amazing future full of joy and excitement for my next chapter and you can, too.

Diane Berg
Age 73

CHAPTER 34

FINDING PURPOSE AT THE ART FAIR

JO DIBBLEE

Have you ever wanted to sell everything, hit the road in your RV, and live your dream? My husband and I did just that; we sold everything in Canada and leaped off the porch. Some said we were crazy. We were entering our golden years, and we were told this was a time to relax. Our haste to live while we can likely terrify some of our loved ones.

It wasn't as though we hadn't thought about it for years, but we had not mentioned it to anyone.

Once we decided, we moved fast. It was now or never. Living fearlessly makes life worth living.

It all began in 2016 in Baja California. We had gone to Mexico to escape winter, fell in love with the culture, people, and lifestyle, and knew we could make a difference.

By 2017, we were thoroughly entrenched and sought ways to give back and serve. And then it happened...

I remember the day like it was yesterday. My life changed for the better that day!

It was a beautiful sunny day in Los Barriles, BCS, Mexico, and we decided to check out the art market that day to support the local artisans. One of the vendors was a nearby orphanage. We had heard so much about these children, and I wanted to learn more about the orphanage and how we could support them.

In short order, we spotted the children. There were 25 children that day. I was so drawn to the children that I sat near their table with our dog. Within minutes, a couple of the girls came over and sat with us, and before I knew it, almost all the children had joined us on the grass.

The children began to play with Mia, our dog, while Michael and I just watched and listened to the laughter. Mia, who loves children, began to show all her tricks, and each time they giggled and clapped, she did more.

And then something remarkable happened. The youngest of the children, Samatha, looked directly at me. She was staring intently at my sunglasses. I thought she would reach over to take them off my face, but no, what she did instead touched my heart and soul. Samantha leaned into me, touched my cheek, and then kissed me. The tears welled up while I told myself, no, you cannot cry in front of these kids. I stood quickly and explained I'd be right back, using a trip to the baño [bathroom] as my excuse. This little one was so tiny. She was not even two years old.

One of the adults told me, "You look like her mother," with that, I could no longer hold in my emotions. I had to take a walk and let my tears fall out. Ten minutes later, a bit more composed, I came back.

We stayed with the children until the market closed. After meeting the children and adults that day, I was convinced I had to start a not-for-profit to serve these children and those in deep need. It was a crazy, ambitious idea I had been concocting for months.

But how? And NOW? I was a fifty-six-year-old Canadian living in a foreign country who spoke little to no Spanish at the time. How hard could it be?

We arranged for the site visit the following week. I don't know what I expected. I had never been to an orphanage before, so I had no frame of reference. When we arrived, I was pleased to see the children were clean and fed, but they needed more necessities. On this day, none wore shoes because they kept their shoes for school. I could tell they did their best to care for the children, but funding was limited. They nearly always ran out of money before they ran out of the month.

One of the scenes that struck me hard was their play area. It had a patch of sand and a few pieces of broken outdoor equipment. Off to the left was the workshop building, where the wares they sold to raise money were made. Immediately, I noticed no safety equipment, yet the children used heavy-duty machines daily. The thought of a child suffering an accident because there were no safety glasses or gloves made me shudder.

Next, we toured the dorms, which may have made me the saddest of all. The boys and girls are separated by a floor in a two-story cinderblock house. And although a caretaker slept in the boys' dorm at night, the older girls cared for the younger ones. Imagine being a young child, waking up at night from a bad dream with no one to comfort you, having been taken away from your parents.

Each bed was perfectly made, but something needed to be added. There was not a single pillow. I thought of those little ones laying their heads down every night. Something so basic as a pillow was a luxury. The bathrooms desperately needed repair, and there wasn't hot water for the showers. Later, we learned water was delivered to the orphanage, and it wasn't uncommon for the tank to run out before the month's end. Two bathroom doors hung perilously to a frame held by wire; the need was real.

There was no personalization in the boys' section, with only minor touches added in the girls' dorm. A memory flooded my mind of my own children's rooms. Each had personalized their rooms with so many little pieces of their lives. A childhood room is a part of growing up, claiming your space, and developing your identity. Yet, there were no signs, drawings, posters, or anything with their names for these children.

I felt sad and a bit overwhelmed. These children had already lost so much. After touring the facility, we sat outside to enjoy the sunshine. The girls loved my phone and taking pictures. Being together and watching them interact with us naturally, I realized how children are shaped to become resilient; all they ask for is love and attention.

They invited us to play volleyball with a vinyl ball over a rope net. Since our Spanish skills still needed improvement, we played a game and used hand motions. We decided Michael would be on the girls' team, and I would be with the boys. We didn't care about the points or keeping score; it was all about the time shared. After a while, we laughed so hard that no one could even hit the ball. In the end, we decided the team I was on had won. Not that it mattered, but there was celebrating and dancing. For a few minutes, all that mattered was the laughter.

After the game, we bought pizza and pop to celebrate, and the kids devoured every bite.

We left the orphanage better humans than when we arrived. These children had served us much more than they knew. I have a few treasured photos from that day, but the emotional impact will forever imprint on my heart.

The idea of Team Humanity Baja was morphing every day. Soon, it became much bigger than I could have imagined and was far more ambitious than anything I had ever done. Seeing the need firsthand further pushed my desire to do whatever I could. It's impossible to unsee extreme poverty and, worse, the longing for love in their eyes and do nothing.

Team Humanity Baja had not only taken shape but was also evolving. We would become an umbrella, grassroots society focusing on four distinct areas and our mission: elevate, educate, and empower, creating sustainable change while respecting culture. I will never forget the day Samatha changed my life.

Helen Keller said it best: ***"Alone, we can do so little; together, we can do much."***

Living our dreams has only strengthened our resolve to live fearlessly, no matter what.

Jo Dibblee
Age 63

CHAPTER 35

A CRYSTAL-CLEAR PASSION

JOANNE SALVADOR

Do what you love and love what you do, It's as simple as that. Everything returns to fill you with joy, excitement, and passion. Age has absolutely no limit on this.

Every great love starts with the taking of a hand, and ends on the day it falls lifeless from yours. I have lived two lives. In the first one, I dreamed my dream, and it was more than I ever could have wished for. It ended on the day my husband died. The life I have now is not the one I wanted, but it is the one I now have. Listen to me then, and I will tell you a story…

Ten years have passed. In one way, it seems like only yesterday, in another, a lifetime ago. I remember it all in great and vivid detail, so much I want to forget, and yet, always want it all to remain in my memory forever. What I didn't realize back then is that what I thought was the end of my life would become the beginning of another one.

At this time, I would only leave the house at night to go for long walks with my sister Susan. I didn't want to run into anyone who knew my circumstances and have to struggle trying to answer questions I didn't want to. It felt safe in the dark, where no one could see me crying.

One particular evening in the early fall on the path we always walked, a huge hill of sand appeared in the park across from our houses. It was put there for construction work. It was a clear night, the sky filled with stars, lit by a bright full moon. The dozens of lamp posts reflected on quartz stones shining brilliantly like diamonds flung upon the sand. It was magical. I decided to try climbing up the hill. With nothing to grasp onto, I kept sliding back down. My sister nearly died laughing witnessing this less than athletic attempt.

When I finally made it to the top, I just sat there and watched as the trees swayed in the breeze, the dark blue and gray clouds drifted by, illuminated by glimmering moonbeams. My first thought was, "All this beauty is wasted on me."

I dared my sister to climb up and watched her follow the same fate of slipping and sliding backward. When she finally made it, we sat up there together and began gathering the sparkling quartz stones into our pockets to take home for our gardens. Suddenly, a police car pulled up and shone a blinding light on us, and yelled, "Get down from there, the park is closed." We quickly slid down the other side of the sandhill and ran laughing all the way home. It was the first time I had laughed in a long, long time. And, it felt good.

I never would have thought this would be a turning point. From that moment on, the beauty of nature became my constant companion. There was magic and enchantment all around me, all I had to do was just look...

I inherited my childhood home from my parents only a few months before my entire life as I knew it was about to unravel. My sister Susan was left my grandmother's house right next door. There is a long winding path that leads between both houses. We used to joke that we could run back and forth in our bathrobes and fuzzy slippers whenever we wanted. This was no longer a joke, it was now a reality.

My childhood home is huge. As I looked around my new surroundings, deep down, I knew my circumstances could have been a lot worse. The little white stucco house I had shared with my husband for 40 years could fit in my new home three times over. Despite this, I kept and still have my old house till this day. Though this was more than I ever had, I would exchange it all in a heartbeat...

Since there was nothing I could do about it, I surveyed my new surroundings. Turning first to the tremendous sunroom in the back. "OK", I thought, "This is quite a blessing." First, I took every living thing from my old house. My tortoises, all my in-house and outdoor plants... I removed them all and set them up here, their survival being most important.

I began creating a sanctuary for myself with my animals and my plants. There was much solace in this. It helped me to retain my sanity and find some peace of mind.

There were other rooms here filled with my mother's antiques. Many of them are massive. I would return to my other house periodically and bring back and combine my favorite pieces with what was already here. I surrounded myself with a mixture of what already existed with my own collectibles, art, books, and classical music. Slowly, I began to appreciate what I had created. Sometimes, upon returning with my own belongings and looking for a place to put each one, an odd sensation would come over me. For a split second, I lost track of time. It seemed like both past and present overlapped and melded together. This still happens even now. I can only say it is a very bittersweet feeling...

I had become somewhat agoraphobic at this point and had never left the house alone. Then, Covid-19 hit, my sister Susan was away and it was a beautiful fall day. The leaves were glowing in orange, yellow, and red hues, swirling around in the wind and falling gracefully to the ground. It looked like they were dancing. I desperately wanted to be out in it. I had seen a post advertising a garage sale and decided it was within walking distance. I thought to myself, "I can do this," Stepping way out of my comfort zone, out the door I went.

Upon arriving, sparkling in the bright sunlight, creating beautiful diffused rainbows, was a tremendous collection of Waterford Crystal. For five dollars a piece, no less. Completely mesmerized, I acquired about 50 pounds of crystal on the spot. I asked the seller if he could help me get it home. "Sure," he said, "I can lend you our wagon." I told him I didn't drive, thinking he meant a station wagon. "No, dear, this!" And he handed me a very old rusty little kids' red wagon and threw all the crystal in it. Adding "Just bring it back right away.'" "Oh, oh," I thought, "this can't be good. " as visions of disaster circled through my mind. I weigh only ninety-four pounds, so fifty is more than half my weight. Seeing no option or alternative, I had to give it a try.

Carefully, I started to pull this incredibly heavy wagon down a steep incline. The wagon started pulling me and I had an extremely hard time holding onto it. So, there I was a seventy-year-old, sort of agoraphobic woman pulling a broken-down child's wagon filled with fifty pounds of crystal. I was ridiculously proud that I had gone out and got everything back home safely. However, this little incident caused me a lot of physical pain, even though mentally it had done wonders. It was actually a very good trade-off. I was in agony for several days. While recuperating, I was haunted by the fact that the precious collection was not appreciated by the heirs at all. While cleaning and placing them in my house, a thought struck me, "Maybe I should teach a class on collectibles and heirlooms?" As I arranged the dazzling pieces, I grouped them together, which ended up resembling a crystal palace or cave, like in Mary Stewart's book *The Crystal Cave*. A treasure trove. So, my class "Secrets of Treasure Hunting" came into being. Continuing Education loved it. The class attracted so many students, there wasn't enough seating. I parlayed it into four more classes. It is a joy to be teaching again.

There are some who live only for and by the special and the unique never for the ordinary or mundane. I was like that once, and now am once again. I have regained this way of living, and it is remarkable.

I always knew, from my earliest and happiest days, when I had nothing yet everything that truly mattered to just do what you love and love what you do. It's as simple as that. Everything comes back around to fill you with joy, excitement, and passion. Age has absolutely no limit on this.

So, why not soar freely like a bird above the clouds as you pass countless people on your journey, in this ever-changing world?

As I drift through the storms and dark clouds of life, I never forget, in those deepest and darkest moments, there is a bit of humor, even enjoyment, to be had. We weigh our tears and our laughter. Life is not perfect, but there are many perfect moments to embrace in it. Everyone has a story that begs to be told. Many of us will become the heroine in our own tale, and this is a wonderful thing to accomplish. We are all capable of writing our very own happy endings. As surely as the sea washes up on the shore, and the moon shines above, the possibilities are endless.

May the winds of destiny carry us so high we will dance with the stars...

Joanne Salvador
Age 73

CHAPTER 36

FROM THE FIRE TO THE DIAGNOSIS

JOYANN GOLD

In casual conversations, we quickly talk about having courage, being bold, or being fearless. In those moments, we say and think we are fearless. I have lived long enough to realize that we see how fearless we are only as the fire becomes personal. It doesn't matter whether the fire is real or assumed! Will FEAR stop us in our tracks, or will we move forward?

"You can face everything as an adventure and be fearless."
JoyAnn Gold

I have had many opportunities to become fearless in my life. I will share a couple of significant moments where I discovered that I was more fearless than I could have ever imagined.

I'm 67, and today is day five of the Enlightened Warrior camp designed to help us move beyond our comfort zones! I've done more to stretch myself physically and emotionally than I ever imagined I'd do. Activities like scrambling up a 20-foot pole, a rope walk, and even being taken to the ground by a would-be attacker where I found myself fighting for my life...or at least it felt that way!

Now I'm being told that we'll be doing a fire walk tonight! "Oh no, haven't I already pushed myself out of my comfort zone enough this week? Maybe I'll just pack my things and leave! But how can I live with myself if I leave? I'm here to become a warrior, and warriors confront their fears; they don't run away!" So, I decided to stay and yet again face my fear.

Another eight hours have passed! It's now evening, and I find myself in the fire-walk line, watching some of the other participants do their walks.

I remember thinking, JoyAnn, "This is a once-in-a-lifetime experience; why would you miss it?" So, I stayed in line, and before I knew it, I was at the head of the line facing a 30' bed of hot, glowing coals. "Oh no… can I actually do this? YES, I CAN!!!" Don't look down, just walk flat-footed swiftly across the coals, was what I was told! HERE I GO…I'M WALKING ON FIRE!"

As you can imagine, I could hardly contain my JOY upon reaching the end of the 30' walk! I truly felt INVINCIBLE! IF I CAN OVERCOME MY FEAR OF DOING A FIRE WALK, I CAN FACE MY FEARS AND DO ANYTHING! I had no idea how much I would lean upon what I had learned about myself during that fire walk later in life.

It was twelve years later, at age 79, I found myself in the hospital due to ongoing chest pain. Following blood work and other tests, my world came to a standstill when a doctor marched in, announcing it was likely I had pancreatic cancer! Immediate shock overtook me! I'm not ready to leave. I've got too many plans and dreams. No, no, no!!! This can't be! But some hours later, upon processing the news, I remembered my fire-walk adventure and the message I'd told myself ever since. "You can face everything as an adventure and be fearless!" I also remembered how my fear of dying totally vanished upon hearing the stories of many individuals having near-death experiences. So, the following morning, after seeing two oncologists, I decided

I was going on yet another adventure—one I never believed I'd go on!

Three weeks later, after completing more outpatient testing, I was in my doctor's office, preparing to handle the bad news. However, he came in with a smile, announcing that while the central duct of my pancreas is exceptionally enlarged, it's not cancerous. What a relief!

While I'm incredibly grateful the initial diagnosis was wrong, it gave me a newfound knowingness. I AM FEARLESS! I can now face anything life throws at me!

JoyAnn Gold
Age 81

CHAPTER 37

SOMETHING MUST BE DONE!

DR. K. MHINA ENTRANTT

I grew up in a family and community of educators. However, my personal career choice was Social Work and Mental Health Professional. I've always had a soft spot for teaching and mentoring children. When I moved to North Carolina, I learned that elementary school children's literacy rate was significantly declining, and 4th graders throughout the area could not pass the state literacy competency test. This information disturbed me deeply, for if a child cannot read and master reading comprehension, their life experiences are more likely to become dismal.

"When you realize a social problem, and your response is 'Something must be done!' it's probably yours to do!" — Dr. K. Mhina Entrantt

In my meditation time, I asked what I could immediately do to help children improve their reading and comprehension skills. I was given the assignment to create a summer camp—**Arts & Academic Enrichment Summer Camp**. The answer started with something I was already doing—teaching Conversational Spanish. I realized how learning a new language organically teaches grammar, words, adverbs, etc. The skills learned in the new language are transferable to English.

The next step was to combine the arts with primary basic learning skills. It was a different approach, and I saw it could work! I began to write on paper what I was given to do. The camp was to cover these subjects: Reading, Reading Comprehension, Arts & Crafts, Conversational Spanish, Intro to Public Speaking, Intro to Music, Intro to Drama, Yoga, and Positive Peer Communication. Within a few days, I had created the format. Also, the camp would provide a free lunch and snacks for the children. I had a budget of $0 to begin such a lofty project!

At the time, I was not looking for a cause to take on. I was still trying to get settled in a new location. The urge to go forward would not leave me alone! I woke up with it; it nudged me throughout the day and went to sleep with me at night. I could not shake the feeling of, "You gotta do this now!" Sometimes, emotionally and energetically, I felt like I had been put in an arm-wrestling championship and had lost. All my thoughts were centered on this. It's not a good time to do this! The urges, nudges, and pushes simply intensified!

"When it's your turn to step forward with logic, excuses, or current status, do not run the show!" — Dr. K. Mhina Entrantt.

I had a great idea but was unsure where it could be "housed." One night, while participating in an open poetry mic, I met a poet; we "just happened" to talk about my summer camp idea. She excitedly said she would introduce me to the director of a cultural center who would be open to the idea. The director and I met. We clicked. We began putting the pieces together for the camp. The director had excellent community connections that he reached out to for supplies, participation, and other resources. I created brochures, posted them on social media, and did radio interviews to spread the word. I recruited educators, parents, visual artists, and peer teens to volunteer.

There was a strong rhythm and synergy of community, always present. The large multi-purpose room was full of laughter, creativity, learning, and modeling. Our children crossed all lines of educational categories—gifted, quick learners, requiring one-on-one support, needing academic support, needing emotional/social support, and autism, just to name a few areas. I saw the camp as a modern-day one-room schoolhouse where everyone was accepted, valued, and encouraged to reach their potential together.

"Children need adults to show up with care, patience, and confidence in their successful learning experiences." — Karen Entrantt

We began with the basics of phonetics and visual associations to stimulate interest in reading. Books that were culturally appropriate and relatable for the children were donated. Their reading and reading comprehension improved significantly. Children who had not experienced success in reading began to fall in love with reading.

The children also enjoyed learning Public Speaking Basics—stand up straight (no wiggling), look at the audience, and tell your story. The children obviously wanted to be heard and knew they mattered in a learning environment. Intro to music was taught by a college student studying music theory and music engineering. The children could play with small instruments, use a microphone, and create original music. Intro to drama allowed the children to learn the basics of character development and stage presence.

Arts & Academics Summer Enrichment also became a space for parents to gather and have meaningful conversations, debates, and information exchanges. My family, friends, parents, community agencies, and leaders donated snacks, lunches, and cases of water for thirsty, hot days.

It seemed like our time together passed so quickly—too quickly! Our summer camp children returned to school, connecting to learning more deeply. I still get reports of their successes. Our teen peers are attending college, studying abroad, and making a difference in their own rights. I'm proud to say I stepped forward to increase children's literacy. I desire to find funding, space, and support to bring Arts & Academics back as an afterschool program.

Dr. K. Mhina Entrantt
Age 66

CHAPTER 38

BEYOND AGE LIMITS: EMBRACING LIFE'S LATER CHAPTERS

KATHERINE MERRITT

"Sixty is when life gives you the wheel and says, 'Now, show us the way!'"

As I woke up on my 60th birthday, I experienced various emotions. The world was buzzing like any other day, but a storm was brewing inside my head. Regrets about past choices and missed opportunities, thoughts of being alone, and the weight of dreams still unfulfilled invaded my thoughts. And if I'm honest, aging scared me "a lot."

It wasn't without good reason. Watching loved ones grow old and frail, especially witnessing my Mom's battle with Dementia, had cast a shadow over my perception of aging. Seeing her frailty and the devastating impact of her condition made me dread what the future might hold for me. It would've been easy to fall into a cycle of fear, resigning to a predestined fate. However, I decided not to let my life's story be defined solely by others' experiences.

I have come to understand that the lifestyle choices we make have a significant impact on how we age. As a result, I decided to educate myself on health and wellness. By delving deeply into these topics, I have made changes to my life that are different from those made by previous generations. My goal is to not only live a longer life but to live it with vitality and to the fullest. However, I acknowledge that making changes can be difficult. The same proactive approach I took towards my health could also apply to achieving unfulfilled dreams that have been on my heart for so long.

During a particularly introspective coaching session, my mentor, Maria, looked at me and asked, "What's holding you back from embracing all facets of your life?" The depth of that question pierced through me. It wasn't just about aging or the familiar fears associated with it. It was my haunting self-doubt, magnified by years of being caught in a loop of unfulfilling roles, which overshadowed my true passions and purpose.

That pivotal conversation with Maria stirred something profound within me. Harnessing her unwavering support and my rejuvenated desire, I began tearing down the walls of self-doubt between me and my dreams. My vision became clear: to empower women, rewrite the aging narrative, and cultivate a community where life's later chapters are a time of expansion and unlimited potential.

Today, I am determined to achieve a lifelong aspiration that I once doubted would become a reality; I am about to launch my online business to empower, guide, and support women as they go through their later years. I intend to create a platform that embodies my heartfelt desire to remind every woman that she is not alone, that aging is a journey full of endless possibilities, and that every day presents an opportunity to learn, grow, and become a better version of oneself.

So, if you, too, sometimes grapple with the challenges and uncertainties of aging, take a moment to reflect. It's essential to approach this period of your life with a positive outlook, to see it with fresh eyes, and to embrace all the experiences it brings. Alongside this renewed perspective, surround yourself with individuals who elevate you, resonate with your aspirations, and wholeheartedly believe in the boundless possibilities that age can bring.

The journey starts with you. It's essential to change and reframe your perspective on aging. As we age, we gain wisdom, experience, and a richness of life that the enthusiasm of youth cannot match. Embrace your wrinkles as signs of the stories you've lived and lessons you've learned. View every challenge as a chance to evolve, grow, and rediscover your vibrant spirit.

Whether they're friends, mentors, or coaches, ensure you have a support system that guides and stands by you through every twist and turn. It's understandable to feel overwhelmed, but please remember that seeking help can make a big difference. You don't have to carry everything on your own.

Facing life's challenges is inevitable, but how we rise to meet them is a choice. With unwavering determination and the strength of a supportive community, we can do more than endure; we can flourish. The journey ahead? It's brimming with untapped potential and uncharted adventures. Age is just a number. The human spirit's desire for knowledge and new experiences has no limits. So, I challenge you:

1. Seize this chapter of your life.
2. Embrace every moment.
3. Redefine what it means to age.

I can't help but feel a sense of excitement. The best part of our story is yet to come, and I can't wait to see what lies just beyond the horizon. It's like standing on the edge of a cliff, ready to leap into the unknown. But instead of fear, feel a sense of exhilaration! Who knows what adventures await us? The possibilities are endless. So, hold on tight because things are about to get interesting!

"Join the revolution: where the spirit knows no age and age knows no limits."

Holding onto cherished memories and looking ahead with awe,

Katherine Merritt
Age 67

CHAPTER 39

FROM FEARFUL TO FEARLESS AT FIFTY

LAURA TAYLOR COX

The young mom sitting near me asked, "Do you mind if I ask you how old you are?" "You can ask." So, she did. I laughed and said, "I said you could ask, but I don't have to answer." She was taken aback, but I just wanted to be a bit sassy. "I'll be 66 in September." Her eyes widened as she gasped, "And you're still traveling?!?" That was when I saw the fear behind her query. It was a fear I was all too familiar with—the fear of getting old.

Somewhere along the way, I picked up a false narrative that when a person gets old, they are useless, have no more life to live, and have nothing left to give except for the inheritance at their demise.

For me, as a young mom, the magic age of oldness was 50. I don't know how I became afraid of the number 50. Maybe it was comments from others who had been there: "The day I turned 50 —that very day! —I needed reading glasses!" "My body started falling apart at 50!" I was bound and determined not to let these things happen to me. So, I decided to "reinvent" myself before I turned 50!

Honestly, reinventing myself became more about aesthetics. Yes, I pressed into goals, but I needed to figure out what I wanted to be and do after my home-educating days. So, I went the easy, measurable route. I got braces! And I used colorful rubber bands! Why should the teenage girls have all the fun? Purple was my favorite. To add a touch of vibrancy to my life, I also decided to get purple hair extensions. It was a small change, but it symbolized my willingness to step out of my comfort zone and embrace my individuality. At the age of 49, I was beginning to not really care what other people might think of me.

However, the date of turning 50 kept getting closer. There was nothing I could do to stop it. Time kept marching on. My anxiety grew with each passing day. The braces came off. I babied the purple extensions. Each day, I got O-L-D-E-R. I realized that I had gotten older every day of my life. We all have! What was different about this run around the sun?

As the days ticked closer to my 50th birthday, the fear intensified. To me, 50 was the nightmare from which there was no escape. After a year of reinventing myself, I was stronger, but the fear of 50 was ever-present. Half a century! A few days before my 50th birthday, I was just going through the motions of life because 50 was too close. There was no more time for reinventing. I was who I was; there was no time left to change that.

I'm unsure how it happened, but an epiphany broke through my fearfulness. All of a sudden, the glory of heaven invaded my closet and the Hallelujah Chorus enveloped me! Or so it seemed. That epiphany cleared away ALL my fear of turning 50 and getting old! This appears very simplistic, and I don't mean to be a downer, but the epiphany said, "If I don't turn 50, that means I'm dead." My next thought was, "I don't want to die, so...50 is good!"

I was able to embrace turning 50. I looked forward to turning 50 for the few days I had left of being 49. And I've loved every birthday since, which is quite a few, and I look forward to every coming birthday. Each year adds so much to the previous ones!

I still have a fear of getting old. Mind you, I did NOT say I have a fear of aging. I want to have as many birthdays as I possibly can. I said I have a fear of getting old. I never want to be one of those "old" people. My mindset around aging is ageless! I feel younger, and I have much less anxiety than I did 20 years ago. I am excited for the adventures that lie ahead and the endless possibilities that await me.

Laura Taylor Cox
Age 67

CHAPTER 40

MIND MATTERS: A STORY OF RESILIENCE, PERSISTENCE, AND FOLLOWING YOUR DREAMS

CINDY MCKEE

And what I do know now is that I can affect outcomes. I have way more power over the quality of my life than I ever imagined.

This is a powerful story of overcoming a life-threatening and potentially lifelong debilitating neurological disease that struck when I was twenty. It shares lessons of mindset and gratitude learned then that have served and continue to serve me throughout my lifetime.

There I was, 20 years old and lying completely paralyzed in a hospital bed outside of Boston, tubes and wires everywhere, and a respirator was doing my breathing for me. This certainly was not part of the plan I had in mind for my life.

I was an Olympic hopeful in the equestrian world, working hard to launch a career of competition, teaching, and training. I had arrived in the area for an event and never reached the competition. I was struck by a rare neurological disease, and I was terrified. A team of doctors gathered to come up with a diagnosis. After a few days, my doctor came into my room to share their findings and a definitive diagnosis with my parents (who had quickly flown up from Philadelphia) and me. If I could have held my breath at that moment, I would have. But when they told us my diagnosis, I barely heard what they said. I didn't recognize the name of the disease. All I heard was that there was a chance I could recover; I might walk again and even be back on my horse!

What they didn't share was that this wasn't necessarily true for everyone. That this disease could leave me on a respirator for a year or more, in a wheelchair for life, or that I might not survive it at all.

All I heard was that there was a chance I could recover so I immediately made the decision that I would.

This was October, and I was determined to leave that hospital before Christmas. When I wasn't being treated with the many, often grueling therapies, I would lie in that bed, dreaming of being back on my horse. In my mind, I was competing again. I was teaching and training for a successful equestrian career.

Day in and day out, in my mind, I ran my hand down my horse's neck. I could feel his smooth coat's warmth and his neck's rippling muscles under my hand. I was riding and jumping and competing again. I could feel it as strongly as if it were actually happening.

I smiled more than I cried. I just knew I was going to get there. And, little by little, I did. I walked out of the hospital under my own steam on December 24th. The tears flowed all around. I had done it. Three weeks later, with assistance, I was back on my horse. Over the next year, with a lot of supportive therapy, I slowly gained strength and flexibility. It wasn't an overnight process, but I was determined.

Eventually, I did have the career I dreamed of. I was teaching, training, and competing again. Not at the Olympic level, but I was doing it. I had many, many months to reflect on my experience and I knew there were lessons in there that could serve me.

What kept showing up for me again and again was the word "gratitude." And it wasn't just gratitude for my recovery. That, of course, was present. It was gratitude for an amazing awareness and appreciation for the human body, its ability to function and to heal itself. It was gratitude for the attitude of all who contributed to my recovery in such a positive way. It was gratitude for my coming through a traumatic experience with a positive outlook. It was gratitude for gratitude itself. A lot of discovery and awareness for a mere 20-year-old!

What I didn't appreciate until many years later, with the newer studies in neuroscience, was that I had contributed in a big way to my recovery. Steve Jobs once said, "You can only connect the dots looking backward." We don't know what we don't know. All my dreams of riding again while in the hospital actually helped me get better. I know now that I can affect outcomes. I have way more power over the quality of my life than I ever imagined ~ physically, mentally, and spiritually. On a day by day, minute to minute basis, I am far greater than my circumstances. And so are you!

Cindy McKee
Age 71

CHAPTER 41

HOW TO PREVENT TECHNOLOGY FROM RUINING YOUR HAPPY DAY OR LIFE!

LUCIE ROSA-STAGI

I've been doing business online since 2016. When I first started, I had no idea what online business meant; I only knew how to copy and paste. I would continually lose things and not know where they all disappeared to; it was very frustrating. So, why did I keep going? Was it my desire to succeed as an entrepreneur? Was it because I'm hardheaded and don't want to be the loser in this game? Was it because I had nothing better to do?

Something drove me.

I had recently been divorced and had just turned 70. I was devastated by this divorce. I saw my dreams fade away. But I knew that I had to take care of myself because no one was coming to save me.

So, everything online requires some tech knowledge. I got that! Then I learned you can always find someone to do the technical stuff. If you have grandkids, you can pay them to help you. How is that for connecting with them?

I didn't let technology get in my way. I became an affiliate of Tony Robbins and Dean Graziosi's new legacy in 2019, entitled "Self-Education Is The New Norm." I loved the concept from the beginning, as everyone, including me, was at 'Google University,' learning and getting the knowledge that we needed to advance in our business and personal lives. I was so successful as their affiliate that in their third year, 2022, they narrowed the affiliate pool to 50 affiliates, and I was one of the chosen ones.

By then, I had formed an online business with three other coaches who were ex-moderators for Tony & Dean. We began Launch Lab Academy, helping Tony & Dean's program students who needed more guidance and handholding. We succeeded because of the support and love we bestowed on our clients. We are now in our fourth year of business. We, like many, learned to pivot with the needs of our clients, and this year's program is a hybrid of the last two or three years' programs.

We are a multigenerational, multinational organization. I'm the baby boomer, and our youngest coach lives in Israel and is 30. He is a Millennial; the other two in Malaysia and Oregon, USA, are part of Generations X and Y. I am the community builder for this team. I am responsible for outreach and finding people for our new programs. I love my work because it impacts so many people's lives and stories, and there is no greater fulfillment than serving your brothers and sisters or your children and/or grandchildren. I love hearing people's stories and featuring people who have inspiring stories. I do that in a series of weekly interviews.

I love my life! I can travel whenever I want and work as many hours as I want. I have many friends online and offline. I have an abundant life, and my message is that if I can do it, so can you.

Lucie Rosa-Stagi
Age 78

CHAPTER 42

I AM GOING TO WRITE MY OWN EULOGY!

MORIAH HUDSON

No matter your circumstances or your situation, you are braver than most because you went through what you had to go through.

And why do you ask? Who better to tell my story than me? I don't want to leave any of the juicy parts out. So, my life is hard but not as hard as many people have had. My life was good, but not as good as many people's. My life is my adventure, and I lived it to the best of my ability.

This story is not about what I did in my life but what I learned. What I learned about the richness and fullness of life, from the mountain peaks to the deepest depths, is what I want to share in my eulogy.

As we move into the third chapter of our lives, hopefully, we will be wiser. After my wife BJ died in March of 2020 at the beginning of COVID-19 after 35 years together, it was the worst four years of my entire life. Grief can consume you, or it can open an incredible path to self-discovery.

I chose the latter. Choose wisely, my friend. There are sensations, sounds, and magnificence that I never even knew existed. Know that you are powerful. That's because you're still here. Your journey, pain, and tears must be shared, as they can be someone else's light in the darkness. And happiness is your birthright. No matter your circumstances or your situation, you are braver than most because you went through what you had to go through. Remember to love one another and be kind; there's enough hate in this world.

As you start down the journey of gratitude, it will all come into focus. You can experience gratitude because it's not about what's happening outside of you but what's happening inside of you. Learn to experience and share your joy. Read a good book. Watch an inspirational movie. Fly a kite. If you have not done it in your lifetime, turn your speakers up to the total volume and dance to the music. Everyone should have blown out their speakers at least once in their life!

Always look for the joy in your life, or you will miss its magic.

"We are all walking each other home," Ram Dass said.

Moriah Hudson
Age 74

EMBRACING EMOTIONAL AND PHYSICAL WELLNESS: MY JOURNEY OF SURRENDER AND LIFE LESSONS

NANCY JOHNSON

Let nature's embrace heal you, hold tight to connections that warm your heart, and exude positivity at every turn. Release those worries, love deeply, and always expect goodness in every soul you encounter.

As I reflect on my now vibrant journey at 65 years young, I had reservations about how much of my struggles to share and decided to leave that for a more extended version. I consider life a journey of lessons to learn from.

My journey has been marked by transformation, resilience, and a relentless pursuit of well-being. I've traveled this path, overcoming challenges, embracing change, and embracing the magic of saying "yes" to life's many opportunities.

My eyes were opened at 16, witnessing how health is a choice, with food, attitude, and more. I made a bold decision to step away from an unhealthy home environment. It wasn't an easy choice, but my need for change was necessary for self-preservation. Drawing inspiration from my mother's work ethic, I embarked on a path that would reshape my destiny. While wrapping up high school, I secured a full-time job, crafting a life where I could support myself and forge my own path. And I played cards on the weekends. Thanks to my uncle, who taught me how to win, it helped support my freedom to do and explore life.

Leaving behind a tumultuous roommate situation due to her drug use and more, I set my sights on new horizons. I headed to California with dreams of the modeling world. While the Golden State introduced me to incredible experiences, I realized that the glitz and glamour of the industry needed to be aligned with my Minnesota roots. With a heart full of memories and lessons, I returned home, forever changed by the healthy food options I'd encountered and a newfound love for travel.

My journey into well-being took a significant leap when I delved into yoga and organic eating at 20. It was a few years down the road that I found myself embracing motherhood and raising a six-year-old son diagnosed with ADHD. Instead of following conventional paths, I explored the impact of nutrition and chemicals, witnessing his transformation as we eliminated sugar and created a chemical-free home. Our shared pursuit of karate boosted his focus and catapulted me into the best physical shape of my life at 33. This was after his dad and I divorced. They say many marry someone like their dad, and in many ways, I did. Another lesson, no regrets, though.

Here's a concise overview of my decades and their unfolding.

In my 20s, I embraced marriage, motherhood, and a demanding corporate role, all while discovering the profound power of meditation, yoga, and more that got me through.

My 30s brought changes in relationships—divorce and remarriage, each chapter adding new layers of growth and challenges.

My 40s marked a pivotal turning point as I transitioned from a 15-year corporate career. After my company offered me an impossible ultimatum, I leaped into entrepreneurship, a path that resonated deeply with my inner entrepreneur. I remember standing in my beautiful empty house I had manifested, as all the moving trucks were pulling away and my divorce was final. I looked up and said I surrendered, and it was like those words said, "Ok, hold on, you're about to live that word."

Venturing into my 50s, aromatherapy became a beloved companion, nurturing not only my well-being but also touching the lives of countless others. Then, a transformative retreat with Joe Dispenza expanded my interest in meditation. I'm a big believer in manifestation, and for years, I followed his teaching on healing ourselves, so when the opportunity came, I said yes! The experience was another pivotal time in my life on my physical and emotional wellness journey.

As I stepped into my 60s, I embarked on a solo adventure to Australia, diving into Neuro-linguistic Programming and Quantum Healing. The journey continued when I returned to the US, taking Spanish and Latin dance lessons. It all started with my saying yes and not overthinking it. What's funny is that I never liked school; I didn't attend college and found my love of learning came to me from being interested.

In the heart of all these experiences, the power of "yes" resonates deeply. "Feel the Fear and Do It Anyway," a phrase one of my inspirations, Wayne Dyer, used, became a personal mantra, leading me to shatter fears and embrace life's daring adventures, from skydiving to scaling mountains and extreme ziplining with my fearless daughter. Next, I have my sights set on giving a TedX talk to share the knowledge I've gathered after returning from another trip to Australia to further my learning.

My journey has woven connections with incredible souls across the globe, underscoring the beauty of human connection. Personal struggles, including the devastating loss of my second husband to suicide, have fueled my mission to champion mental health awareness alongside my daughter.

Reflecting on my mother's yearning for more learning opportunities and juxtaposing it with my own path, I've understood that life's twists and turns are our most invaluable lessons. Every choice and every challenge has sculpted me into the strong and resilient woman I am today.

Can we talk about defying age labels? Trust me, mindset is the elixir of eternal youth. I've embraced life with unwavering passion, coining the phrase "33 and holding." This philosophy embodies pursuing passions unapologetically, staying connected to nature, adopting healthy habits, and nurturing positive self-talk.

So here's my invitation: dive headfirst into your dreams with unwavering fervor. Let nature's embrace heal you, hold tight to connections that warm your heart, and exude positivity at every turn. Release those worries, love deeply, and always expect goodness in every soul you encounter.

As my journey continues to unfold, I stand here as an open book, ready to share the transformative power of holistic well-being and mind-body coaching. Remember, your life's worth is immeasurable, and each of us is destined to live fully and freely.

Sending you all my love and boundless positivity,

Nancy Johnson
Age 65

CHAPTER 44

THE QUIET CONFIDENCE OF SELF-ESTEEM

DR. SALLY L. CLELAND

Memorable are the life lessons taught in story form. I learned well from the stories told by my first role model and mentor: my father. Each story had unique guiding principles and values. Whether he shared stories on trust and honesty, or authenticity and genuineness, or standing strong when facing adversity, my dad's lessons were grounded in maintaining healthy self-esteem.

Self-esteem is an inside job—the original "never-ending story." It is a myth that once we "have" it, we always "have it." No, we must dedicate ourselves to maintaining and building it every day as we grow through our lives. Self-esteem is at the core of our personalities, and it arises through self-validation. It is the essential backbone of success. Success is predicated on a desire for success and an expectation of success.

Once we accept and embrace that we have lived more years than we have years left to live, we know the value of healthy self-esteem. We are the "wisdom keepers"—in our homes, workplaces, and communities. Not only wisdom of our skills, talents, and abilities but also wisdom related to attitude—attitude towards life, attitude towards others, attitude towards ourselves. We are redefining retirement - we are mentors, trailblazers, historians, and creatives; we are contemporary pioneers and re-envisioned suffragettes with new objectives; we are a new breed of entrepreneurs, leaders, collaborators, contributors, and advocates; we are empire builders. We will not go "gently into that good night" - we will be loud and strong!

As women at this stage of our lives, we are challenging the standards of beauty, sexuality, perpetual impact, and what is possible. We are projecting our value and are committed to meaningful longevity; we have a purpose. A significant contributing factor to who we are and what we can do is our self-esteem and its power. Here is a story to exemplify.

A young Clinical Psychologist sat nervously in a dreary interview room furnished with only a stocky wooden table and two chairs. The room was like a cage - iron bars on four sides. His next interviewee was a Death Row inmate. The burley, gruff convicted murderer was brought in wearing leg irons and handcuffs and plopped down on the chair opposite. A prison guard stood outside the door. Twenty minutes passed, and there was a guard shift change. For a few moments, no guard stood outside. This gap in protection did not go unnoticed by either the young interviewer or the inmate.

This intimidating, scar-faced, heavily tattooed prisoner leaned over the table towards the timid, bespeckled, and meek-looking psychologist and said, "I'm not answering anymore of your f****** questions. I'm bigger than you, I'm stronger than you, and, hell, I'm even better looking than you. I could pick you up and squeeze your head through those bars."

The novice psychologist was scared. He then leaned toward the prisoner, replying: "You are bigger than me and stronger than me, and I'll even go as far as saying you may be better looking than me. No doubt you could pick me up and squeeze my head through those bars, BUT if you think I'm just going to lie down on the floor and let you mop it with me, you are mistaken—before this is all over, you are going to know you were in one hell of a fight!" Silence. The prisoner leaned back into his chair, saying: "What's the next f***** question?"

That young psychologist was my father. This event from his early professional life is a lesson about the quiet confidence of self-esteem. Throughout my life, I have regularly applied this life lesson, which has served me well. One such occasion is as follows:

While attending a high-profile corporate meeting with several VPs and higher managers, I awaited my turn to contribute my expertise; that is why I was invited. It was an arduous meeting where senior decision-makers gathered to determine a critical aspect of the company's future. I was one of only two women in attendance.

A decision was made to send me and my immediate boss to Ottawa to meet with our governmental regulatory body, which "oversaw" compliance and safety; we were to represent the company's interests and present documentation supporting our recommendations.

As the meeting concluded and people began to leave the room, one of the VPs said he expected my boss (a man) and I would do a "good job" as company representatives. My boss's boss glibly said, "Oh, I'm sure they will, but I certainly hope they are staying in separate hotel rooms!" Much laughter followed. Having heard this sexist, condescending, and dismissive comment, I immediately turned around, addressing all, but directed my gaze to the man who had made this remark, "Well, actually, since you cut 25% off our travel budget this year, we decided to share a room to keep the cost down!" I turned and exited! As I did, I heard my boss's boss say, "I am sure she is only joking!" He recognized the inappropriateness of his comment AND that I had courageously and confidently "called him on it." Later, he spoke to my boss, asking him to apologize to me on his behalf. He did not dare to apologize directly to me.

No further public sexist, condescending, or dismissive comments were directed at me or uttered at my expense by this individual during my tenure at this company. As my father had taught me, I stood my ground, stood on my principles, and stood up for myself, irrespective of potential consequences, confident as I stood alone against a dragon. This was neither the first nor the last occasion upon which I relied on the quiet confidence of my own self-esteem.

No matter the circumstance, how dire the situation, or the setbacks or missteps, those with healthy self-esteem know that "standing" triumphs over tyranny.

Standing strong, you can be quietly confident and ready for anything, no matter your age. Any friggin' questions?

Dr. Sally L. Cleland
Age 74

CHAPTER 45

HOW I ESCAPE AGEISM

SUSAN FARLING

"I silently thanked all the vibrant women, the researchers and writers, men and women, who have helped me to have realistic positive expectations for my future, for possibility, meaningful growth, exploration, good health, loving relationships, joy and awe in this third phase of life."

I remember the shock that ran through my young body when I heard his words. He was my dad, my father, and I adored him. I was five years old.

It was his birthday, and we stood and looked out our living room window.

He sighed.

"It's my 50th birthday," he said.

"My life is over."

I was incredulous. How could he say that? Didn't he love the trees, the mountains, and the ocean? What about the dog? Our cabin? Me?

Wasn't I worth living for?

I was silent that day in 1950, but I am silent no longer.

Today, I'm part of a revolution that's brewing—an upswelling of voices of people challenging cultural stereotypes with their lived experiences, devouring a growing mountain of research that debunks ageist myths and enthusiastically informing everyone listening that the claims of ageism—of inevitable decline and decrepitude, of diminishment and depression—simply do not have to be true.

I see the impact of ageism today in the attitudes of two of my brilliant and accomplished colleagues. One recently turned 50, and the other 60 within months of each other. Both are worried—anxious that they will be perceived as less than they have been, diminished, less attractive, less desirable, less dynamic, with less to contribute, on their way to "over the hill."

I get it.

Ageist assumptions are baked into our language and our institutions. None are exempt: education, medicine, advertising, entertainment, finance, industry, government. As the World Health Organization says, ageism is pernicious and pervasive, more rampant globally than sexism or racism.

I didn't escape it.

Now that I'm in my late seventies, I remain vigilant to counter the ageist self-limiting beliefs that slide through my ageist myth-busting filters and dim my vitality and enthusiasm for living.

Those myth-busting filters have been created in part by the brilliant, informative, and fascinating-to-me writings of people like Ashton Applewhite (*This Chair Rocks: A Manifesto Against Ageism*), Margaret Morganroth Gullette (*Ending Ageism or How Not To Shoot Old People*), and Dr. Becca Levy (*Breaking the Age Code: How Your Beliefs About Aging Determine How Long & Well You Live*).

These women join a chorus of voices of authors, researchers, and scientists, all stating that it's our underlying beliefs, our conscious attitudes, our thoughts, emotions, feelings, and, importantly, the actions we take that determine in large part how healthy we are, how long we live, and how much happiness, a sense of purpose and meaning, contentment, contribution, and joy we have in our lives, even as we live longer in aging bodies and experience age-related losses.

Without this dynamic flood of evidence countering the dominant age-phobic cultural narrative, I wouldn't feel as optimistic as I do as I approach my eighties. For many years, ageism had me hooked.

I didn't have grandparents. The only person I knew as a child who was old was childless "old lady Pete," who would peek out from behind her curtains to watch us as we kids made our way home from school for lunch. Among ourselves, we would mercilessly make fun of her.

The teased hair, mini-skirted version of myself was vaguely contemptuous of the women I saw who were twenty years older than me, who, to me, looked desperate as they flirted with professors or later showed up looking as though they were in a wind tunnel. My story to myself was that when I aged, I would do so gracefully, not like them. I wouldn't dye my hair or try to look younger than I was. At that time, I thought older people were boring, tiresome, uninteresting, and unattractive. I was thoroughly indoctrinated with my society's ageist tropes. It never occurred to me that if I was lucky enough to live a long life, I, too, would join the group I was shunning.

In my early forties, I became close friends with two very different, extraordinary women. One was a decade older than me, and the other was two decades. We loved each other, and they taught me life lessons born of their hard-earned wisdom that serve me today. Finally, I was engaging without prejudice with lively, accomplished, worldly older women, happy to share the laughter and tears of deep friendship.

Around that time, white hair began to thread through my dark hair. I was asked one too many times if I was my daughter's grandmother. For the next twenty-seven years, I dyed my hair. I told myself that I would embrace my silver when I turned seventy. At times, I had flashes of awareness of feeling invisible, erased, and oddly embarrassed, as though I should apologize for my age.

Barely conscious, internalized ageism was lurking and taking its toll.

When I turned seventy and stopped lowlighting, I felt liberated and relieved to have let go of a ritual that had become tiresome.

I began to recognize, name, and counter the ageist myths that I was confronting in myself.

The years passed. One morning, I woke up, stretched, and was startled to see the skin of my arm drape, wrinkle, and fall toward my elbow. It seemed to have happened overnight. There was no doubt. I was in the land of the old—middle old, but old nonetheless.

I silently thanked all the vibrant women—the researchers and writers, men and women—who have helped me to have realistic positive expectations for my future, for possibility, meaningful growth, exploration, good health, loving relationships, joy, and awe in this third phase of life.

The other day, my almost three-year-old granddaughter was sitting on my lap, examining the prominent veins on my hands. She rolled the largest back and forth, then said, "They look like trees, gran-gran."

I agreed with her and, once again, thought about how my dear dad, who died in his early sixties over fifty years ago, would have enjoyed this beloved child.

Susan Farling
Age 79

CHAPTER 46

HIGH FIVE BEAR

SUSAN "SUEZEE" FINLEY

My heart was pounding, my breath was heavy, and I could no longer continue. I collapsed on the side of the mountain. I couldn't believe I was so wrecked.

I was in a group of 5 being led by an amazing Shaman, for a healing workshop in Woodstock, NY. He invited the workshop attendees to join him on his 6 am hike up to the monastery before our 9 am class.

I jumped at the chance and woke up at 5 am just to prepare the questions I wanted to ask during the walk.

I was so pumped for this chance to talk with him practically one-on-one.

All was well as we started up the road, I kept pace, thinking it would eventually slow a little. But it didn't, it increased and so did the incline of the road. After about 35 minutes, I started to have difficulty keeping up and watched in amazement as this magical Shaman appeared to mysteriously glide up the mountain road with such ease and grace as he puffed on his cigar.

He literally left me in a puff of smoke.

I lost ground quickly, I hung in there as long as I could because there were so many questions I wanted to ask if only I could catch my breath, which, sadly, I could not. I slumped over.

They looked back when they no longer heard the pitter-patter of my exhausted feet and my Darth Vader-like breathing. I smiled and waved stoically, "I am just going to sit here for a while, on this rock, I will catch you guys on the way back."

Well in my mind that's what I said but in reality, it was probably more like "Rock, wait, here, ugh."

When they were out of sight, I rolled off the rock and flattened myself to the ground in complete and utter defeat. I looked up at the sky, which seemed about 2 seconds away from opening up and pouring down on me. I was feeling completely inadequate and disappointed in myself.

If I had the strength, I would have kicked myself!

There were so many questions I wanted to ask about spirit animals and soul retrieval and the meanings of the different ceremonies… but where was I?

Sprawled out on the side of the road and feeling like a total failure. I went to take a sip of water and ended up just pouring it on my face. Yep, that type of day .

The sound of rustling and twigs snapping quickly snapped me out of self-pity mode. I suddenly remembered the huge bear population in Woodstock. My friend had told me the night before that if you see a bear, it's "your medicine." The bear is there to give you a message. I thought how nice, but what if the bear didn't get the memo and was thinking more along the lines of me being breakfast or lunch?

That thought caused me to jump to my feet and begin my long lone walk of shame up the road to the monastery to catch up with my group.

Boom! A memory, Tony Robbins crashed my pity party in his undeniably raspy voice. I could hear him saying, "Don't compare yourself to others, just compare yourself to you yesterday."

As I started to think about yesterday, I remembered it was not that long ago I was crippled by lupus. Getting out of bed was an ordeal and when I did, I possessed only 3 hours of energy a day.

No! This was not a walk of shame like I originally proclaimed it to be. It was a symbol of how far I had come, how much I had healed, and I had completely forgotten about it.

As I saw myself in this new light, not as a failure but as a victor, my strength surged back, my heartbeat steadied, and my gratitude grew!

I continued on up the hill,and made it to the monastery, but my group was not there. I searched the grounds and as I went towards the side entrance, I spotted a bear coming down the side of the mountain about 100 feet from me.

I gazed at him. He stopped and stared back. This time I was ready for my message, I'm not sure what I was expecting, but he seemed ready too.

I wondered what he had to communicate. Suddenly, he stood up and lifted his right paw, being mesmerized, I shadowed, high-fiving him right back!

That was my medicine, …That high five, was my message, my pat on the back for coming through so much, and I needed to acknowledge it!

We often forget all the great things we have done, I invite you to remember your greatness and never give up.

SueZee Finley
Age 61

CHAPTER 47

FULL-CIRCLE BEAUTY!

TERESE PARKIN

The truth is that we are all born beautiful, with God-given beauty. When I was called names at 7, when I had anorexia and couldn't see my actual image at 17, and now, at the age of 66, I have been on a path to remember this without needing the approval of others. Understanding my inner and outer beauty has taken many years and experiences.

I felt my beauty depended on what others said or thought about me for a long time. I felt that if the "pretty people" who seemed to have it made and easily liked me, I would be enough. I'll share one of those times with you. I was 7 years old, having fun with my friends on the school playground. The boys were doing boy stuff, and the girls played a game with me. I swung the tetherball with gusto, playing this fun ball game with my girlfriends. The blacktop was hot, and the sun was bright. Out of the blue, Eddie and Mike started a chant. "Look at you, Buckwheat; Terese looks like Buckwheat!" My stomach flip-flopped, and I turned bright red! The other girls laughed nervously, just turned around and walked away, leaving me alone on the playground. All alone. With that insult, my fun day ended—just like that!

I did not know what to do or say or how to respond to those mean words. I knew no one wanted to play with me if I looked like a character that didn't fit in with the rest of the group. I felt sad and ashamed. I felt like there was nothing I could do to be accepted. Do you remember Buckwheat? His big eyes, big ears, and big teeth didn't seem to fit in his tiny face, like me. I am sure many of you have been called names by kids. This rejection was so devastating to me that it affected me for a very long time.

At 17, I stared at my reflection in the full-length bedroom mirror. What MY eyes saw was an overweight, not very pretty girl. My Mom slipped into the room and saw me grabbing my scrawny belly fat in disgust. She said, "Terese, what is going on?" She was so worried and knew that I was barely eating. The next thing I knew, I was sitting in the doctor's office. The worried doctor sat me down and grabbed my bony, thin hands in his. He said to me, "Terese, you are too frail. Why, you barely weigh 100 pounds! If you continue like this, you may never be able to have kids." Oh no! Wait! I felt sick and shaky. Me, not be able to have kids? But having kids was all I ever wanted! This cannot be! This jolted me to the core, and something clicked inside my head. Could my actions take away the possibility of having a family? No!

That day, I chose my journey back to eating healthy. I am 59 and am attending an empowerment event. We are asked: "What is your greatest obstacle stopping you from living the life you are yearning for?" I knew right then my answer. I turned to share with the woman beside me, and we both said, "You go first." I took the first turn, looking at this beautiful blonde woman and seeing her big heart. "I don't feel confident, I don't feel beautiful, and I just want people to like me," I said with tears in my eyes. Denise grabbed my hands and said to me tearfully, "YOU don't feel confident, beautiful? YOU don't feel that way? That's me! That's exactly how I feel, too! Oh my gosh, I can't believe we feel the same way! I feel not worthy." It hit me that many of us here in this room felt the same way. I felt compassion for myself and others. I didn't have to "fit in" after all. I finally recognized what I hadn't seen before about what I thought about love. That somehow, having others admire my beauty meant that they loved me. I now know that my opinion of myself is the most important. No matter my weight, appearance, or circumstance, I always have Divine beauty in me and I want you to know that you do, too.

Will you join me in making a difference and living an Ageless, Beautiful Life?

Terese Parkin
Age 66

CHAPTER 48

DARE TO BE AGELESS: EMBRACE NEW TECHNOLOGIES

WINNIE ANDERSON-BROWN

In 1962, on a warm, sunny day, teachers were locked in a meeting. The time had come for students to be promoted to a higher grade. What could be so urgent? Why did the teachers need to meet at that time? These questions occupied my nine-year-old brain. The meeting could not be a long one. We were given work to do while the teachers had their meetings. I was uneasy. I was doing my work but couldn't help hearing the principal's voice saying those fateful words.

"SHE IS TOO YOUNG. WE CANNOT PROMOTE HER TO A HIGHER CLASS."

I was crestfallen. They had to be talking about me. I had skipped the first two classes, then spent two weeks in a higher class and was promoted to the class above. I was promoted twice after that. I was the strange little girl who could recite a poem with twenty-three stanzas when no one else in the class had memorized it. Indeed, I was the subject of discussion.

I was not surprised when my teacher told me I had to do another year in her class. They would allow me to do the placement examination for high school. Still, I was too young to attend high school, so I would remain at elementary school even if I passed the placement examination. I did pass the placement examination for high school. Still, I remained at elementary school, did the placement examination for high school a second time, and was awarded a full scholarship.

I knew that I had done nothing wrong, but I could not articulate it then. I knew that something was wrong. I was treated unfairly. It was clear that the problem was bigger than my teacher, the principal, and my school. There were people outside of my school who would not allow me to be promoted.

The words **"YOU ARE TOO YOUNG"** kept ringing in my ears long after they were said. That day, I told myself that, as a little girl, I had to go along with what I was told, but something was wrong with using my age to stop me from being promoted.

I resolved then that, as soon as I could make my own decisions, I would not allow anyone to use my age to deter me from doing anything I wanted.

I dismissed age and only used it when society demanded it. As far as I was concerned, I had freed myself from the shackles of age.

I had no interest in my age or anyone else's. To make matters even worse, I later discovered that the month my mother told me I was born was different from what was on my birth certificate. This further strengthened my resolve to disregard this thing called age and just live my life on my own terms.

That little girl still lives inside of me, with the fearless determination to ignore societal norms regarding age and be an ageless ME.

During the recent pandemic, COVID-19, I was listening to the radio one day, and I heard someone imploring people to pay close attention to the elderly because they need support. I was compassionate for this vulnerable group and imagined how some could be lonely and sad. Then it was as if someone tapped me on the shoulder and said, "Excuse me! You are numbered among the elderly." You are sixty-eight years old! I had a good laugh and counted my blessings.

I still don't belong to the sad, lonely group. As a laughter yoga teacher, I do all I can to bring laughter and joy to others.

I had to figure out at what age I did various things in order to share them. Although I was singing when I was five years old, I recorded and released my first single in 2021 when I was sixty-eight years old. In 2022, I released three new original singles, which are available on most digital platforms. That same year, I started playing the drum set at church.

What brings me the most joy is a project I initiated with the Jamaica Society for the Blind. We are partnering with Bethel Temple Apostolic Church in May Pen, Clarendon, to provide training and support for the blind and visually impaired. My vision is that all the services available in the island's capital will be made available at this location. The project is in its second year and going well.

At 70, my current adventure is with Artificial Intelligence (AI), specifically Large Language Models (LLMs) like ChatGPT, made available to the public on November 30, 2022, Google Bard, Bing Chat, and others.

I asked ChatGPT if it would encourage people over 60 years old to use ChatGPT and to give reasons for the answer provided.

Here is the answer:

- "Yes, I would encourage people over 60 to use ChatGPT for various reasons.
- It can provide a platform for engaging in conversations, answering questions, and even offering companionship.
- It is a tool that can help one stay mentally active, learn new things, and connect with others, which can be particularly valuable for seniors who might face social isolation."

A word of caution is also given. "Just remember, like any technology, it's important to use it in moderation and prioritize real-life interactions."

Finally, I asked ChatGPT to share its views on the AGELESS STARS PROJECT and got the following response:

"I think that's a fantastic and inspiring project! Challenging societal views on aging and showcasing the joy and accomplishments of women over 60 can have a positive impact on perceptions and stereotypes. It promotes inclusivity, celebrates life's experiences, and encourages a more diverse and nuanced understanding of aging. Their efforts could inspire people of all ages to appreciate and learn from the wisdom and vitality that come with advancing years."

I am inviting everyone who has never used ChatGPT or any other LLM to go to www.openAI.com and open an account. Don't be deterred by age.

Winnie Anderson-Brown
Age 71

CHAPTER 49
DANCE WITH DELIGHT
WINNIE ANDERSON-BROWN

What is that old lady doing?
Can't you see?
She is dancing with delight as if she is with the Stars.
That old lady should be saying her prayers.
She is close to dying.
"The young **may** die, but the old **must** die."
Well, I bet she is dancing her way to the great beyond.
We can't beat that!
So, let's join the Dance.
After all, we, too, **must** die, young or old.
Let's **DANCE WITH DELIGHT**

Winnie Anderson-Brown
Age 71

CHAPTER 50

THE HOUSE FLIPPER WHO FLIPPED HER HEART

BONNIE L. SENFTNER

When we walked into the room, the mother hid behind the bedroom curtain. I saw the toes of her shoes sticking out from the bottom of the drape and then noticed a pair of little brown feet beside her. She didn't want us to know that they were in the room.

We are house flippers, and the woman and her husband were in the process of losing their home. The husband allowed us to view the property's layout before we went to auction later that day. Upon entering the house, the scarcity and lack of furniture were shocking. One extensive buffet in the living room was devoid of anything in it, and beside it was an infant carrier on the floor, which also apparently served as the bed for the baby in the family. There was nothing else in the living room or kitchen. The refrigerator displayed bare shelves, and only one tattered, old queen-size mattress lay in the bedroom where the mother and child hid.

My heart broke when I saw her feet and those of her child beside her, hiding from the reality of losing their residence. They had not paid in months, and now their property was on the auction block.

I gently urged her and the child to come out from behind the curtain. I knew their plight. As a nurse, I had more compassion than the average house bidder since flipping homes is a business, and most competitors would not be sensitive to the fact that this was a family in need. I counted six children, including the infant, but one caught my eye in particular: her six-year-old son, who hid with her to support her in her time of distress. Their fear dissipated when they came out gingerly from behind the curtain. I spoke to them in my broken Spanish, ensuring everything would be okay. The young boy ran to his siblings in the front yard. They were skipping rocks and conversing with each other. They had no toys to play with. They happily called their father Papi, and I could feel the energy of the love that they all had for each other. There were no material things to occupy their young minds. No toys, and indeed no electronic devices. Just themselves.

Something about the six-year-old boy, though, tugged at my heartstrings. We had a four-year-old son at home and were unsuccessfully trying to adopt another baby. Adopting newborns was starting to feel impossible, and we were frustrated about the situation until that day when my thinking changed after meeting the six-year-old boy who hid behind the curtain. Not having anything material but the essentials of a roof over his head and hopefully enough food to eat, he still had so much joy that it exuded from him. It is hard to explain the apparent connection. Still, I could easily take him into my home if he were adoptable. Suddenly, my thinking changed regarding the absolute need for a newborn.

My husband then did something unwieldy and unbelievable in the business world. He agreed with me to try to persuade the other house bidders not to bid against us, as I explained I wanted to help the family. It was a miracle that they all agreed. No one bid against us, and the house was ours. He believes it was because they didn't want the house, but I believe it was divine intervention.

I took my husband shopping with me and bought hundreds of dollars worth of groceries and toys for our now new tenants. We knew of a job opportunity for the husband and shared the good news with him. We helped them set up a plan to stay in the house and pay rent, which was doable with the new job. We visited them once a month, and their life was much better. A local charity provided beds, and I would see the special six-year-old boy each time we visited. Sadly, one day, we went home to check on them, and it was oddly quiet. There was no answer when I knocked on the door. We learned from neighbors that the mom had packed up the children and moved to a shelter. Despite our attempts to help them, the father did not change his ways and remained involved in drugs. The family was gone.

Around that same time frame, we learned of a three-year-old boy who needed a home. Because of that six-year-old boy, my heart had changed. It became an easy yes to agree with a child who was already here and needed help.

I have never forgotten that six-year-old boy and what he taught me. How can we, as potentially adoptive parents, discriminate against age just as many folks discriminate against age when we are older? Everyone wants a newborn, but some wonderful kids are older and need homes. Often, they are products of parents who have made bad choices, but they, the children, are loving and good and need forever families and love from the right people.

Perhaps I didn't flip a home the day I met that six-year-old boy, but the experience flipped my heart. Let us open the curtain of our minds and know that every child, regardless of age, deserves to be loved.

Bonnie L. Senftner
Age 72

PART THREE
FABULOUS

We ask ourselves, "Who am I to be brilliant, gorgeous, talented, fabulous?" Actually, who are you not to be? ~ **Marianne Williamson**

CHAPTER 51
MAGNIFICENT AGELESSNESS
JANA LEE GATTUNG

The feelings of growing ageless are magnificent.

Flavors are sweeter and more intense,

Sights are more stunning,

Sounds are both more soothing and exciting,

Friendships are deeper,

Family has more meaning.

Every sunrise brings hope and joy,

While each sunset brings peace.

Adventure and curiosity are more important than ever.

Time and experience become magnified.

Growing Ageless is a gift to be savored every moment of every day.

May you grow into your magnificence and embrace it!

Jana Lee Gattung
Age 61

FROM TRIUMPH TO DESPAIR TO DIVINE AWAKENING: THE CATACLYSM OF 2020 AND THE RESURRECTION OF MY SOUL'S MISSION

DR. ANGELIKA CHRISTIE

"In the shadowed abyss of our deepest pain, we often stumble upon the most radiant glimmer of our inner strength."

"Angelika, have you lost your mind?" The incredulity in my husband's voice shocked me, his eyes wide with astonishment. Drawing a deep breath, I clarified, "I wish to grow the reach of my message by speaking from the grandest international platforms." His skepticism, laced with disapproval, threatened to derail my ambition, yet my stubbornness and unyielding spirit prevailed.

Soon, I was electrifying audiences at Carnegie Hall, Rockefeller Center, West Point, the prestigious Harvard Business Forum, and others.

The accolades poured in, and a bit of celebrity status seduced me with its glittering appearance. Prosperity started flowing effortlessly.

A euphoric high consumed me, strengthening both my confidence and ego. I felt invincible. Until the universe decided to ground me. COVID-19, in its first fierce wave, knocked me off my pedestal in March 2020. Every fiber of my being felt the brutal onslaught.

The months that followed were a blur of pain and perseverance. A whisper from my soul beckoned me to heal, yet the louder voice of my ego, ever so audacious, urged me to press on. I set a date to re-launch my business in May 2021.

Fueled by determination, I prepped for a well-marketed live webinar. But that fateful morning, my body and mind waged a silent rebellion. Mid-presentation, my world spiraled into chaos. A mini-stroke, witnessed by 27 women, their faces etched with deep concern, stopped me harshly. Only 20 minutes later, sirens blared as an ambulance sped me to our local hospital; it was my first-ever ambulance ride.

Yet, adversity had just begun waving its subtle warnings. As I tried to rebuild my business, doubt and exhaustion seeped in, only to be punctuated by the crippling arrival of shingles. I, the paragon of strength, was unraveling. Intuitively, I was no longer aligned with the outer' business as usual' matrix.

Clueless and in my darkest moment, I cried out to the Divine, "What do you seek of me?" The unmistakable response: "Be still, listen, and embrace your mighty I AM presence."

I finally returned to heeding my own teachings. My journey from that point was a profound voyage to another, deeper level of self-discovery, where the battle between ego and divinity was once more tested and peeled away. Eventually, the omnipotent I AM within emerged triumphant.

In my extensive library of books, one little book kept coming up. "The Impersonal Life" was the book I was guided to study again. Underlined text on yellowed pages from having studied it extensively so many decades past made me buy another copy so I could read it with fresh eyes. After a year of daily meditation and contemplation on each chapter, my path was clear. Align with God's Impersonal Life and Impersonal Love as He guides my desires to serve.

By 2023, the universe acknowledged my newfound alignment, showering me with a dream opportunity to connect with my European roots as Executive Director for a section leading the Global Win-Win Women Organization. However, it was not God's will for me because my ego's seductive voice promptly returned, leading to further health challenges.

The pivotal realization? I had to shed my personal desires and surrender to Divine guidance to truly serve. Amidst external tumult and inner tempests, I found clarity and serenity. I finally surrendered every thread of personal wanting yet listened by becoming more sensitive to my God-Alignment.

Divine intervention introduced me to a visionary (a woman I immediately recognized as my soul-sister) embarking on a global movement for women aged 55 and above: "The Golden Life Community" and "Worldwide Golden Connections." My purpose became clear: facilitating their self-empowerment by guiding these incredible women to live their highest Body-Mind-Spirit potential.

My final life purpose is clear. I couldn't be more excited to begin living the last chapter of my incredibly colorful life by serving women I cherish. It is the mature woman who must remember her unapologetic power and magnificence so that she inspires others to become pillars of a new consciousness and lead the way. This is how we restore God's plan for Earth.

Takeaway for the reader:

Glamour and worldly success can be intoxicating. But it's ephemeral and never defines you. Your true essence is like an uncut diamond; it gleams brightest only after enduring the fiercest trials. Discover that inner gem. Synchronizing with the Divine is the ultimate power, leading to optimal well-being and profound bliss.

Dr. Angelika Christie
Age 78

CHAPTER 53

ADVICE FROM A NONAGENARIAN

ANNE LORIMOR

I love kids! I don't like discourtesy, meanness, or arrogance when you find it, but I am predisposed to like kids. They are so ingenuous, so lacking in artifice, and so very genuine until people or society get hold of them. I'm always happy to encourage kids to be their best selves and lead lives they love. They help keep me young. I'm pleased to offer advice for children, teens, and even adults.

My first **piece of** advice would be to keep yourself fit and healthy in body, mind, and spirit. All of life is better when you feel great. Challenges are met more easily. Keeping yourself bursting with vitality means eating healthful foods in suitable quantities, which may differ for each person. Eating disorders can be so very devastating, and if you need professional help, then find ways to get it. For most of us, it helps to remember, "Food remains in your mouth for only a few moments, in your stomach for a few hours, and a lifetime on your hips." It has always helped me to eat slowly, and if I still feel hungry at the end of a meal that I think is sufficient, to wait a half hour. Mostly, I feel satisfied, but if not, I eat a low-calorie fruit or vegetable, preferably with a lot of fiber.

Exercise is an essential part of keeping fit. Finding an exercise that suits you is crucial, so you will stick to it. I love climbing and hiking, and if I don't get jumping jacks, I can enjoy many exercises that a personal trainer would assign. Unlike many trainers, I believe in gradually working up to your potential so that you won't be stiff, sore, and in agony. I have been so fit for most of my life that I can climb a mountain or take a long bike ride without feeling sore or cramping. Set up a sensible exercise regime suited to you, then do it! However, if you miss one, be kind to yourself. After all, tomorrow is another day. Don't be like some people who throw up their hands and quit if they are imperfect. Hang in there!

My second **bit of** advice is to become financially literate and learn to handle your money well. You should live below your means and pay yourself first. Set aside whatever amount you can; I suggest 10%, but you can work up to that if necessary. That will be for your contingency fund because there will be unexpected expenses and emergencies. When you have saved a safe amount— some experts say 6 months' salary—then you can begin investing in property, stocks, mutual funds, business opportunities, whatever your advisers, your reading, and your temperament cause to feel right for you. It seems so much more sensible to save for what you want rather than to put it on a credit card and end up paying much more for everything, or perhaps even having to go bankrupt, where others suffer too.

I speak in concrete terms for a young child, and they can be as young as 6 or 8. If you get a dollar, put a dime in a piggy bank for charities, spend 3 dimes, put 3 dimes in a savings account to earn interest, and 3 dimes in a subaccount to save for something you want. With today's inflation, I would start with $10 and say dollars everywhere I said dimes. I think allowing yourself some spending money in the equation is essential. I often failed to do this and felt deprived when it wasn't necessary.

Set aside another amount for your church and/or your charities; again, 10% is customary, and it can become much more when you reach the financial status where you are genuinely comfortable. Then consider the rest as what you must live on. If you think it's not enough, find a higher-paying job, but one that you enjoy. Take a second job if needed, but don't let it destroy your desired lifestyle.

Learn about passive income and entrepreneurship. Find a way to make your hobbies pay off. Suppose there is something that you really want. In that case, it is amazing what you can demand of yourself for a short time without doing yourself permanent damage. Immigrants often demonstrate this. Life is before you. You can do what you dream, but don't live paycheck to paycheck or bury yourself in debt.

My third **piece of** advice concerns giving. Get deeply involved in a cause greater than yourself. You can do it as a volunteer or donor on someone else's project that speaks to you, or you can see a need and create a means of meeting that need. Children and very young people have conceived and carried out projects to alleviate hunger and increase learning opportunities for the disadvantaged or succor abused, ill, or neglected pets. Learn from people who are doing the kinds of things that you see need doing. There is a great deal of need in the world, and I see it as essential to find a cause that moves you.

My fourth **bit of** advice is more abstract. It is essential to develop and embrace your own core values and live by them. Integrity, generosity, and reliability are fundamental to me. You can learn from people you admire, from reading, and from movies based on strong values. It's easy to be blinded and dazzled by glitter and glamour, but it is far better to form friendships or romantic attachments based on strong and enduring values.

My final kernel of wisdom can be stated briefly: When you have found your focus, never, **ever** quit; but pivot **when** necessary. Again and again, I see persistence mentioned as a quality required for success, and I see it as a vital factor in my own life. However, I have often found adapting or making changes necessary without losing sight of my goal. My Kilimanjaro Climbs for a Cause had to be postponed, and significant changes were made. Still, I accomplished the climbs, achieved a Guinness World Record, and gained attention and support for my charity, Creating Exciting Futures.

In summary, my advice to children, teens, or adults is basically the same:

1. Keep fit and healthy in body, mind, and spirit.
2. Become financially literate and manage your money well.
3. Get deeply involved in a cause greater than yourself.
4. Develop and cherish your values and live by them.
5. When you have found your focus, never, **ever** quit, but pivot **when** necessary.

As Auntie Mame said, "Life is a banquet," and we don't have to be one of those poor outcasts who are starving to death. We can live so that our lives are exciting, productive, generous, and loving, and with the result that we can make a difference. The ripple effect of our influence on others can make the world a better place to live and to love.

Anne Lorimor
Age 94

CHAPTER 54

FIND YOUR WHY

BARBARA J. MORRIS

"Finding your path, your why, is really about finding and connecting to self-love. When you love yourself, the journey becomes so much clearer, easier, and joyful."
Barbara J. Morris

I asked myself recently why I am writing a book (of which this is part). After all, I'm in my late 70s! I discovered there are several reasons. When I first thought about the possibility of writing my memoir, I had in mind who I would be writing it for. It was women who were feeling stuck, were entering their 50s, and thought it was too late for their dreams to happen. However, when I closed my eyes and dropped into my body and heart, it felt like I needed to write for a younger generation. Those still trying to find their way in a world that is not always welcoming. I want to help them find their true essence so they can show up authentically and impact the world. They need to know there is no reason to fear aging; it is a natural progression and can bring a new kind of joy to one's life when you stay open to possibilities.

I want to help the younger generation circumvent the traps we tend to fall into, derailing our lives. After writing this, I want to benefit both categories of women. I'm undoubtedly receiving personal benefits, like increased confidence in my writing ability! It is helping with my spiritual growth, too. This is about striving to be the best human being I can be in this earth suit. And it's about challenging myself. When we avoid challenging ourselves, no matter our age, we do ourselves a great injustice. Without challenges, we don't learn to stretch and grow. We stifle our creative abilities and can become stagnant.

A saying goes something like this: *If you are not growing, you are dying.* Do you know people like that? They do the same thing day in and day out and think they are living a happy life. I guess that if you look deep into their eyes, you will not see any spark. We need things to spark and make us want to do and be more. It's like our muscles; they atrophy when we don't use them. Use it or lose it, right? I think we all know this.

If my writing this book (or even just this segment) changes even one person's life for the better after reading it, then it will have served its purpose. Of course, I would love to think my story will help many more than just one, but that is not up to me. I release my ego and allow for the success or failure to come. For me, it's not a failure, no matter the outcome, because I am receiving so much in writing it. All is good with my soul.

How wonderful it feels to know that! Each person has their own path and journey, and how they respond to me expressing my essence and vibration, and my story is for them alone. And so it is. Finding your path, your why, is about finding and connecting to self-love. The journey becomes much more straightforward, easier, and joyful when you love yourself.

Yet many of us have a hard time loving ourselves because we sometimes judge ourselves harshly. As an example, you might be overweight like I was and still am. If you are like me, you may think others won't take you seriously or may not even see you. Don't let that define you! Our souls yearn to be seen and heard. You are so much more intelligent than you give yourself credit for. You have family and friends who love you just the way you are. I don't believe that God makes any mistakes when He creates us. You need to find that love deep down inside you where you have stuffed it for too many years.

Each of us has something extraordinary to share with the world, regardless of our appearance or age. I could give you many examples of happy, successful people, but the list would be too long for this space. They don't fit "the look" that today's society wants us to subscribe to. That something special that only YOU have is chomping at the bit to be let out! Many of the things we judge ourselves for are just downright false beliefs we hold on to.

Believe me when I say there are ways to move you from them to that self-love that will transform your life. Others have found their way out to let their light shine, and I want that for you, too! What will your world look like when you learn to forgive yourself, appreciate yourself, and love yourself? I feel in my gut that your light will shine so bright when you get to this knowing for yourself.

Barbara J. Morris
Age 77

CHAPTER 55

A SPRING IN MY STEP

BARB LAUBMAN

I realized that getting older didn't have to mean giving up on the things that made me feel alive. It was simply an invitation to explore different avenues and deepen my understanding of myself and my capabilities.

Throughout my life, I have been known as someone who loves physical challenges. From a young age, I eagerly participated in sports, pushed my limits, and continuously sought new adventures. Whether climbing mountains, running marathons, or engaging in intense workouts, my body was always in motion. It felt like I was invincible, and nothing could ever hold me back.

However, as the years passed and I entered my sixties, life threw a series of unexpected challenges my way. Accidents began to happen, affecting my knees, wrists, and shoulders. These injuries left me devastated, feeling as if my active lifestyle had come to an abrupt end. The thought of not being able to do all the activities I once loved caused me to feel frustrated at getting older and unable to do the level of activities I had once done.

During my lowest point, a wake-up call came knocking at my door. I could either succumb to despair and let my injuries define my life, or I could embrace the challenge, adapt, and find new ways to stay active.

With renewed determination, I embarked on a journey of self-discovery and adaptation.

I sought guidance from physical therapists and experts in the field, eager to learn how to modify my exercise routine and activities for longevity.

I discovered that it wasn't about giving up on my passions but finding creative ways to continue pursuing them while caring for my body.

One of the most important lessons I learned was the power of pivoting and changing my mindset. Instead of mourning the loss of certain physical activities, I focused on the ones I could still do. I delved into yoga, eccentrics, and hiking, which offered a low-impact way to keep my body moving without causing further damage. Gradually, I started to appreciate these new experiences and the joy they brought me.

Something incredible happened as I embraced this new approach to fitness and well-being. The depression that had once engulfed me began to lift, replaced by a sense of gratitude and excitement for the next phase of my life. I realized that getting older didn't have to mean giving up on the things that made me feel alive. It was simply an invitation to explore different avenues and deepen my understanding of myself and my capabilities.

As I strolled through the park today, I noticed a spring in my step that wasn't there before. My knees may not allow me to run marathons anymore, but they can still carry me to beautiful places. My wrists may not tolerate the strain of intense workouts, but they can still hold a paintbrush or strum a guitar. And my shoulder, though a little weaker, can still embrace loved ones in warm hugs.

Life throws unexpected challenges our way, but how we respond to them genuinely matters.

I have understood that every setback is an opportunity for growth, a chance to redefine ourselves and discover new strengths. By adapting our exercise routines, modifying our activities, and changing our mindset, we can navigate the twists and turns of life with grace and resilience.

So, let us not be discouraged by the hurdles that come our way. Instead, let us embrace them as catalysts for personal growth and transformation.

Barb Laubman
Age 70

CHAPTER 56

PARADIGM SHIFT

BONNIE L. SENFTNER

As there really is no space and time, age is just a number, and the chronological number is an illusion.

"Wow, I'm impressed!" I exclaimed. You're 83 years old and just learning how to dive!" I stared in awe at the gentleman who looked like he had stepped out of the book The Old Man and the Sea with his pure white windblown hair and weathered skin. The scuba diving class consisted mostly of twenty-somethings, and he seemed a bit out of character.

"Young lady," he replied, with a sparkle in his eyes. "I only learned how to swim when I was 70! Don't ever believe that you are too old for anything!"

What words of inspiration I have carried with me through each subsequent decade of life! The surreal thing about aging is that even if our body shows signs of it, like creaking knees and wrinkles, or we notice physical things diminishing, like not being able to plop down on the ground, sit cross-legged, and then jump up quickly when we are ready, we always seem to stay young in our heads.

I remember our Aunt Stella, who attended an all-class reunion and called all her classmates (who were in their 70s) "kids." Yes, in her mind, they were still those teens she knew way back when.

When friends would start to bemoan their decadent birthdays approaching, whether they were turning thirty, forty, or fifty, I created my own words of wisdom that I would share with them: "Chronological aging is God's cosmic joke, as we never become old like the old people were when we were young." It is so true. So now, in my seventies, I go back to my reunions and still think of my classmates as kids. We somehow never get old in our minds unless we fall victim to the hype that we are supposed to believe we are old. It is all about our mindset!

What is the hype? Society encourages people to believe that it is all right to get out of shape because we are getting older. It's permissible to be overweight and settle for being fat and frumpy because we are over a certain age.

One of my callings is to help people avoid this harmful and false mindset. We can all age gracefully with class and style if we change our thoughts about aging and believe we can achieve and be anything we want (except chronologically younger)!

In my twenties, I thought people were old. I remember thinking how "old" our parents were when we were in high school. Most of the parents were in their forties.

I remember a few of my friends having a crisis when they reached thirty. They feared they needed to accomplish more compared to others. Or worrisome were those who were not married and did not have children. Even worse was noticing physical changes, like the first wrinkles or gray hair! I had a roommate in my thirties when I put myself through nursing school. She was the same age. She would look into the mirror and say, "Beauty Queen, is that you?" We would laugh and laugh, thinking we were getting old, as we saw a wrinkle crop up here and there and noticed our bodies were not like the fitness gurus we were in our twenties. She once told me, "When I was younger, men in their cars would happily honk as I crossed the street; now they try to run me over!"

Wham! And then the big 4-0 hits. That was the first decade I personally struggled with getting older. I called one of my best friends from high school and said, "I cannot believe we are now our parents age when we were in high school!" This whole aging thing created a little trauma response in me. I bought a card that said, "I ran into an old friend from high school the other day, and she looked marvelous! She hadn't gained an ounce and didn't have a single wrinkle. So, I ran into her again!"

Even though I did not like the chronological number, there were a lot of benefits to being older. I had more confidence in who I was and what I believed. After facing different challenges and curveballs in life, I learned that most of what I worried about never materialized, and in the rare case that it did, things always had a way of working out somehow. My travel experiences with being older and better financially established allowed me to start traveling the world and developing more empathy and understanding for people with diverse backgrounds and perspectives. People are pretty much the same wherever they go. Everyone wants to love and be loved; family and friends mean everything to them and are the highest priority for most people.

When I turned fifty, I was so traumatized that it took two years to settle into that decade before I could admit that I was in my fifties. *That is when I finally realized that aging is just an illusion. As we learn, we remain young in our minds if we have the proper mindset. We eventually understand that we are letting in one of life's biggest secrets. As there really is no space and time, age is just a number, and the chronological number is an illusion.* Pick any time you feel like you are, and that is the magic of it. I am twenty-eight!

Turning sixty was not as bad for me as turning fifty, but I did not like mail ads for hearing aids, AARP membership, good gracious, and burial plots!

Studies show that people who see aging as a potential for personal growth tend to enjoy a happier life and better health in their seventies, eighties, nineties, and beyond than people who view aging with helplessness and decline. In this decade of life, most people can retire and have financial freedom. Suppose they have been wise enough to eat correctly by eliminating processed foods and refined sugar and have kept up physically by working out and building muscle, which deteriorates the older we get. In that case, studies show they are significantly happier than their middle-aged counterparts. However, one of the best rewards is slowing down, savoring life, and giving back to others. Martin Luther King said, "Life's most persistent and urgent question is, *'What are you doing for others?'*" Being retired allows one to have time to volunteer for charities that they believe in. My personal ones are organizations that help foster children, sex-trafficked victims, and animals.

However, one of the most significant benefits of aging is finding peace. There is a well-known rule called the 18-40-60. At 18, you worry about what everybody thinks of you; when you are 40, you don't care what anybody thinks of you; when you're 60, you realize nobody's been thinking about you. People spend their days worrying and thinking about themselves, not you.

So, no, those with an ageless mindset are not sitting in our rocking chairs reminiscing about the past. We find great comfort in living in the moment and planning our future. Many find immense joy in becoming mentors for younger generations by encouraging them to develop a positive mindset about getting older.

Embracing every decade with the wisdom imparted and learning to be grateful for life's lessons and blessings is a message those of us who are chronologically older want to share. The greatest gift is finally realizing that life's most significant purpose is to love and be loved in return.

And did you get what you wanted from life? I did. And what did you want?

"To call myself beloved, to feel myself beloved on the earth." ~
Raymond Carver

Bonnie L. Senftner
Age 72

CHAPTER 57

THE CIRCLE OF LIFE: THE ECHO OF LORRAINE'S LOVE AND LEGACY

CATHERINE SCHWARK

"Let us be the authors of compassion, for in our smallest deeds, we script a legacy that whispers hope to the hearts of the future." -- Catherine

In my thirties, I was employed at the Minneapolis Veteran's Hospital. Two days a week, this tiny 5-foot tall, 71-year-old, wavy, silver-haired ball of energy named Lorraine bounced into my office. She always came in wearing the brightest, biggest smile and carried herself with the most joyful spirit. Star beams radiated from her eyes, and her aura was otherworldly. She was the volunteer assigned to me; in my eyes, she was indispensable. She often surprised me when she questioned if she was 'really' doing anything purposeful. She was more helpful to me than the paid staff, and I enjoyed her company more, too.

Lorraine's husband, Niles, a tall 77-year-old WWII US Veteran, also volunteered at the hospital. They'd been together since she was sixteen. Their family legacy was impressive, with nine children, thirty-nine grandchildren, and seventy-five great-grandchildren.

Their dedication to service was apparent. On the days they volunteered, their alarms were set for 5:45 a.m. After a quick bite to eat, they traveled over two hours, transferring onto multiple city buses before arriving at the VA. Rain or shine, they were punctual and committed and never missed a day.

Their bond was evident, too. At the end of the day, Niles would come to our office to pick up his beloved bride of 55 years. He'd poke his head around the doorway and say, "It's time to go, honey." Niles would wait patiently for Lorraine, and together, they would walk hand-in-hand through the hospital corridors and the ginormous parking lot to the bus station pavilion. Their enduring love was palpable.

But life threw a curveball. Niles was hospitalized for heart complications. Even during his stay, he managed to surprise me. Sneaking around the hospital, he collected over a hundred business cards for a family scavenger hunt I mentioned in passing. Despite my shock and concern for his well-being, Lorraine, with a chuckle, reassured me that it made him happy. Thanks to him, I won that hunt.

But shortly after his discharge, Niles passed away.

Lorraine's resilience shone through her grief. She continued to volunteer, her spirit undimmed. However, the thought of her commuting alone on those dark, cold Minnesota afternoons was unbearable. I began driving her home.

Our car rides were filled with heartfelt conversations, laughter, shared stories of our families and faith, and a little office gossip.

One day, as I mentioned my desire to quit smoking and the high cost of a treatment program I couldn't afford, Lorraine, without hesitation, offered to cover the expenses. I initially resisted, thinking of how she could use that money within her large family. Yet, her insistence and a deep sense of caring in her voice compelled me to accept. I later wondered if, at one time, Niles might have been a smoker and if this was her way of ensuring someone else didn't face the same fate.

I attended the program, but shortly after, a mental health crisis kept me away from work and the world for years. I never saw Lorraine again. I never got to explain my sudden absence or express my gratitude for her generosity and its profound impact on my life. Lorraine and Niles Quinn showed me what enduring love looks like. They displayed the benefits of selflessness and service.

Lorraine's resilience in the face of loss taught me that we truly get to decide how we will show up.

As I venture into the Third Act of my life, I'm driven to pay forward Lorraine's kindness. I'm on a mission to set up the Quinn-Schwark Foundation, a beacon for those affected by addictions and trauma, a testament to the enduring power of human connection, love, and the profound ripples one act of kindness can create.

The one lady in the Third Act of her life who believed she really wasn't contributing much has led this lady in the Third Act of her life to carry on her legacy.

Catherine Schwark, AKA Catharine From Minnesota
Age 63

CHAPTER 58

FRIENDSHIPS

CIS AHEARN

Nothing that was said or done will ever dull the beauty of friendship. Life is that way.

When I first met her, I hated her. What followed was an incredible 25-year friendship, and then it ended. This happens in friendships. We can look at them as evil events or be grateful for the gifts within them. Here is that story.

We worked at the same hospital in Burlington. I didn't even know who she was until the man of my dreams took me to dinner to tell me he'd met "the girl of his dreams." It wasn't me. So, all I could feel was loathing. Yet, life had another plan for me.

We all parked in the same place and walked the 200 yards together to work, rain, snow, or shine. For whatever reason, she and Dane always ended up walking next to or close to me, and she was very chatty. She asked me about work, what I was doing on the weekend, if I had cats, and so on. She was very curious and friendly.

I wanted nothing to do with her. She was cute, cheery, funny, and she was with him. Yet, she would not let up. So, one day in late January of 1985, she wanted to know what I was doing on the weekend as we walked into work. I said, "Celebrating my 30th birthday at the Daily Planet," and she said, "Oh, great, what can we bring?" She invited herself and him to my birthday party!!!! I thought, how am I going to explain this to my friends?!?!?!

It wasn't on my birthday that our friendship started; it began the next day when she called and asked if I wanted to go cross-country skiing with her. That day!!!! Brownie points for spontaneity!!! From then on, we played whenever we could in the snow. She'd call up and say, "When are you off work? I have a bottle of champagne. Let's go...." Since Dane was always on call, we were off to explore somewhere at least once a week.

The wedding was the hardest for me at the time. Yet, because we were friends, I inherited a family of sisters (I had no sisters) and a fantastic variety of life experiences through her and Dane and then her children. We all traveled to ski resorts and beaches together, took diving trips, met in Europe, and more. I was there when she and Dane separated and got back together when her babies were born and when she got cancer.

Over time, I became increasingly curious about spiritual thinking, self-empowerment, and healing for myself and others. I dove into self-awareness and loving others. And a gap was created. Whenever I would share my enthusiasm about what I was learning, she would ask, "Why would you want to explore that?" When I became a part of Tony Robbins's world, Dane found reasons to diss Tony and the inspiring world I'd stepped into.

Suddenly, staying upright in my thoughts and sharing was a constant battle. The relationship began to crumble.

I felt like I had to hold my arms up to defer the blows of my life choices. It wasn't until later that I realized I was being judged for having different thoughts than our group. I was in a defensive position whenever I shared how awesome I felt, so I stopped sharing.

The friendship ended right after my mom passed. I really needed some love and connection from my friend, and she didn't come. Then Dane and I had words one day; the next day, she wrote and said the friendship was over. I was too tired and sad about my mom to want to defend even those silly words, so I let it go. In one short year, I'd lost all my support systems.

Here's the thing: *if it "doesn't kill you, it will make you stronger,"* which is what became of me. I was suddenly not my mother's daughter, a best friend, or a burden to others; I was becoming who I had always meant to be. There were no obstacles. Suddenly, doors and ideas opened for me.

Today I look back and feel nothing but pure Love and gratitude for that friendship. A quote that Tony Robbins says came to mind for me, " If you want to take the island, then burn the boats". I had to walk away. Be okay with doing what needs to be done. Take the gifts and leave behind any pain. I still think about some of the funny things she did where I'd end up howling with laughter. I remember the gifts.

It's been almost 10 years since then. We still text Happy Mother's Day to each other, and when her mom passed, we texted quite a lot. I felt that I wanted to be there for her. And I still hold out that one day, when we're old, she will put down her sword, and we will be friends again. Because I have.

Nothing that was said or done will ever dull the beauty of friendship. Life is that way.

Cis Ahearn
Age 70

CHAPTER 59

THE SPIRIT OF LISTENING – LESSONS

DEBI LYNN

As her kids slumbered peacefully on those beds, she was filled with a feeling of safety and optimism.

The 26-year-old woman stood at a crossroads, overwhelmed by the decision she had to make. Her young children depended on her, and with only $100 in her pocket, no job prospects, and nowhere to call home, she knew she needed to make a change. Despite the fear of the unknown that awaited her, she took a leap of faith. She left behind her difficult past in Oregon, setting off on a bold journey to Texas in search of a better life.

Having faced adversity and heartache in her young life, this high school graduate had already experienced the pain of losing a child. *Despite her hardships, she held on to a glimmer of hope, believing that a new beginning awaited her in Texas.*

Upon reaching Texas, she sought refuge in a small, humble apartment made possible by the kindness of a church she had joined. The compassionate members of the church took her and her two children under their wings, providing much-needed support and assistance during these trying times.

Feeling the warmth of her newfound community, she worked to create a stable home for herself and her children. Through the church's thrift store shopping spree, they secured a comfy couch and solid bunk beds for her little ones. *As her kids slumbered peacefully on those beds, she was filled with a feeling of safety and optimism.*

However, she knew that she needed to become self-sufficient to create lasting change. The church recognized her determination and eagerness to improve her situation, so they rallied behind her in her quest to find employment. They provided encouragement and networking opportunities and even offered to babysit her children while she attended job interviews.

Realizing the importance of acquiring new skills, she took the initiative to enroll in a trade school that offered introductory word processing courses. She was eager to expand her horizons and open new possibilities for herself. *Studying while balancing her responsibilities as a mother was challenging. Still, she persisted, motivated by the dream of a brighter future for her family.*

Days turned into weeks, and weeks turned into months. The tenacity and hard work of this young woman did not go unnoticed. Through determination, she landed a job as an office assistant, utilizing the word-processing skills she had acquired. With a stable income, she could provide for her children and gradually build a better life for them.

As the years passed, this once-struggling mother continued to blossom and grow. She never forgot the kindness and support the church had shown her and vowed to pay it forward. In her newfound stability, she started volunteering at the church that had given her a helping hand.

She wanted to be a beacon of hope and inspiration for others who were going through tough times, just as she had once been.

The story of this young woman's journey was met with a mixture of emotions from the people in her community. On the one hand, many were inspired by her bravery and determination to make a better life for herself and her children. However, others were more skeptical, believing it would be impossible for someone to turn their life around. But when they got to Texas, the sun seemed brighter and the air sweeter for this remarkable woman and her children. People embraced them with open arms, showing that with love and support, anything is possible. This inspiring tale became a testament to what can be achieved against all odds and a reminder of hope in even the darkest times.

Debi Lynn
Age 67

CHAPTER 60

OUR AGELESS, TIMELESS LOVE

DENISE YONKERS

The true essence of a person lies not in their years but in the depth of their character and the light of their spirit.

The greatest blessing of my life was the twenty-seven years of love and companionship I shared with my best friend and late husband, John F. Yonkers. *I could not have celebrated life without him! It was as if we were transported by the Heavens to meet at this one place in time on that warm June afternoon in 1985 when we first met. It was like a dance of fate; few things compare to the magic of a beautiful, loving relationship between a man and a woman.* This was the beginning of our relationship, which eventually led to our marriage. It is my story of our two souls, bound by love, trust, and affection, that transcend the boundaries of time and space.

Communication nurtured the foundation of our relationship. *Open, honest, and compassionate conversations created an environment where we both felt heard, valued, and respected. We were beginning to build our future. Trust is the cornerstone of a flourishing relationship.* Trust is not merely about faithfulness in fidelity but also about having confidence in each other's decisions, intentions, and abilities.

We created an environment where trust could thrive, allowing us to explore the world with a sense of security and assurance. We honored our differences. We cherished the value of each other's presence in our lives. We expressed gratitude for the little things that often go unnoticed but contribute to our happiness.

We invested time and effort in understanding each other's emotional needs, fears, and desires.

We loved being together and sharing our lives together. Vulnerability was met with empathy and tenderness, strengthening our emotional bonds. Small gestures of affection and genuine interest in each other's well-being were the building blocks of our emotional intimacy.

Since we were older when we married, we decided not to have children but to satisfy our need to nurture by adopting our pets. Our pets brought us great joy, happiness, and laughter. We celebrated triumphs and provided comfort during times of sorrow, recognizing that personal growth is part of the journey. We encouraged each other to pursue our passions, dreams, and ambitions.

Laughter filled the air when we were together as we found humor in the simple joys of life. ***Our burdens were light in each other's presence, and laughter became a healing balm that mended wounds and strengthened our shared connection.*** Amid times of challenges and hardships, our love stood unshaken and resilient.

We remembered our commitment to one another and let our love serve as a guiding light, illuminating the path through life's uncertainties. Through the highs and lows, we kept holding each other close, knowing that our marriage is a cherished gift that grows more valuable with time.

In the end, this beautiful, loving relationship between a man and a woman is a testament to love's transformative power. Through the highs and lows, the laughter, and the tears, we wove a tapestry of love that transcends the limitations of this world. *John passed away from cancer in 2013.*

In the symphony of aging, I learned the art of accepting the passage of time, the changes in my body, and the ever-changing versions of myself. With grace, I shed the expectations of my youth, realizing that beauty is not confined to youth's energy but flourishes within our authenticity. I endure life's storms with resilience.

I learned to love myself unconditionally, cherish every moment, and find joy in everyday miracles. I embrace the beauty that is within me. I sing and dance the dance of grace and acceptance; I revel in the fullness of my being, understanding that I am a timeless soul illuminated by life's journey. *My memories become treasures, guiding me through time and unfolding the cherished experiences that shape who I am.*

The beauty of aging taught me to discover the true value of each moment and to live in the present; for now, it will become the foundation for my future memories. *I am creating the next chapters of my life, creating my new future, sharing my passion for venturing out and exploring new exotic, foreign places, and living my dream of flying without fear.*

I honor and salute you, John F. Yonkers. I am filled with immense love for the great memories and your endless love and devotion to me, our pets, our families, our friends, and the people we served. My heart is continually filled with gratitude and love for the time our lives aligned with each other here on this earth.

I wish you, the one true love of my life, to dwell in a place of light where you can feel God's true, pure love for all eternity. A place of refreshment and peace. A place where evil cannot dwell ever again. A place where sickness and disease are no longer present. A place where there is no hatred or war. A place where there is unity, not division. *A place where our souls will align once again to dance with grace and to the vibration of our new symphony.*

Denise Yonkers
Age 69

CHAPTER 61

MANIFESTING A DREAM...MINE!

DOLLY KENNEDY

Dancing makes me happy, and at 98 years young, I even feel sexy. The best part of all is that it keeps my entire body healthy!

My mother was a courageous, 18-year-old young woman who affectionately named her newborn baby girl ... "Dolly!" (legally, Yvonne M. Smith!) 3/2/26. Her beloved baby girl grew up in Buffalo, New York, attended local schools, and upon graduating from high school in 1943, this 17 1/2-year-old entered the US Cadet Nurse Corps, a government-funded program intended to attract young women to the nursing profession, a worthy and much-needed cause.

The program's parameters involved a three-year commitment, e.g., living in the hospital dorm, attending classes at the University of Buffalo, and working in the hospital simultaneously. At that time, there were no orderlies or assistants to care for the patients, and the "probies" (student nurses) were expected to assist with 20 or more patients.

Dolly completed her training in three years; however, New York state law required applicants to be 21 when applying for the state board exam. Dolly's "California Dream" plan was placed on hold for three months, and those three months were crucial in finding a companion. Mary (her roommate of three years) chose to join her en route to California. They both had relatives there. Mary would stay and work in a doctor's office (her uncle), and after a short visit, Dolly intended to travel to Hawaii and start a nursing career at Queens Hospital.

At that time, Queens Hospital offered passage back to the mainland after being employed with them for one year! It sounded like a plan; however, the Love Bug intervened!!!

Dolly was introduced to a charming young man, her soulmate! She repeatedly delayed her trip, and after a year, Paul (the handsome young man) asked Dolly to stay in California and marry him! Her answer? "Yes! If you promise to take me to Hawaii." However, she didn't say WHEN!!!!

Paul agreed, and 18 months later, they were married on September 11, 1948.

Fast-forward 25 years and seven "offspring." Paul presented Dolly with tickets to Hawaii! OMG, after 25 years, he remembered! That was an amazing anniversary gift. How could I possibly show my appreciation?

I'll tell you, but first, you must promise me you won't tell a soul. You won't, will you? It did take some doing; however, I was determined! For three months, I secretly took mid-eastern dance lessons.

When we arrived at our hotel in Hawaii, Paul sat down with a cool drink, and I excused myself for a few moments.

I quickly donned my "passion pink" costume, turned up the volume on my tape recorder (that survived security), and gave my first performance... for an audience of one!!!! Needless to say, Paul was impressed with HIS anniversary gift!

Would you believe I continued dancing and taught mid-eastern dance at the University of Phoenix Adult Education for two years? We had so much fun!!!

Dancing makes me happy, and at 98 years young, I even feel sexy. The best part of all is that it keeps my entire body healthy!

Let's turn up the music, Ladies! Smile, and let's dance!

Dolly Kennedy
Age 98

CHAPTER 62
CONNIE, MY INFAMOUS MOTHER-IN-LAW

DIANE BERG

Her teachings have influenced how I approach life, with a sense of adventure, fearlessness, and the belief that we should pursue what brings us joy.

My mother-in-law, yes, mother-in-law, was one of the most influential people in my life. She was full of piss and vinegar. She had an incredible sense of humor and could captivate an audience with her exciting stories, singing, and dancing. She sang "Bird on a Gilded Cage" by popular demand and swung her roaring '20s beads at her 80th birthday party.

I learned so much from her, like cooking and playing bridge, but the most important lesson I learned was living life to its fullest. She lived a full and vibrant life, surrounded by countless friends and family. People who knew her remember her fondly and often speak about her with admiration and a smile. To this day, I hear her many quotes being repeated over and over again. Like: *"As we get older, we are who we are, only more so."* In other words, make sure you cultivate your good qualities.

Her impact on how I live my life is immeasurable. She taught me to seize the moment, follow my passions, and go for the gusto. Another saying of hers was, *"There is only one time on the clock of life, and it is NOW."*

If you feel stressed, you are living in the past. If you feel worried, you are living in the future. When you feel happy and content, you are living in the present moment.

I can still envision her lively presence, making everyone laugh and smile with her infectious energy. She knew how to entertain and had an uncanny way of engaging everyone in her presence. Whether sharing her fascinating stories or belting out a song, she knew how to captivate an audience.

But it wasn't just her entertainment skills that made her influential. She taught me practical skills, too. I can credit her patient teachings with my culinary abilities and proficiency in playing bridge. She took the time to pass down her knowledge, ensuring I had the tools to enjoy simple pleasures like gardening and socializing. She had a heart of gold and always took food to someone who had lost a loved one or just needed a home-cooked meal to brighten their day.

Yet, her wisdom and outlook on life resonate with me the most. Her quotes, often filled with humor and a touch of wisdom, have become my guiding principles. *Her teachings have shaped how I approach life with a sense of adventure, fearlessness, and the belief that we should continuously pursue what brings us joy.*

"I carry her spirit within me, even though she is no longer with us." Her impact continues to serve as a reminder to live life passionately, embrace opportunities, and face challenges head-on. I treasure the memories and lessons she shared and strive to honor her vibrant spirit by living life to the fullest, just as she did. So, here's to my extraordinary mother-in-law. Her stories, laughter, and teachings will always hold a special place in my heart. May I strive to be half as good a mother-in-law as she was!

Diane Berg
Age 73

CHAPTER 63

RETIRING ON MY TERMS

ELIZABETH LUPACCHINO DONOHUE

At 70 years YOUNG, I am still working and enjoying each and every day more than the last.

You are telling me that I need to retire at 65; why? I don't want to, so I'm not going to! There is no way we would have heard these brave, forward-thinking words uttered by our mothers. When retirement age came, there were retirement parties, planned vacations, and all kinds of celebrations marking the end of the journey.

Well, I am not going down that road; I am creating my own road. At 70 years old, I am still working and enjoying each day more than the last. Most of my friends are my age and have been retired for years. They look at me and wonder why

I'm still working. Financially, I don't have to, but I enjoy what I'm doing; I'm making a difference in people's lives and my own, and it is keeping me young!

I hear them complaining about being bored or not knowing what to do. My mindset is that I am still young and energized, and I will continue doing what I enjoy. It is not work; it is how I can give back and help others.

I am a certified hypnotherapist who works with women with forgiveness issues. I have worked with clients for over 25 years in hospitals and private settings. And now, I am also working with women online. I saw an incredible need when Covid hit to be able to reach out and help even more people. These women may have said or done something they regret or may have had things said or done to them that they need to forgive so they can cut the cords attaching them and allow themselves to move on! To become the woman they were meant to be.

I have my own story about forgiveness, which brought me to where I am today. If I had not experienced verbal abuse in my marriage and gained the strength to get a divorce, I would not know what it is like to forgive and move on. I would not be married to the wonderful man I am married to today.

Listen to your own heart. What do you want to do? Just because it is what other people are doing does not mean it is your right decision!! Be your own person. If you are not ready to retire, then don't! Hang in there, create, and follow your own journey.

Elizabeth Lupacchino Donohue
Age 70

CHAPTER 64

LIVING MY 20S IN MY 50S

JOELLYN WLAZLOWSKI MARTIN

"Faith is taking the First Step when you don't see the Whole Staircase" Martin Luther King Jr.
I wanted to find new love in 3 years! I wanted to know what it felt like again to be in love. As silly as that sounded, that is what I wanted.

What we did back then: if we were not going to college, we married. I had 3 sons born in 1976, 1980, and 1986. I loved being a Mommy. One of the many advantages of being a younger mom was that I was also a young grandmother, becoming a "Nana" in 2000 at age 45. At the time of the divorce, there were 7 grandchildren, and since then, one more, making 4 boys and 4 girls. Oh, how I love and adore them!

I had contemplated divorce a few times over the 34 years that ultimately ended in 2008. It was an amicable divorce, but it was still difficult on my grown children. Now what? This is when life got very interesting! I was no longer a wife; my children were having their own children, and I was starting over at age 54.

As scared as I was to move into an apartment, I was also a little excited. I had never lived by myself before! On the first day of moving in, I met another newly divorced woman, who I did not know then would play an essential role in my single life. A few days later, I met another woman who was also newly divorced. We became somewhat like the 3 Musketeers.

There is something strange about divorcing—the friends I thought I had disappeared except for my BFF. I had to find new friends. Due to the stress, I suppose I don't remember many details. Still, my new friends and I started to have great conversations about our families and what plans we were trying to make to move forward. I did not want my family to worry about me. I felt that I needed to be brave for them more than for me. I did keep a journal about some of those conversations. We talked about how great it would be to share with other women. We were ahead of our time. Little did we know that we could have been Podcasters! What a hoot that would have been.

It can take 3 to 5 years to move on, get over, whatever you want to call it from a divorce. Having lived life a certain way for so many years was not going to be an easy change, even though I wanted to. I wanted to find new love in 3 years! I wanted to know what it felt like again to be in love. As silly as that sounded, that is what I wanted.

People told me to go take some classes and focus on myself. I was focused on myself but in other ways. I got a personal trainer, worked out 3 times a week, and walked almost every day, and soon, I would add dancing...lots of dancing. Working out and dancing are things that I wish I had continued with. Those few months were the strongest and best I had looked in years!

Except for 2 things! Having 3 babies, big babies, with my first being a cesarean, my stomach I thought needed more work than exercising could fix.

I felt very self-conscious about starting dating. I told one of my friends, and she laughed! Then she told me with a straight face that men would not care about my stomach and that I should get implants. I was shocked! Even though I liked the idea, I thought that I would never do that! After a couple of weeks, I made an appointment with a plastic surgeon. I dragged my BFF with me. She was in total denial that I needed to do anything. Of course, she never saw me naked either, at least not before being in the doctor's office. During the appointment, the doctor draws out what he thinks I need on my chest, and I am laughing at this point. What the hell am I doing? I am still not sure, so I have my BFF come into the room. She takes one look and says, "Yes, you need to get this done." All of that breastfeeding had taken its toll. Now we are both hysterically laughing!

One of my new friends suggested that I start dating online. What the heck is that? I had only heard of two other people who had tried, and wasn't it dangerous to be meeting strange men? Well, she says, "How else are you going to meet any?" She gets me started with my profile, and I wind up being on 4 different sites. Oh my... this is going to be a full-time job. Back then, in 2009, it was all innocent fun. There was no swiping left or right. I had to read the profiles. Of course, it did not take long to learn that after seeing a few of these men in person, they looked nothing like their picture! I did have a system set up so that someone would always know where I was. I would get a text or a call a few minutes into the meetup and give a code word if everything was OK or not. I never felt in danger, but I did have times when I knew it was not the right dating person for me and had to end it because I had an emergency and needed to leave. That was the easiest way. No hurt feelings.

What I learned during that time was that there were lots of men who were lonely and hurt and just wanted to talk. I had several lunches and dinners like that. It was not just about hookups. Now, that is not to say that there weren't any! Both of my new friends loved dancing. One was into country western, and one was salsa. Since I have always loved to dance and did some ballroom, I learned quickly with country western. When dancing with a good dancer, I was floating in the air. I loved the faster turns and twirls. The salsa was not my thing, but my new friend was an excellent dancer. My first time going country dancing, I was scared to death. What if someone asks me? My friend did not tell me that it was ladies' night and there were many single men! We were only there about 15 minutes, and this guy started hanging around us. My friend noticed him first and said, "I don't think he is going anywhere!" OMG, he asked me to dance. I did not trip or step on his feet, so I survived!

We know that some people come into our lives for a reason, a season, or a lifetime. "Those two women were my lifeline for the first several months." I ended up leaving the apartment and keeping in touch with the ladies for a while. Still, eventually, they moved away, too. I looked again with my BFF to find a new home for me. I wound up having a condo built, and I just loved it. As someone once told me, I lived there for about 2 ½ years, having the world by its tail. By the end of 2010, I was ready to stop dating for a while. It was coming up on my 3-year window, and I felt defeated in not finding love.

One night, I got this message on Plenty of Fish. Is it still being used today? I was not planning on meeting this guy, but after our first conversation, he seemed nice enough and kept leaving me messages. I agreed to meet him for lunch. I walk into the restaurant, and he is sitting in the booth. I am thinking, "No, I don't think so." I sit down, and he starts coughing. It was evident that he was not feeling well. I eventually told him that I thought he should go to the doctor and that he might have pneumonia. He says that he gets this every year. Good grief! We make it through lunch, and he gives me a present of this gorgeous scarf. I now think that it was very generous and lovely! It was time for me to go, and he said he would walk me to my car. Of course, that was

OK. While walking next to each other in the parking lot towards my car, I got the strangest feeling! It was a sense of calm and connectedness, and I thought this guy might be OK after all. As I got into my car, he walked over to his truck, which was not far from my car. He stood outside his door, smiling and watching me drive off. The next day, he called me after he had gone to the doctor to tell me that he had bronchitis, which was better than pneumonia.

Since I had become such an expert...Ha! Ha!... at reading men by this point, I asked him for his address and said that I would be dropping off chicken soup! A way to a man's heart is indeed through his stomach. I found love at the beginning of December 2010 and reached my 3-year goal of being married the following New Year's Eve 2011. Every anniversary when we go out is like having a big celebration with people we don't know! We had many good times getting to know each other during our dating time. He had also been divorced for a few years with one adult son. It was all so new, exciting, and a little strange.

When I told my husband that I would be a part of this collaborative book, he told me, "Do not forget to talk about the shoeboxes." I was surprised that he remembered. You see, with the few men I had dated, I kept a shoebox of memorabilia and had one for him, too. Of course, the other boxes are long gone, but his shoebox has grown and grown. What seemed like the beginning of a fairy tale in 2012, only 3 months later, tragedy struck. Our lives would not be what we had expected for the following decade, but we survived to tell the story. For right now..."All is Well with My Soul!"

Joellyn Wlazlowski Martin
Age 69

CHAPTER 65

LESSONS FOR A MAGNIFICENT LIFE

JANA LEE GATTUNG

Lessons Learned In My Treatment Rooms And In Life
Please remember that life is a choice, living is a choice, and joy is a choice that is all up to you!

As a Licensed Acupuncturist, I have been honored to treat many people over the last 26 years. Most people usually enter my clinic as a last resort, desperate for help. Some issues are minor, while some patients have been diagnosed as terminal by their MDs. But ALL have a story to tell, and part of the healing that takes place in my treatment room is giving them a place to be 100% heard. I have a true God-given gift as a Healer, but I am not seeking praise. Every person seeking my help has also profoundly impacted how I look at life, especially those I helped transition into the next plane of existence. The following are "Lessons in Life" that I have gleaned from my time with patients and Family, common threads that have stood out as secrets to a happier, more fulfilled life. It seems only fitting that I share them in this book celebrating life, aging, and the joys that come with it. I hope you find them as precious as I have.

Lesson 1 – Decide to be grateful for at least one specific thing every day! This became homework for almost every one of my patients, especially those who didn't have enough joy in their lives. One of the great things about being a healthcare practitioner is seeing people with worse issues than your own. That in itself made me grateful every day. Many people get caught up in their "stuff" so much that they don't see the beautiful things happening around them. When you aren't living in gratitude and awe, life can be a dark and joyless place. Gratitude lifts us into a higher vibration, into the light and out of the dark. Medically speaking, those who live in gratitude daily have a better healing prognosis, shorter healing time, and fewer ailments. Get yourself a huge pad of sticky notes. Every day, while looking in your bathroom mirror, write something you are grateful for, even if it is the violet blooming up through the crack in your sidewalk. Place this on your mirror and add to it daily, making a ring around your mirror. Read ALL of them every day, and only take the old ones down to replace them when you have completed your ring. I guarantee this alone will supply more joy every day.

Lesson 2 – Forgive whoever, for whatever, sooner rather than later! Several of my patients had to convince me of this, as I have a narcissistic family member who has terrorized me my entire life, and I was convinced I shouldn't need to forgive them. What I experienced and witnessed from others is that holding negative feelings towards a person can create illness in your body and more negative experiences for yourself. "Poor Me" isn't a state of health, joy, energy, or anything good. When I forgave this family member, it indeed was like the weight of the world had been lifted from my shoulders and the sun had come out from behind a cloud. If you have a hard time with this, as I did, write an in-depth letter to them explaining how they made you feel and why it's in YOUR best interest to forgive them, then burn the letter. As the ashes replace the words and wisp off, let your hurt wisp off as well. Forgive often! Not for them, but for you! Life is too short to hold on to negativity.

Lesson 3 – Surround yourself with friends and Family as much as possible! Scientifically speaking, the happiest people who tend to live the longest are those with extended Family living with or near them and seeing their friends daily. If you're too busy, unforgiving, and tired to spend time with others, I would rethink what's most important to you. I was lucky to have been raised around my grandparents, and I lived near my parents once I became a parent, so my children got the same benefit. I didn't know at the time that I was helping my parents' health, but I did know they had threatened my life if I tried to move away with their grandkids! Children raised amongst generations are better adjusted and grow up with fewer issues than children in a one- or two-parent home, relying upon after-school programs. So, it's a win-win for the children and grandparents, and the parents learn forgiveness!

Lesson 4 – Don't Retire, at least without a backup plan! People who retire and don't fill their days with meaningful activity don't live nearly as long as those who do. Again, it's scientifically proven and one of the most significant contributors to my never wanting to retire. Just think of all the knowledge locked up in that "not so young" head of yours! Are you going to let all that, along with all your experiences that make you truly you, just fade into oblivion? Some people out there need to hear what you have to say and would find your knowledge extremely helpful. Think about all the things you have put off doing that bring you purpose and joy. NOW is the time to delve into those. I don't care how young you are; people need more joy in their lives and to spread it into the lives of others. You are a treasure trove and have a purpose far beyond your career. Find it, feed it, do it! Your longevity depends on it!

Lesson 5 – Always tell the truth KINDLY if you need to say anything at all! Yes, just because you are telling someone the cold, hard truth doesn't mean you need to be cold and hard when doing it. Truthfulness is always the best way to go when you need to say something, but delivery is everything. My older patients have all said that unless it NEEDS to be said, sitting quietly and holding judgment in your heart is the best way to go. Especially with a little smile on your face that makes everyone wonder what you know they don't!

Lesson 6 – You can never express your love too much! This, to me, is the most important. Maybe it is because I have worn my heart on my sleeve since embracing my Healer purpose in life. I love people; I truly do. I can see past what many judge them for, keep it to myself, and show them the unconditional love some have never received. Maybe that's just a Healer's gift, I don't know. But even with my children, Family, and friends, I tell them I love them A LOT! The older I get, the more the tears seem to accompany these words because I deeply feel them. The people I treated at the end of their lives said and did the same when those words crossed their lips. I didn't wait for my life to end to let my loved ones know how deeply I care. I don't care if they think I'm a little crazy; I am! But whenever those deep and meaningful conversations come to a close, or even a short hello, I end them knowing that if I never see that person again, they know how deeply I care for them, which makes my soul happy!

Lesson 7 - Don't wait for more time or a Pain-free/Fatigue-free day to go out and do things that bring you joy! The hardest thing in my life was losing loved ones out of the blue. Death is coming for each of us, and none of us knows when, but there were times when this lesson hit hard, especially with my mother. My Dad had been chronically ill for 15 years. My mother took care of him to the point of exhaustion and bitterness. She refused to take a break and see her Family six hours away. I could tell things were becoming unbearable, no matter the help she was given. A few weeks later, she dropped to the ground at the kitchen sink, gone, before she hit the floor of a brain aneurysm. Granted, that is a great way to go for the ones going, but for the ones left behind, not so much.

THIS experience was one of the biggest catalysts in my life for a change. No longer was I going to wait to do things; no longer was I going to work myself into the ground. I now slow down and stop at all the places passed up on road trips, read the signs, eat at the little dives, take off my shoes and dangle my feet in the water, and spend as much time as possible with those I love. At the time of this writing, I am in my 32' Class A motorhome, and I have driven halfway across the country with my two dogs as co-pilots and towing my pickup truck. I hook up and unhook myself! I have been to Texas to see my youngest son, and I am now in Tennessee to see my oldest son, his wife, and my teenage grandson. My grandson still thinks his grandma (me) is a badass and tells me so often. With autoimmune and structural issues, I don't always feel like a badass. But I can tell you this: that never stops me - EVER! This trip, he and I have gone sightseeing, hiking, and learning about the Civil War and Native Americans; toured caverns; been to the IMAX; the aquarium; his 4-H Chicken Show; and, my favorite, Zip Lined through the forest on an eight-tower line!

We have had deep and meaningful campfire talks, and I have eaten things I usually wouldn't. Some of my doctors will be mad that I took such risks. I am just tickled that I got the opportunity to laugh, play, and be a "kid" with my grandson, who loves me so much! And I will continue to do these things until I am unable to, and then I will find other things to do that will take their place. *When you reach a certain age, you just need to decide to do what you want, when you want, no matter what!*

For heaven's sake, steal the car keys and sneak out the door if you must! None of us know when it's our time; life is so short. ENJOY LIFE NOW before it's too late.

These are a few essential things I have learned in the 61 short years, but they help make my life feel well-lived. I genuinely hope they have made you think, laugh, and think some more! Start here if you are missing something in your life and can't put your finger on it. If you are already living well, start here anyway! It can't hurt, but it can add years and meaning to your life. You can always reach out to me; I'm easy to find!

Please remember that life is a choice, living is a choice, and joy is a choice that is all up to you! May you always choose to live long and magnificent.

Jana Lee Gattung
Age 61

CHAPTER 66

THE STORY BEHIND MY SMILE

JOYANN GOLD

"I now wear a smile that's coming from the inner joy of loving the woman I've become. It's no longer a pasted smile covering up the pain, fear, or sorrow." — JoyAnn Gold

Have you ever wondered what is behind a person's smile, or do you take it for granted that it is just a smile—a nonverbal communication of pleasure, delight, or agreement? For me, my smile today is hard-won and intentionally worked for. I grew up during a time when I learned to mask my most authentic feelings with an acceptable or expected smile. I became really good at hiding my feelings with a smile. I will now share with you how I regained the power of my smile—no more second-guessing or crowd-pleasing. When you see me smile now, it is from the bottom of my heart and full of joy.

"You'll Find That Life Is Still Worthwhile...If You Just Smile" — Nat King Cole

"Oh... there's another one!" Those were the words of the doctor following the birth of my twin sister. I was the surprise second-born of identical twin sisters. From then on, I took on the role of being second as I learned to crawl, walk, talk, and do just about everything a bit later than she had. I often felt so disappointed during our elementary school years as I'd received an A- when she got an A. It became clear that I was second best, so I just smiled to cover up my feelings.

During those years, our mother, a farmer's wife with three daughters just 17 months apart, often felt stressed with all the work, both on the farm and with her three children. To help her be happier, I usually didn't express the disappointment or sadness I was feeling. Instead, I just wore a smile and pretended everything was ok. I really never learned to love myself.

At age 20, I received a phone call telling me my fiancé had died in a car-train accident! That fateful call hugely impacted my life for the next 30 years, making it challenging to honor or love myself. You see, my first thought after receiving that fateful call was: "Oh no... I've killed my fiancé!" It was just four months before our wedding, and I was a junior in college.

The evening prior to his death, I had a conversation with him suggesting we postpone our wedding for a year. The reason was that I would need to transfer to a different college to complete my senior year, and the program wasn't nearly as complete.

As you can imagine, my fiancé was very disappointed that I'd even suggest a wedding postponement. Not wanting to hurt him, I agreed that we'd go forward as planned, and I'd transfer colleges. So after he left that evening, I felt extremely disappointed in myself that I'd hurt him as I had by asking for what I wanted. I wished I'd not even suggested the idea and was eager to apologize to him the next day. That opportunity never arrived.

Following his death, it became my secret, shared with nobody, that I'd suggested postponing our wedding. I simply buried my emotions along with him, went back to college, and wore a fake smile to conceal both the grief and guilt I was experiencing. Even though I was told it was an accident, I always believed our discussion the evening prior may have contributed to it.

During this time, the song "Smile" by Nat King Cole became a constant refrain, offering some peace as I played it repeatedly in my mind. *"Smile...though your heart is aching, even though it's breaking, when there are clouds in the sky, you'll get by if you smile through your fear and sorrow, and maybe tomorrow, you'll see the sun come shining through for you. Light up your face with gladness, hide every trace of sadness, although a tear may be ever so near. That's the time you must keep on trying. Smile, what's the use of crying? You'll find that life is still worthwhile if you just smile."*

For the next 29 years, I lived with the motto, "Life will be worthwhile...if you just smile!" And while I did enjoy a good life, it was mostly an outside job as I lived in my head rather than in my heart.

Most of my happiness during those years came with the joy of raising my daughter and from my interior design business as I helped women celebrate and enjoy their homes. Even with those joys, I still often felt empty and continued to wear a fake smile. I remember asking myself over and over, "Is that all there is?" I couldn't feel real passion or happiness and, at times, even questioned if I wanted to live.

Fortunately, I was introduced to the idea that I needed to love myself before I could truly love my life or anyone else. So, prior to my 50th birthday, I began the incredible adventure of diving into personal and spiritual growth. That took me to countless trainings, workshops, retreats, etc., which helped me evolve and grow from doing life from my head to a more heart-centered approach.

And my smile grew more authentic through the years. I stopped singing "If You Just Smile" from a place of emptiness but rather from a joy-filled heart. At 73, I was at a speaking engagement telling the audience my new motto was, "Free to be me...at seventy-three!"

However, I still had work to do with falling in love with myself, so at age 75, I began an intensive practice of mirror work that I learned from Louise Hay. I finally saw my inner child, that little four-year-old who wasn't ever allowed to express her emotions. For months, I held up her photo every day, looking into the mirror as I expressed my love for her. In the beginning, there were tears of sadness for not loving her.

As I continued the daily practice, my love and joy grew. I actually found myself enjoying the woman I saw every time I looked in the mirror. Instead of finding fault with her, I smiled at her.

I now wear a smile coming from the inside out. I no longer need things on the outside to make me happy as I have fallen in love with the woman I've become. My smile is no longer a pasted smile covering the pain, fear, or sorrow. Today, I can honestly exclaim, "I love my life!"

My question for you, dear reader...what's behind your smile? Is your smile authentic? Or are you wearing a pasted smile covering up your feelings of hurt or sadness? If so, I want you to know it's never too late to fall in love with yourself and your life. And you will discover *Life Truly is Worthwhile!*

JoyAnn Gold
Age 81

CHAPTER 67

NOISE WAS MY CHOCOLATE

JO DIBBLEE

I distinctly remember a time when I was proud of my ability to multitask in the noisiest of situations. I would pride myself on being able to read a book while the TV was blaring, with my children playing rambunctiously down the hall and the dogs barking while chasing the hissing cats. Everyday chaos was usual and welcomed.

How was this so? How could I filter all that was happening around me—to read and digest what I was reading? A better question is why. Why was I doing this? I had become a master at creating and managing noise. The more, the better. For years, I would never be alone in silence with my thoughts.

I used noise as a coping mechanism. If I bombarded my mind with noise—so much so—I wasn't afraid. I was fearful of being found and discovered, and therefore, I felt safer. I feared silence; the noise was my best friend, my go-to, my comfort food—if you will.

I used noise, much as someone might use chocolate, cake, potato chips, or more destructive substances to distract oneself.

I don't know when or how noise became my coping mechanism. But I did see that I used noise as a way to hide. For decades, the last thing I wanted was to be alone in silence with my thoughts.

It baffled me when I overheard others speak about meditation and silence and how much they loved it; I couldn't understand why. I liked Yoga and Pilates until the instructors would spoil it with the need for us to be silent. What was this need to be silent about

Why did we need to go inside and reflect? After all, I was doing my darnedest to keep myself from being alone with my thoughts.

But that all changed when I wrote my memoir at forty-five. Silence no longer scared me. The more I wrote, the more I craved the peace and release silence offered. I found myself seeking ways to get quiet—just to BE.

Initially, it was awkward, but I relished the moments of silence over time. It takes time to let go of harmful self-protection habits, just as it does when we use unhealthy coping mechanisms to cope. It took time to shed my irrational belief that silence was deadly and replace it with the understanding that being silent is a gift that heals, allowing time to reconnect with our heart, purpose, and soul.

Today, at sixty-three, I live free of my need to fill the void and understand that anything is possible when we stand for what we dream and believe. *Thank goodness I did not stay locked in my jail of fear and instead embraced the wisdom of age, healing, and time.* Our pasts do not define us, but they are a chapter in the patchwork of our lives.

Jo Dibblee
Age 63

CHAPTER 68

ECHOES OF AGELESS WISDOM

KATHERINE MERRITT

"If wrinkles could talk, they'd tell tales of laughter, tears, and years well-lived."

In a society where youth is often idolized and revered, I find a deep sense of inspiration and admiration in older people's wise and gentle smiles. Growing up, I never saw a boundary between the young and the old. Instead, I came to deeply value the knowledge, wisdom, and insights born from a life with rich experiences.

There is something extraordinary about the unique perspective and insights that only come with age. We can all learn from listening to the stories and experiences of those who have lived long and full lives. Growing up, I found the elders in my community to be a great source of wisdom and knowledge. I found their stories incredibly fascinating and was always eager to hear more. I valued their insights regardless of age and learned a lot from them.

Looking back, I now realize how much those friendships meant to me and how much I gained from them. As a young child, I was always excited to make new friends. I often knocked on my neighbors' doors, hoping to find new friends to play with. As fate would have it, I usually made unexpected new friends who taught me much more than I ever expected. Those memories will always hold a special place in my heart.

During my door-to-door visits, many people would share their personal stories with me. One encounter that stands out is with Mrs. K, who greeted me with a warm smile and offered me homemade treats. She wore a traditional house dress from the 60s and a well-used apron. As she shared stories from her youth, I listened attentively and was in awe of her larger-than-life presence.

One day, while riding my bike, I noticed Mr. B sitting alone on his porch. I stopped to visit with him, and to my surprise, he introduced me to the Chinese Checkers game. Even though I haven't played the game since, the memories of that moment, filled with laughter and discovery, remain vivid in my mind. In my early twenties, I worked at a nearby retirement home. It was there that I found the most happiness through interacting with the residents. Even on my days off, I often returned to visit them because I was drawn to their incredible stories and wisdom. I loved spending time with them on the front porch, listening to their fascinating tales of the past. One resident, Ms. Julia P., held a special place in my heart. Our trips to a nearby restaurant always brought a smile to her face and a twinkle in her eye. Later in life, at a Premier Retirement Home, my love for the older generation remained strong. While I found my work fulfilling, my days were made even more delightful by the beautiful companionship of my colleagues, Mrs. B and Mrs. M. Despite being a decade or more my senior, their wisdom and friendship brought me immense joy and brightened my days. I still clearly recall Mrs. B, at 70, jumping onto a bike and riding it through the corridor. Our laughter echoed through the building. That scene, frozen in time, captures the significance of living agelessly.

I also fondly remember residents Bill and Wanda—a married couple whose love story embodied ageless love and joy. Despite their advanced age, their youthful spirit was very contagious. Family gatherings were often filled with laughter and tales from the past. Spending time with the elders was my favorite part. They would share hilarious memories and, at times, share about the challenges they'd overcome. I could hang on to their every word for hours, always ready to hear another story. Being a caregiver for my Mom during her final years was an experience that revealed my own vulnerabilities. While her progressing Dementia was one of the toughest challenges I may ever face, it has also blessed me with some of the most cherished moments we would share. We laughed so hard for hours, watching comedies that had us laughing joyfully.

During those times, I saw a playful side of her I hadn't seen in a long time. She was a woman now free of the burdens of her past, of the memories of pain, regrets, and struggle. It was as if the disease, in its cruel way, had erased the years of pain she'd endured, allowing her, perhaps for the very first time in years, to be genuinely happy, if even for a minute.

Visiting a museum named 'Magic Wings' was an unforgettable experience. Surrounded by butterflies of all shapes and colors, we both experienced a feeling of enchantment and freedom. I was often reminded of how timeless the human spirit can be. *Moments of joy, laughter, and love can be found even in the most difficult circumstances.* During these challenging times, I gained a newfound appreciation for my Mom's strength and kind heart. Our unbreakable bond only grew stronger in these moments.

Now, at 66, I am entering the age range that fascinated me as a young girl. The roles have quietly transitioned. Through all these experiences, I discovered truths that transcend time. I learned that people could form deep connections regardless of age difference and that everyone has a unique story to share. I've seen love that remained youthful and spirited. During my challenges with my Mom, I have come to appreciate the strength of the human spirit to find joy and resilience in difficult times.

As I now embrace aging, my gray hair represents a life full of experiences, wisdom, and lessons. Life is not just a passage of time but a journey of self-discovery and love, with stories waiting to be shared. I have come to appreciate the significance of connecting with others, finding happiness in the small things, recognizing the value of every individual regardless of age, finding fulfillment from helping others, and the critical role of listening, truly listening. All the beautiful souls I had the pleasure to meet throughout my life had lived long and meaningful lives, and their stories held great significance. Every word in this story has been influenced by the souls and moments that have touched me deeply. Every person I have encountered and every story I have heard left an unforgettable impression on my heart.

Consider this: *Your story could be the inspiration that someone else needs.* Please cherish your memories, learn from the big lessons, and even embrace those gray hairs. Share your unique journey with others, take the time to listen to theirs, and never let age determine your worth. *Celebrate your path, and who knows, you may inspire someone else to appreciate the beauty of their journey.*

"Time moves forward, but the Echoes of Ageless Wisdom remain steadfast and unwavering."

Katherine Merritt
Age 67

CHAPTER 69

YOUR CHOICES...YOUR EXTRAORDINARY LIFE!

LUCIE ROSA-STAGI

I remember not having any control over my Life as a kid. I was at the mercy of my parents and the adults around me. Yet, I was aware that adults made terrible choices, as I experienced hurtful feelings and saw these same hurtful feelings in other members of my family.

As a kid, I was aware of this, although it was not a term used much back then in the fifties. I might have described myself as observant, alert, or even astute about my surroundings. I knew my 'gut' had much to do with my decision-making abilities. A strong force within me guided most of my steps, moving me toward a future in which I only knew what I didn't want to happen; I couldn't quite analyze or figure out what I wanted.

And because I couldn't articulate what I wanted, I got what came to me and dealt with it, thinking someone else, maybe God (that big man in the sky at that time of my thinking life), was in charge. I was just like a puppet having to play this game called Life.

I remember how much the book *Siddhartha* by Hermann Hesse affected me in my first year of college. It awakened a new journey within me. My Life became a series of manifestations without understanding that I could manifest whatever I desired. Looking back, I can see that clearly now.

Without ever reflecting upon it, I was described by my family and others as courageous, adventurous, and living a life filled with fun, joy, and passion. I was never bogged down with a job that described who I was or coming from a place that limited me. However, I certainly had my 'limiting beliefs' about who I was and understood that where I came from and society's image of what 'women should be like' limited me a whole lot.

I can't remember exactly when I woke up from this dream and became aware that we can create our own destiny, and it's all about the choices we make in Life. BIG EPIPHANY! Blew me away...

Lucie Rosa-Stagi
Age 78

CHAPTER 70

WHO IS YOUR EARTH ANGEL?

MORIAH HUDSON

If I had one story left to tell in my life, it would have to be about my maternal grandmother. You see, she was my angel. With my covert narcissist mother and my father, who was gone traveling most of the time until he started molesting me, Grandma Hall taught me how it felt to be enfolded in angels' wings.

Her hugs were the only kind and loving physical contact I had growing up. I can remember being held in her arms, and it was always like lying on a warm cloud and being enveloped. No matter what I did or what I got in trouble for, I always knew it didn't matter to her. She taught me unconditional love. She taught me that it was okay to be me. And in so many ways, she helped me stay alive through those difficult years.

I remember so many stories and so many good times we had together. As a young girl, I remember getting to go to her house in North Hollywood, California. You would expect North Hollywood to be ritzy, but Grandma's house wasn't.

It was just a shack that had yet to fall. I remember the bedroom being the central portion of the house. There was a semi-working bathroom. The kitchen counters were made of wood and had fallen into disarray, and you couldn't use them any longer. But what always amazed me was that the living room and dining room floors had collapsed, and tall grass was growing through the floorboards. I used to tell Grandma Hall I'd be willing to get a lawn mower and mow her living room and dining room as a kid. And then I would laugh hysterically, impressed by my own humor. Grandma Hall and her three small children had lived in that shack for years. My grandfather had died when my mother was only eight. It was a tough time for Grandma Hall to raise three small children.

The shack had a wonderful screened-in front porch, and we spent many hours laughing and talking. She spoke, and I listened. She was the first storyteller in my life and a great one! You see after the children were grown and gone from home, my grandmother made her living as a nanny. She also had the opportunity to work with some of Hollywood's great directors and producers. Before flying was a big idea; they went cross country, and it was a train ride. And she had gotten her own sleeping quarters and would take care of the small child.

And she could do amazing things to entertain children. I remember her being able to take a handkerchief and shape it into a baby in a crib. She taught me how to do the hand signs: "Here's the church; here's the steeple; open the door, see all the people." She also had the most beautiful whistle. It sounded like Burl Ives. I remember thinking that someday, when I grew up, I hoped to whistle like that. I loved listening to it!

Unfortunately, that never happened.

The best memory I have of Grandma Hall is when she came to visit when I was about eight or nine. My mother decided to go out and do some shopping since she didn't have to worry about what I was up to, which was usually bad, according to my mother. Grandma Hall decided we should make some homemade noodles for dinner. Now, we're talking about it from scratch. She thought that would be very nice for my mother since she disliked cooking. So let me paint you the scene.

Grandma Hall was probably in her 60s. She wasn't tall, but she was a full-sized woman with beautiful platinum gray hair, which she kept pinned up on top of her head. And Grandma Hall and I were a lot alike. A lot clumsier than we were careful. So here we are making pasta, and flour has a way of getting away from you. So, to say the least, we had a lot of flour everywhere.

We were rolling out the dough, and of course, you need more flour. And we were laughing and giggling and having such a great time. And then we got to cut the noodles. I was too young to realize we had to dry the noodles. So, we carefully laid out all the little noodles all over the kitchen, the counter, and the stove. Then we covered the table. Then we had to put tea towels in the washer and dryer to lay noodles on them. And everywhere there were noodles.

And the funny thing about the kitchen was that it had a red linoleum floor. But that day, it wasn't red any longer. We had slopped so much flour everywhere that you couldn't see the red at all. All you could see was white. White on the floor. White on us. White on the counters. White on the table. White was everywhere. I remember we laughed and giggled so much that I had tears running down my face. I felt like I had died and gone to heaven, feeling free for the first time in my life.

And then she walked in and screamed, "Oh my God! What have you done?" My mother was home. We both froze at the same time. We tried to explain that we would clean everything up and that we were trying to make dinner for the family. But we were both humiliated and banned from the kitchen for the rest of the visit. But my mother could never steal that joy and freedom I felt for that short period.

Grandma Hall taught me to be a kind woman with a loving heart. Nothing was ever beneath her. I remember that, as young kids, my brother and I would play marbles on the floor. Grandma was not one to sit in the chair and just watch. She was the old woman gingerly who would get down on her knees and lie on the floor so she could shoot marbles, too. She always wanted to be involved, not just sit and watch.

I don't remember the story, but my family has passed it down from generation to generation. It was back in the day. In the 1940s and 1950s, the National Park System was a big event. And if you were lucky enough, you could go camping with your family.

I was only two years old when we went to Yosemite as a family: my parents and my older brother, my uncle and aunt and their two young daughters, and, of course, Grandma Hall. So, the adults pitched their own tent, and they pitched a tent for Grandma and the kids to sleep in.

Even then, they had a problem with bears in the park. In all the commotion, somebody had left out the sugar on the table. And the bear found it. The story goes that the bear headed into the tent that had my grandmother and the babies.

She barricaded herself between the bear and us. The bear began to swipe his arm into the tent to get in. Grandma was screaming at the adults to get rid of that bear so it wouldn't get the little ones. I guess nobody came to the rescue because I was told that Grandma got really upset and slugged the bear in the face. I guess he got tired of the hassle and finally wandered off. She showed me how to be a strong woman and protect my family.

Grandma Hall taught me not to be afraid to try new things, not to let anyone tell me how much I could love someone and another important lesson in my life.

The greatest fear my grandmother had was that she would get dementia or Alzheimer's and lose her memory. I remember her telling me that the whole time I was growing up. I didn't understand anything about mindset at the time. What we focus on is what we create.

At 81, she had a very mild stroke, but her memory was gone. She didn't know who she was anymore. She was just lost. I was 21 years old, and I was devastated. She gave me so much, and now I couldn't give her anything back.

What we focus on is what we create.

So, with all her love, strength, and kindness, she gave me one of the most important lessons of my life: What we focus on is what we create. It took me a long time to understand that. Now, in my 70s, I realize it's one of the greatest gifts she gave me.

Now, I know I don't have to create my own fears. And I get to remember the incredible times we had together. The laughs and giggles made us have tears running down our faces. And the complete joy of knowing how it feels to be enfolded by an angel's wings by my earth angel! And now my earth angel is a celestial angel, and she teaches me how to fly!

The only thing that holds more power than 'I love you' is 'I got you.' From the Heart Speaks.

Moriah Hudson
Age 74

CHAPTER 71

UNCONSCIOUS INFLUENCE: HOW OUR MOTHER SHAPES US

NANCY JOHNSON

The Gifts and Challenges of Aging Well - Nurturing a Positive Mindset, Perseverance, and a Humble Spirit

In the radiance of my mother's 94 years of life, I reflect on the journey we've traversed together, illuminated by resilience, positivity, strength, purpose, and, above all, love. Listening to her words and writing, I was humbled by the undeniable truth that the threads of influence run deep, connecting generations in a beautiful tapestry of shared experiences and lessons learned.

Let me begin by affirming that the adage "the apple doesn't fall far from the tree" is more than a mere saying; it is a living reality I've come to understand with astonishing clarity. Hearing my mother's words recounting her life, I now see the resilience and unwavering positivity that have flowed seamlessly from my mother, through me, and onward to my precious daughter. Please join me in hearing my mother's story, intertwining her 94 years of life with my 65 years of lessons, love, and growth.

At 94 years old, my mother continues to exude a vibrant and humble spirit that defies the passage of time. We both hear we look younger than our years, and I know it's not just genetics. I'm excited to share what I know has profoundly shaped my life from hers.

Lessons, like heirlooms, are passed down through generations.

Her story has weathered countless storms, surmounted hurdles, and transformed heartaches into steppingstones. Her journey was marked by profound losses, from her mother's early departure from her life to the battle with her own health challenges. Then came the shattering blow of her father's untimely departure through his own hand, which imprinted upon her a steel resolve and an unyielding spirit.

An unintended blessing arrived with my parents' marriage at 21. Though often ensnared in tensions, our home harbored a quiet refuge in the pages of "The Power of Positive Thinking" by Norman Vincent Peale. This literary companion became her steadfast ally during daily bus rides to work, its wisdom seeping into her consciousness until its pages crumbled and fell apart. Ironically, my father's reluctance to allow her behind the wheel of a car meant to confine her gifted her with uninterrupted moments in communion with the book's teachings.

Amidst societal norms that consigned women to domestic roles, my mother embarked on a journey that led her to a prestigious secretarial job. But my father's reservations about her interactions with male colleagues redirected her path to a 28-year tenure at G & K Services, a living testament to her adaptability and inner strength. It wasn't until I reached adulthood that I truly appreciated that I had never heard her utter a single complaint about working full-time, managing a household, and raising three children. Despite enduring harsh winters and waiting at the bus stop in sub-zero temperatures, she never once voiced a grievance.

Mom also instilled in me the importance of balanced meals. My father's battle with diabetes and deteriorating health cast a spotlight on the importance of mindful eating. In her kitchen, an oasis of nourishing choices, she crafted dishes infused with love: vibrant vegetables, succulent fruits, and her renowned pies. Her passion for gardening, baking, and pursuits like biking and walking seamlessly integrated well-being into the fabric of our lives. She rode her bike until she couldn't.

Retirement's embrace at 68 offered her a respite from the mounting challenges posed by my father's fading health. Within the tapestry of her retirement plans, a desire to volunteer at the Veterans Administration emerged. To her surprise, my father championed this endeavor. She realized adjusting to being home was a challenge for both. Following Dad's departure, she embraced her newfound role as a volunteer with renewed vigor, a purposeful dedication that breathed life into her days. The canteen at the Veterans Administration became her haven, a space where her reserved demeanor gave way to conversations that flowed effortlessly. Eleanor, a kindred spirit, became a cherished friend whose companionship transcended even after her passing. The Veterans Administration loved her so much that they hired her, and eventually, she had to retire from there.

A lesson that resonates through my own life's journey is the gift of genuine connection. My mother's ability to invest time in meaningful conversations, making others feel treasured and heard, has imprinted upon me an enduring lesson. This skill, honed by her, has been a cornerstone of my career, allowing me to truly understand and empathize with the journeys of those I counsel. It's an undeniable truth that everyone craves to be acknowledged and heard.

Age, it seemed, held no dominion over my mother's embrace of life's adventures. Around 70, she took her maiden flight to Arizona to visit her brother. She then surprised us all one day by hopping onto the back of a motorcycle alongside my nephew. At approximately 75, she said yes to ride with me on a roller coaster perched atop a Las Vegas hotel. Her unwavering openness to novel experiences left an indelible mark on me: if she can do it, so can I.

Yet, amidst all the lessons, one stands as a beacon of her character – the magic of kindness. Her words, "Look at the good things about someone; everybody has some good things in them," encapsulate a philosophy that has shaped the contours of my heart and guided me to become a better person.

There are so many stories I could share for you to understand what Mom endured, and I decided she always finds the positives, so that's my intention here. My mother, at 94, remains a luminous wellspring of inspiration, a living testament to the transformative power of a positive attitude. Her story, a legacy of strength and compassion, has woven itself into the very fibers of my being. As I share her narrative, it encourages me to pass along what can help others. My daughter and I ponder embarking on mother-daughter retreats, a journey that celebrates life, beauty, and kindness inside us all. We have met and learned from so many beautiful people. It's a profound beauty that speaks to the heart of our existence—the ability to touch lives in ways that surpass our understanding.

In closing, Mom's journey, for now, let us celebrate the gift of life, find splendor in the stories of others, and sow seeds of kindness, for in doing so, we partake in a legacy that resonates far beyond the confines of years.

With love and boundless gratitude to my Mom Ardis.

Nancy Johnson
Age 65

CHAPTER 72

THE JOY OF BEING IS THE JOY OF LIVING A CONSCIOUS LIFE

SHIRLEY TURNER

"Like a Lotus Flower, we too have the ability to rise from the mud, bloom out of the darkness, and radiate into the world."

I'm sitting in my bedroom on my meditation chair next to two large French doors leading out onto a sparkling blue swimming pool and a beautifully well-manicured garden. I can feel the start of spring coming; the sun's rays are beaming onto the carpet in front of me. It's deliciously warm and comforting. This is my favorite spot.

I'm pensive as I admire the gorgeous vista outside, peaceful and incredibly still. It's like time is standing still. I'm aware of my breath and chest's gentle rise and fall as I inhale and exhale. I hear the birds chirping in the trees outside. I feel blissful at the moment.

For a short while, there are no thoughts; I'm simply present in the moment with what is.

I began to ponder a question that I had been recently asked: "What would the younger me ask an ageless Sage?" So many things start racing through my mind. I feel the excitement as I anticipate what it would have been like to know the answers to my struggles at an earlier age. Things would have been so different, I think. Yet, without the struggles, would life be as radiant and exciting as it is now, entering a time when the road ahead is shorter than the one, I'm leaving behind? Would I know the light without knowing the darkness? Without the pain, would I know the exhilaration of the freedom and fulfillment I feel now?

When I think of life, I relate so much to the metaphor of the Lotus Flower, symbolic of how we can get through all the obstacles and adversities that life throws at us, shine through the darkness, and blossom into the fullness of a brighter life and a brighter future. Beautiful, free, fulfilled, and abundant in so many unassuming ways.

Many years ago, I woke up one morning from an induced sleep in a psychiatric ward in a private hospital. It felt deathly quiet, hostile, and cold. I could hear the distant humming of the fan above my bed. Patients lay in adjacent beds, covered in white sheets, asleep, motionless, curled up in fetal positions, lifeless.

I can't remember the exact day, month, or year. Still, I remember that I was severely depressed, horribly scared, lost, and desperate. I had absolutely no idea of a way forward. I felt incredibly alone, even though I was surrounded by people in the ward and in life. I felt desolate.

I had suffered childhood and teenage trauma. I had nothing left in me other than shame, guilt, fear, regret, and deep, silent desperation. I was also suffering from humiliating panic attacks and a debilitating social phobia. Life scared me.

My doctor, a psychiatrist, was standing next to my bed. He was a short, slender Jewish man with thick, wavy black hair, bushy eyebrows, and a solemn face. He was wearing the symbolic doctor's white coat. He was about to put another needle in my hand, putting me back into an induced sleep. Luckily, I was conscious enough to know that this was not an answer to my pain; it was not a solution to my state of being. I said a firm NO to that needle. He was taken aback, shocked, and surprised. I explained that I wanted to know WHY I was like this and HOW I could get out of this deep, dark hole. I wanted to know WHY and HOW. These questions have empowered me and moved me in unimaginable directions.

Never settle for the opinions of others; you know what is best for you. I was referred to a psychologist.

The next day, Michael, a psychologist, sat across from me in a large, empty room. I was sitting on a high stool in the middle of the room, in a hospital gown, feeling bare and exposed. Michael was a young man, also Jewish; his smile was gentle and caring. He had soft blonde curls that adorned his gentle face, and he spoke in a soft, caring voice.

After being discharged, I continued to see him at his private practice. He took an interest in me and my condition, and I began to feel seen, heard, validated, and supported. I felt safe in his space, a feeling that was very foreign to me. People generally frightened me, and I had huge trust issues. In fact, I wanted to escape from people; I wanted to run as fast and as far away as I could. I wanted to hide.

We all need a "Michael" in our lives. Someone who accepts you for who you are, your imperfections, and your vulnerability without judgment or labeling. Someone who holds a safe space for you to be you.

Perfectly imperfect.

And so, my healing began. It was the start, and there was a long road ahead. They say, "When you start to walk the way, the way opens up," and it certainly did. I came across a documentary of Tina Turner's life story of how she overcame the trauma of an abusive relationship by following the principles of Buddhist philosophy. This led me to the same path.

I found a Buddhist center near where I lived and contacted them. On my first visit, I learned that suffering is part of life and that there is a way out of suffering. This is the core principle of Buddhism, emphasizing mindfulness, compassion, self-reflection, and ethical living. I thought I had hit the jackpot. And I did. I had found the answers to my WHY and HOW questions. I found my path to freedom.

It didn't just happen. Just like the Lotus Flower that takes time to grow through the mud and darkness, it was a process of awakening from an unconscious, dysfunctional state to a state of conscious awareness. I am not saying for one minute that I am awakened or enlightened. Still, I began to see and experience the benefits of mindfulness, conscious awareness, and present-moment living. I consumed myself in the teachings and started embracing and living the principles of Eastern philosophy in my daily life. Working consciously with body, mind, and soul. This way of life provided valuable insights into human conditions. It offered practical wisdom for living a meaningful and fulfilling life.

And the way kept opening for me.

My most significant AHA moment was coming across Eckhart Tolle's book "The Power of Now." It changed my life profoundly and intensely. I learned and embodied "Conscious Living."

The pearls of wisdom I gained are:

We cannot change the past, what happened or didn't happen, or what you did or didn't do. But you can choose to be free, live, and love now. No matter what.

The best way to care for your future is to care for the present. The end of suffering happens when we look inside rather than for external cues to dictate our happiness. What a liberation to know that we are not our thoughts; we are the awareness of our thoughts, and we can change our thoughts just as easily as we change our clothes. When we live in the present moment, we are free—free from the stresses of the past and fears of the future. Stillness and peace arise. Life isn't about what happens to us but how we respond. A conscious life means better choices, which results in better outcomes. It means more joy, more ease, more love, more freedom, and a life of fulfillment. Self-acceptance, self-love, and self-belief. It also means less stress, less anxiety, less fear, less guilt, and regret. Less shame. It means letting go of the past and embracing a brighter future. Not missing out on precious moments. Forgiveness is so much easier.

It's never too late, and you are never too old to be who you wish to be. To live the life you wish to live.

Today, I get up every morning free from the grasp of mental/emotional suffering. I get up with a zest for life, vibrant and excited about my day and future. I laugh, travel, have fun, and enjoy my friendships and beautiful family. Over the past 16 years, I've built a successful business in the health and wellness industry. I've also started a new career at the young age of 63, coaching ladies to find meaning in the midst of life and guiding them to personal freedom and fulfillment. I live life with purpose, meaning, and passion. Life is great. No drips are needed!

My motto is to die young, late in life. I want to leave this life with no regrets but much to be grateful for. It's up to me.

Shirley Turner
Age 64

CHAPTER 73

THE MAGIC OF FINDING LOVE AGAIN

SUNSHINE DEB

"Our love story is a testament to the power of self-discovery and self-improvement. It's a reminder that you attract the person you have become."

I'd like to share a story with you today that's deeply personal and filled with lessons about self-discovery, growth, and the magic of love. As I embarked on my journey of self-development, I began to understand the importance of self-care on physical, mental, emotional, and spiritual levels. Learning to love and honor myself was a crucial part of this process. It led me to a profound realization: the ability to be content and joyful in our company is a significant accomplishment. Not everyone can comfortably spend extended periods alone. Through this journey, I discovered that as we work on ourselves, we become the person we aspire to attract.

Loving and accepting ourselves inside and out can bring immense joy, appreciation, and gratitude into our lives.

Love, in all its forms, can act as a magnet, drawing magic into our lives. My personal journey took me through a long-term relationship in my early twenties. After eight years, I realized that, as much as I wanted it to be, he wasn't "the one." He was my first love, and while there was physical attraction, I needed more than that. Despite family approval and societal expectations, I couldn't ignore the feeling that something was missing. The pressure to stay in that relationship was overwhelming, and I struggled with it. However, I knew it was essential for both of us to move on with our lives, even though it would be painful.

After this relationship, I embarked on a soul-searching journey. I realized that I wanted to be in a relationship because I wanted to, not because I needed to fill a void. I needed time to grow and develop personally. I'd observed the challenges my siblings faced after rushing into marriage and family life, and I was determined to create something different. For over a decade, I took a deep dive into personal growth, doing my best to fill my own cup and taking care of myself from the inside out so I could be there more fully for myself and others. I learned to enjoy my own company and appreciate the moments of solitude. I transitioned from being a fitness instructor to a personal trainer and eventually a Life Enrichment/Wellness Coach, helping others enrich their lives in a similar way. As I worked on myself, I realized I was ready to find my person—the one I could move through life with.

My criteria had evolved beyond physical attraction; I sought a deeper connection. I wanted someone with similar interests who could engage in meaningful conversations and share life's journey. Years passed, and my ex-boyfriend had moved on, married, and started a family. Meanwhile, I hadn't found anyone yet. At times, self-doubt crept in. But life had its own plans, including caring for my ailing mother, which delayed my personal journey. Sometimes, you have to hit rock bottom before something beautiful blossoms.

I learned to release expectations, humble myself, and allow life to unfold.

I remember a particularly challenging day around the upcoming holidays when I broke down in tears after returning home to chaos, feeling vulnerable and defeated. At that moment, I questioned if I would ever find love again in this lifetime, especially at the level to which I sought. But I collected myself and realized that this moment of vulnerability had cleared the slate. With a clear mind, I knew precisely and clearly what I wanted.

Sometimes, you must learn and experience what you do not want to see clearly what you do. It was the holiday season. All I wanted for Christmas was to meet someone who was compatible with my heart. On December 15, 2007, I met my soulmate, my person, and our journey has been magical. On our first date, it felt like we had known each other for a lifetime. In fact, another couple we crossed paths with that evening assumed we had been dating for years. Our first kiss as we parted ways to head to our cars as the evening ended was magical. As our lips met, delicate snowflakes began to fall, creating a moment of enchantment.

A few months later, while in the heart of New York City at one of our cherished restaurants, I posed a question to him. I asked, "Can you see yourself getting married, and if so, what does that look like?" His response was a resounding "yes," as he described his vision, he effortlessly walked right into the image I had secretly held in my heart. It was another one of those magical moments, as a single tear of joy slowly traced down my cheek.

The culmination of our love story arrived the following year when he popped the question in that very same restaurant. From that moment on, we embarked on planning the dream destination wedding in Italy, where my grandparents had once embarked on their own journey before arriving in America. Neither of us had ever set foot in this beautiful country, but I held a vision in my heart. It was a vision inspired by the captivating movie "Under the Tuscan Sun," starring Diane Lane. After a painful breakup filled with betrayal, she found love again in the most unexpected places.

The film painted a portrait of Italy that was nothing short of beauty and love. I yearned to get married in such a place, but the location remained a mystery.

Still, I couldn't let go of the dream, so we booked an inviting venue and took a leap of faith. Our wedding in Italy unfolded as pure magic, surrounded by the awe-inspiring beauty of God's creation. The ceremony included a truly enchanting moment: the musical notes of "The Prayer" by Celine Dion and Andrea Bocelli filled the air. This moving song was sung half in Italian and half in English, resonating as the sun descended. As we were officially pronounced man and wife, the distant church bells rang out, their sweet-sounding chimes echoing throughout the village. It was a universal confirmation, a symphony of joy that made the moment even more special and magical. In that sacred place, surrounded by the breathtaking beauty of nature and the harmony of music, our love story continued to unfold, reminding us of the profound joy that life can bring when hearts are united.

Following the discovery of a breathtaking venue, an intriguing twist awaited. As we journeyed through Positano, Italy, where we got married, the chauffeur turned to me and asked, "Have you ever seen the movie 'Under the Tuscan Sun'?" With a nod, I confirmed. Then, in a moment of serendipity, he revealed, "This is where they filmed that unforgettable love scene." Chills coursed through me, and tears welled up—pure magic. Our entire Italy wedding was a dream come true, where dreams and reality blended seamlessly into a beautiful, magical tapestry.

Our love story is a testament to the power of self-discovery and self-improvement. It's a reminder that you attract the person you have become. My husband and I share a deep connection on many levels. He is my soulmate, and I am his. I've learned through this journey that there is always time to find love, do the work on ourselves, and become a magnet for love and magic. The joy of love can fill our hearts and souls, making us feel forever young.

A personal note to the reader...

As you embark on the path of self-discovery and self-improvement, you will find that the love you give yourself sets the foundation for the love you will attract from others. I hope this letter finds you embracing the beauty of personal growth and self-care, for it is through these transformative journeys that the magic of finding love truly begins.

Sunshine Deb
Age 62

CHAPTER 74
DREAM WEAVER

SUSAN "SUEZEE" FINLEY

I have three daughters: a witch, a bitch, and Peter Pan!

I can still hear my mom's words reverberating in my mind like it was yesterday. It was her comical but accurate way of describing her three unique daughters:

My eldest sister Joanne was deemed the "Witch". She was a crystal ball gazing, tarot card reading expert in all things supernatural; 13 years older than me, she started college the same day I started kindergarten. Janet, 11 years older than me, was the "Bitch,": the rebellious, havoc-wreaking, trouble-making, attention-seeking middle child (most of us are familiar with the breed). Oh, and allow me to introduce myself; I am Peter Pan, and I will forever be the baby of the family and a long-time resident of Neverland.

If Neverland truly existed, I surely would have been assigned a zip code there.

I was born a dreamer and spent more time inside my head than in the real world. In fact, I spent my first four years hanging out inside a bright yellow laundry basket, pretending I was floating high over rainbows, in the sky over exotic lands, with butterflies swirling around me, giant bright colored flowers blooming before me, and singing, dancing magic mushrooms. (No, I was not dropping acid; I was only four, and with that imagination, I never had to). My rose-tinted view of the world did not change as I grew older. I loved everyone I met. I felt lucky, blessed, and grateful for how my life unfolded. My wild imagination led me into the art world, where I made my living as a sculptor and doll-maker.

I had a good run until age 33, but everything seemed to change after uttering two unfortunate words–"I do" in church, at the altar on May 18th, 1997.

Those two words triggered a cascade of events that caused my rather abrupt exit from Neverland and my quick descent into the real world.

A less friendly world plagued with anxiety, ill health, and fear.

I woke the day after my wedding sick with a 103 fever because of some awful virus that barely improved in time for the honeymoon cruise we set off for seven days later.

I spent my honeymoon in agonizing unexplained discomfort on a ship that set sail on such rough water even the crew was sea sick.

I believe those rough seas were a metaphor for the next two decades ahead.

A week after my honeymoon return, I had an emergency appendectomy and bouts of ill health. I used to joke with my husband that if the lemon law applied to newlyweds, he could turn me in and get a new bride.

I healed myself from my health issues,but in the following decade, I became the caregiver for four family members and saw three of them through hospice.

Both my dad and brother-in-law got stomach cancer, my mom got diagnosed with dementia, and my husband got…

A 25-year-old girlfriend (he went the fastest, right out the door!)

My life became a rollercoaster of emotions, divorce, unpredictable emergency ambulance rides, surgeries, hospitals, and family fights. I felt like I was living inside the Whac-A-Mole carnival game. I was the mole and life was the giant foam mallet, and it was going for a top-shelf prize. Every time I came up to breathe, ba-boom, that hammer came crashing down on my head; no matter where I went or what I did, I felt there was no escape. No peace. No time. No fun. No relaxation. I was trapped in some warped parallel universe of hospitals, dementia, and death.

But being a tenacious little creature, much like our little Whac-A-Mole friend, I took a moment (after I admittedly had a full-blown screaming, foot-stomping pillow-punching tantrum) and thought to myself, if I was a character in a novel, how could I write myself out? Only one thing popped into my mind….

Alien abduction!!!

Sadly, no spaceship came for me, but that did not stop me from dreaming about it. Whenever things got unbearable, I would hold that image in my head. Somehow, the ridiculousness of it helped me laugh and break the pattern of falling into despair.

I honestly believe the only reason I didn't have a nervous breakdown was because there was simply no time.

My dad passed first, and shockingly, my sister's beloved husband, Al, passed only four years after my dad, and mom not long after Al, she almost reached 90.

I never had time to process all the grief and because I thought I was Superwoman, I continued without rest, till I was hit with two autoimmune diseases, Lupus and Sjogren's, leaving me feeling like Superwoman wearing a Kryptonite necklace.

Before I was hit with said Kryptonite, my sister Joanne had three nicknames for me (four if you include Peter Pan): Packhorse SueZee, Toolbelt SueZee, and Energizer Bunny SueZee. I became my sister's handyman, grocery carrier, and whatever else she needed after her husband, Al, passed away.

Joanne felt all alone and vulnerable in the world, and she was my motivation to keep going. My new mission was to reclaim my health as fast as possible so that I could continue to be there for her.

It was not an easy journey, but I am grateful for it, as it is what brought me into the realm of sound therapy, giving me a new passion and career.

Even though it was the hardest time of my life, there were lessons learned, great big lessons. My health did suffer, but going with the "Universe is conspiring to help me theory," it is why I became a sound therapist, and the magic of sound therapy is what carried me back to Neverland!

I jokingly refer to it as that because what I was experiencing back in my younger days, B.M. (Before Marriage) was a oneness with the universe that you could only get when you are doing what is congruent with your soul, when you are doing the work you are meant to be doing, when you have a mission that makes your heart sing and an attitude of love and gratitude.

All that came back to me when I became a sound therapist and started my Happiness Now Network . I would have liked to have discovered it without the years of pain and anguish, but it seems when you are not paying attention to your life lessons, they get harder. So listen up, Universe, I am paying attention, and expect only fun, happy things to come my way!

And for you dear reader, I wish clear skies and butterflies!

Xo,

SueZee, AKA Peter Pan
SueZee Finley
Age 61

CHAPTER 75

LOVE KNOWS NO AGE

TINA TAYLOR

"In the album of my heart, the pages dedicated to the memories with
my grandmother
are the most treasured and cherished."

We all have had best friends during different phases of our lives that we will never forget. Whether we met our best friend when we were very young or older in life, it doesn't matter because we will never forget that one person who loved and accepted us unconditionally and was always by our side in the good times and in the bad. We will never forget that one person with whom we shared our lofty dreams and goals, and they never once told us how ridiculous we may have sounded, even if we did.

Unfortunately, my best friend of 35 years is no longer with us, but her spirit is alive and well. Her light continues to shine brightly in the beautiful memories that will forever be a part of my life and in the lives of everyone who knew her.

My best friend, Anne, was independent, sharp, witty, generous, kind, classy, sassy, outspoken, and a true Badass in every sense of the word. She had silver in her hair and gold in her heart; oh, I should mention, she was 61 years older than me. You see, my very best friend, Anne, was also my grandmother, whom I affectionately referred to simply as "Gram."

I am now close to the same age Gram was when I was born. Because of her, I will always live my life with an ageless mindset. Our priceless relationship can easily be summed up with the simple phrase, "Love knows no age."

Gram was so much more than just my grandmother and best friend; she was also my fun companion, mentor, confidant, and partner-in-crime.

My parents divorced when I was 10, and my brother and I lived with my dad. Gram (my dad's mother) became like a second mother to me. I spent almost every weekend with her from the time I was a young child through high school. This was my choice!

My grandfather died before I was born, so Gram loved and appreciated my companionship just as much as I loved and needed hers.

Gram was influential to me in so many ways: She attended as many of my school functions as possible and always told me how proud she was of me. Gram took me shopping for my first bra. She took me for haircuts and to doctor and dentist appointments. Gram always made me feel beautiful, even though I was an awkward and overweight child and teenager.

We had a standing lunch and shopping date almost every Saturday afternoon. Gram would always buy me quality clothing and teach me the importance of spending more money on a well-made item so that it would last for many years.

Gram would take me to plays, musicals, and the ballet. She taught me how to act like a lady who displayed proper etiquette and good manners and always stressed the importance of showing appreciation and gratitude.

Gram also often told me how imperative it was to develop a strong backbone so that no one could easily take advantage of me. It was equally important for me to never downplay my abilities or "dumb down" my intelligence for ANYONE!

Throughout the years, I picked up some of Gram's unique slang terms that she would use instead of the "S" word, "B" word, or "F" word. If someone did something to offend her, she would simply look them in the eye with a very straight face and then emphatically tell them to, "Kiss it!" (A much more polite version of saying "Go to Hell!")

My heart feels like a treasure chest filled with the priceless memories of my time spent with Gram—priceless memories that will be with me for the rest of my life...

Gram loved to play cards because it kept her mind sharp, so she also taught me how to become an outstanding card player. And I don't mean the card games that kids typically play, such as "Go Fish," "Crazy 8's," or "Concentration." I learned to play much more sophisticated games such as "Gin Rummy," "Casino," and "Spite and Malice."

Gram taught me how to become a "card shark" and how to spot other "card sharks." I was a quick learner and became a good card player. How good? Good enough to finance my first trip to Florida at age 12 with the money I won from playing cards with Gram, my bachelor Uncle David, who lived with Gram, and Gram's elderly "boyfriend," Harry, who had LOTS of money!

During our trip to Florida, we went to Disneyworld, and Gram went on the scary Space Mountain ride with me. She was 73 years old at the time and absolutely FEARLESS. What a fantastic role model for me to have!

I have many happy childhood memories of Gram and me attending the Wisconsin State Fair together during the summers and feasting on a "well-balanced" meal consisting of fried chicken, "roasting ears" (corn on the cob) dripping with butter and, of course, the famous Cream Puffs for dessert. (Was it any wonder why my thighs kept getting bigger and bigger?)

I will forever remember Gram's famous RBF's, Root Beer Floats made with frozen vanilla custard from the Pig & Whistle restaurant in Milwaukee, Wisconsin. (Again, not great for my thighs!)

Gram and I spent countless hours watching her favorite television shows together, which included game shows, "Bowling with the Champs," "ABC's Wide World of Sports" (especially the skating competitions), scandalous talk shows (Phil Donahue, Sally Jesse Raphael, and Maury), the "Tonight Show with Johnny Carson," and "Mary Hartman, Mary Hartman," the very risqué adult nighttime soap opera.

And after a long day, we would fall asleep together while listening to talk radio shows and Radio Mystery Theater.

The smallest things meant the most to both of us. Material possessions were never very important to me, especially as I got older. I cherished quality time with Gram, my very best friend. And then, as the aging process continued throughout the years, our roles began reversing.

I was now taking Gram for her hair appointments, doctor appointments, and dentist appointments. I treated her to lunch and took her shopping on Saturdays. I was the one who held her hand as we crossed the street to make sure that she wouldn't fall. I was the one taking her to plays and to the ballet. I was the one who complimented her and made her feel beautiful when she looked in the mirror and saw an old woman staring back at her.

And I was the one who made sure that she felt loved, appreciated, and needed.

When I left for college, I made sure that I called Gram every day just to let her know that she was in my thoughts and that I loved her. Gram's first question was usually a sarcastic, "What's the dirt?" meaning "gossip," and we would then fill each other in. *We always found things to laugh about, which brought a smile to our faces and ended our conversation on a positive note.*

As Gram continued to age, she began using a standard response when I would call her to ask how she was doing. She wouldn't say "fine" or "I'm okay." Instead, she would say, "I'm still here, Tina." I wish I could call her today just to hear her voice and that sarcastic reply, "I'm still here, Tina."

Gram passed away at the age of 96 . She lived a very full and vibrant life. I miss her daily and am thankful for all the memories and the valuable lessons she left me with.

Because of Gram, I will always focus on the unlimited possibilities in life instead of the apparent limitations that may present themselves as the aging process evolves. I will embrace each new day as a gift to be cherished.

I will always approach my life as one grand adventure, whether that adventure is planned or happens spontaneously. I will always have a thirst to learn more, be more, and experience more.

To me, a dream has no expiration date. Dreams can be pursued at any stage of life, even if the means to pursue them may change.

As long as I have a breath in my body, I will find a way to focus on what I have and can contribute.

I will be open to sharing what I know with members of the younger generation who are receptive to learning what I have to offer and equally receptive to learning from them. At the end of the day, we are all human beings who have the same need and desire to feel loved, acknowledged and appreciated.

One of my goals in life has ALWAYS been to make my Gram, my BFF (Best Friend for Life), proud of me and the woman I have become. Because of her, I will remain strong, independent, tenacious, and loving. And I will always keep my outrageous sense of humor!

I will always focus on making each day the best of my life. I will refuse to be put away on a shelf like an old, tattered, dusty, and outdated book just because of a number assigned to me. I will become an AGELESS BESTSELLER and forever be a walking, talking billboard of what is possible in life, because that is precisely what Gram would have wanted me to do.

And if ANYONE should ever try to make me think differently, I will just look that person directly in the eye, with a big smile on my face, and then politely tell them to "KISS IT!"

Tina Taylor
Age 61

CHAPTER 76
THE DAY THAT CHANGED THE DIRECTION OF MY LIFE

VICTORIA MCRAY

"At any age, we can rewrite the narrative to make our lives richer, healthier, and more fulfilling. This philosophy is what fuels my purpose and brings joy and honor to every day."
"We do all this to honor ourselves, the gift of life, our wonderful bodies, and, above all, to honor the divine."

In the story of my life, a pivotal moment altered the course of my existence. In a short period, my entire perspective on life changed. At 24 years old, I found myself in a hospital room, bathed in the harsh glow of artificial lights, trembling from fear and the chill of the room.

My heart raced, and I was overcome with fear as the medical staff hurriedly tried to determine if I was suffering a heart attack. Earlier that day, my biggest concern was writing the last thank-you notes for recent wedding gifts and when to do my college homework. The possibility of a heart condition did not fit into my promising life, and this all felt surreal.

Yet, after being released that night with no answers and having this episode dismissed as a panic attack, this nightmare continued.

As these symptoms persisted, each brought on by the erratic behavior of my heart racing, slowing, or skipping beats, each episode was as raw and frightening as the last.

On each emergency room visit, the staff quickly ran tests and asked a series of questions before sharing that nothing appeared "abnormal." They continued to dismiss my concerns as panic attacks and sent me home.

During those months, instead of feeling the excitement of my newly married life, uncertainty overshadowed my happiness.

As I sat in college classes, I wondered—would it strike there as I sought to learn? When I drove my car, I thought of what I would do if it happened while driving. The worst thoughts came at night. Would I silently die in my sleep?

I had never been in poor health, and I could not understand what was happening to my body. Each occurrence brought more uncertainty and apprehension.

This medical journey was a labyrinth of hospitals, doctors, and specialists. Followed by tests and the agonizing wait for answers. Months passed, leading to a diagnosis of "mitral valve prolapse." I was thrilled to have an answer and medication! However, the medicine was ineffective after a few hours, and symptoms returned. I reported this to my doctor, who advised me to simply increase my dose to 2 pills daily. I was happy to have my life back on track and to be able to focus on school, work, and home life.

After a couple of months, it occurred to me that I would be taking these pills for the rest of my life. This realization created sadness and loss over the good health I had always enjoyed. I had never thought of myself as unhealthy, yet at the age of 24, I needed medication for life.

I wanted to know if there was anything I could do to improve my heart and heal my body in any measurable way.

These events occurred in the '80s, when most doctors were men, and we trusted doctors as authority figures. It was very uncommon to question their diagnosis or decisions.

At my follow-up visit, I mustered up the courage to meekly ask if I could do anything to improve my situation. At first, the doctor dismissed my question. Then, as he was exiting the room, he turned from the door and flippantly replied, "Maybe if you get your heart stronger, it will help."

Those hasty words changed the course of my life!

Those words ignited a spark of hope within me. I resolved to explore every avenue to heal my body. It was a path with no roadmap, but I pursued it with unwavering determination.

Six months later, I had done it! I was off the medications and had more energy and stamina than I thought possible. I call this the day I became "the hero of my own life."

That was many years ago. I am a woman in my 60s, but that experience defined my life. *Due to that frightening, uncertain time, I have focused on living a healthy life for many decades.* I even became a fitness instructor in my 50s to help others improve their health.

Fast forward to today.

During the COVID lockdown, I started a Facebook group for women over 50. I intended to share ideas on aging well to help others stay healthy and mobile during this uncertain time.

But as I connected with these women, I realized that many of them struggled with weight issues. These issues affected their quality of life. This extra weight caused them to have low energy, low self-esteem, medical problems, and overall aches and pains.

All of this affected their ability to be mobile, sleep well, and live rich lives.

Growing older was something many did not see in a positive light as they wondered "what pains and medical issues would show up next."

Then, I knew I had to shift the group's focus from aging well to sustainable weight loss. This brought me out of retirement and caused me to embark on a new mission: to coach women on "31 Sneaky Ways" to achieve their desired weight without resorting to the temporary reduction from traditional diets.

My belief is simple: God intended us to live with joy, contribution, and meaning at every age. We all have the power to become heroes in our own lives. *We can rewrite the narrative at any age to make our lives richer, healthier, and more fulfilling. This philosophy fuels my purpose and brings joy and honor to every day.*

In closing...

This book represents a noble mission and an invitation to join us as catalysts of change. We aim to reverse the "stigma" and negative perceptions surrounding aging.

Our purpose is to illuminate the joy, freedom, and wisdom that retirement brings and publicly state how deeply we embrace this phase of life.

For some, this means dedicating time to causes and careers driven by choice, not necessity. For others, it's about living each day exactly as we desire, whether through enjoyable hikes, scenic bike rides, enriching travel, immersive reading, or more moments of deepening relationships. We fully embrace the beauty of this life stage.

With this in mind, we commit to living life to the fullest, waking each day with optimism and vitality, eating nourishing meals, embracing a love for learning, nurturing social connections, and fostering a sense of gratitude.

We do all this to honor ourselves, the gift of life, our beautiful bodies, and, above all, to celebrate the divine.

Victoria McRay
Age 67

CHAPTER 77

YOU ARE NOT DONE YET! LIVING A LIFE YOU LOVE AT ANY AGE AND AT ANY STAGE

CINDY MCKEE

"The very nature of life requires us to grow. To stretch. To get uncomfortable and be better than we are today. That's where passion and joy live." -- Cindy McKee

This is both a cautionary and inspirational message about how I found myself, unintentionally and unknowingly, becoming a much lesser version of the person I knew myself to be—physically, mentally, and spiritually—as I approached age 70. I had to ask myself powerful questions and embark on a renewed journey of growth—one that has me rediscovering my joy, passion and delight.

Our story of spiraling down came on slowly. After downsizing and moving across the country to AZ, the pandemic hit. My husband Bob and I decided we only needed one car for a while, as we really weren't going anywhere. But we missed our family and friends and began a journey back across the country in our RV when no one was flying yet.

Before I knew it, Bob was doing most of the driving. He was a retired captain for a major airline and used to sitting in the left seat, which was fine with me.

Once back home again, I had surgery on both wrists and an elbow and besides the driving, he took over cooking, cleaning, etc. as well. Even after I had recovered, we habitually shifted more responsibility to him. I was doing less without realizing it. His love language is acts of service; it all felt natural. Even for someone used to being a hard worker, I became accustomed to this way of doing less. We were bumbling along, I was serving my coaching practice, and we were enjoying life in the desert and playing golf. Life seemed good.

And then a significant shift happened. Bob learned of a fabulous aviation opportunity and landed an excellent flying job. After five years of doing everything together (and him doing a lot for both of us), we were back to my needing a car and taking back my old responsibilities.

No big deal, right? It turns out it was! Not that I minded—not at all. What I discovered was that I had, little by little, lost my sharpness and my spatial awareness. I had lost an innate sense of freedom and independence. We were used to deferring to each other, consulting with each other on just about everything, and being dependent on each other.

I had lost my identity. And I didn't even know it. I had spiraled down without realizing it. Bob's return to aviation was the best unplanned shake-up that could have happened to us. On Bob's side, he realized he'd grown stale. He'd lost his spark without having a part of his life devoted to contribution, without being required to use his fantastic brain and get back into his body while performing intricate flying skills. Our survival-based brains, which we all have, were telling us we were okay. We were putting one foot in front of the other, going about our days, tending to responsibilities, and doing things we liked to do. But we weren't being challenged. We were comfortable. Too comfortable.

The very nature of life requires us to grow, stretch, get uncomfortable, and be better than we are today. That's where passion and joy live. There is excitement and fear or discomfort when we continually move into new territory. It is here that we get lit up. I chose to rise to the invitation to reclaim who I knew myself to be, to lean in with intention and to create new and flourishing growth.

Your story will be different from mine.

Have you gotten too comfortable?

Are you living a spiraled-down life?

When was the last time you challenged yourself?

Have you felt the joy and passion of trying something new?

When were you last excited to get out of bed in the morning?

Take an honest inventory. Let the stories in this book inspire you. And do something different. We are not done yet! We all have a lot of growth, contribution, and excitement to experience in these "encore" years. I'm smiling at the possibilities, and I hope you are, too.

Cindy McKee
Age 71

AFTERWORD

Now that you have read our stories, emotionally and energetically sat by the fireplaces in our hearts and Ageless Dens, how will you expand your life?

In this book, we, the Ageless Women, responded to a universal call to make known and demonstrate to our communities, younger generations, and the world at large the personal and social values and benefits of living an Ageless Life.

Contrary to popular opinions and beliefs, there is a bountiful, fulfilling, and satisfying life to live as a 60+ Ageless Star. Life does not end as we celebrate our expanded decades of experiences; it expands, blossoms, and becomes centered on possibilities we could not have imagined in previous years. We have a deep understanding of who we are and what we desire to do and be at this stage. We dismantle well-established perceptions of social labels and expectations of "getting old." We go beyond what others presumed was the final frontier for us.

It is our aim to inspire, motivate, and compel our readers to be open to new ideas, possibilities, and expressions of life. It is impossible to read these powerful stories and not be *stirred to go forward* and have your own experiences of an Ageless Mindset.

Through our stories of transparencies and vulnerabilities, sharing raw truths of successes, failures, and get-back-up steps, we light the torch on the path for others. We stand in the dignity of our choices, decisions, outcomes, and life lessons.

How are we equipped to talk about Agelessness? Our stories are tried and true; *we have lived it*. We have not aimlessly lived through decades of life waiting to be put away or silenced. Each story is like a blueprint, showing how the writer was able to lay the foundation bricks of life and womanhood. We have succeeded when we were expected to fail, picked ourselves back up from dark places, stretched small resources, and triumphed in the face of social messages, beliefs, and talking points about the un-usefulness of women when they "become a certain age."

We have defied, surpassed, and overcome all the odds stacked against us because of our age and the assumptions of what that means. When we became grounded and centered in the truths of our progressive, ageless mindsets, we left footprints on paths for those who would come behind us.

Let us become your Ageless Sages and Empowering Expansion Squads.

Writing our stories in Ageless Voices is our way of creating new paths with direction signs, rest-stop signs, detours, closed roads, and new construction ahead signs. We knew there would be others after us, trying to sort out the messages and experiences of womanhood, and we wanted the road to be smoother than it had been for us. We celebrate and honor those who come behind us, realizing their own Agelessness.

On the newly paved roads, we also left a few life-lesson signs as reminders that during challenges or apparent obstacles, we should be willing to grow, pivot, and explore new interests and possibilities. Finally, we intentionally left nuggets of gold between every story's sentences. When your heart is at peace, you will find them; it will feel like we shared those gold nuggets just for you because we did.

Let the Wave of an Ageless Mindset have a ripple effect within you and around the world...

Dr. K. Mhina Entrantt
Age 66

Ageless Stars Bios

The purpose of life, after all, is to live it, to taste the experience to the utmost, to reach out eagerly and without fear for newer and richer experiences. ~ **Eleanor Roosevelt**

Dr. Angelika Christie

I picture a world where the mature woman is outrageously happy...

finally, putting herself first, doing what she loves, following her passion, creating new meaning, following her intuition, having no regrets, rejecting manipulation, stepping out of clichés, being proud of herself, and generously giving of her wisdom.

Women deserve to do what excites them.

Because happiness is a beacon of light, guiding her through the years of freedom that lie ahead, illuminating the path to a fulfilling life.

As a Naturopathic Doctor, Relationship Coach, and Reiki Master Teacher, I have been helping mature women solve their health, self-realization, and relationship challenges for over thirty years. What does this mean?

So, rather than feeling old in her body and unhappy with herself and in her relationships which could lead to loneliness and depression, she experiences radiant energy that gives her a zest for life and the security of a loving relationship with herself and whomever she wants to spend her precious life with.

I believe that women deserve to be outrageously happy. When women are happy, everybody wins.

Angelika Christie ND, RMT

info@angelika-christie.com

+1-242-359-5550 (Bahamas)

WhatsApp: 305-343-8324

https://angelika-christie.com

www.baronessangelika.tv

Live every Saturday at 3 PM ET

https://winwinwomen.tv/show/your-radiant-life-after-45

Join my FB Group here:

https://www.facebook.com/groups/radiantlifeafter45

Anne Lorimor

Anne Lorimor is not your typical great-grandmother, sitting in her rocking chair. At 85, she climbed Mt. Kilimanjaro, the highest mountain in Africa as the oldest woman. This climb was to benefit her cause of empowering disadvantaged children and youth. In July 2019, she climbed again to set a Guinness World Record as the oldest PERSON, to climb the highest free-standing mountain in the world. While this is a monumental achievement in itself, Anne is not doing it for herself. Again, the purpose is to gain attention and funds for her cause.

In 2016, Anne founded Lorimor ChildEmpowerment Foundation dba Creating Exciting Futures to show children their options, give them the tools to reach their full potential and then pay it forward. Each child is encouraged to give back by, in turn, helping others. Anne says, "My life is about helping kids in every way possible. To empower kids can create a ripple effect that benefits all of us." Her motto is, A hand up, not a handout.

You can learn more about Anne and the Cause by going to CreatingExcitingFutures.org.

Barbara J Morris

Hi! I am Barbara J Morris, a lively 77 year-old, at this writing. I was married young and together we have two beautiful daughters. The marriage lasted 19 years and, believe it or not, we remained friends until his death at age 70. I spent about 19 years with my second husband (are you seeing a pattern here? LOL). After two divorces I moved to Colorado and that's when my life changed! Feeling lost and mostly alone I was so very fortunate to find new friends that lifted me up and helped me to see the real me. It led me to my purpose at the age of 63, so you see it's never too late. It turns out that my purpose is to help women to learn to forgive themselves, appreciate and love themselves. And that has been the underlying premise for the rest of my life. Learning to apply all that I have learned over the years in order to help women struggling (struggle is an option, not a necessity) has given me much joy, particularly when I watch those women blossom into their own purpose and living a joy filled life. My newest mantra is: How can I help?

Reach out to me at my email address below and let's connect. bjmorris47@gmail.com

Barb Laubman

As a role model and contributor to the ageless movement, Barb Laubman exemplifies what it means to live an ageless lifestyle. From her lifelong dedication as an extreme athlete to now embracing her seventies and beyond, she eagerly anticipates all that the future holds. She radiates joy, purpose, and authenticity in everything she does—a true embodiment of ageless living. As a transformational coach and Reiki Master, Barb has a unique gift for helping women over 50 reconnect with their inner strength and create lives filled with peace, fulfillment, and self-discovery.

Her playful spirit and boundless curiosity are contagious, whether she's exploring nature with her beloved dog or savoring the beauty of the present moment. With intention, kindness, and a deep belief that every stage of life offers fresh opportunities to grow, thrive, and inspire others, Barb lights the way for women ready to embrace their own ageless journey.

https://www.facebook.com/blaubman/

https://www.linkedin.com/in/barb-laubman-13061b17/

blaubman@gmail.com

Bev Walkner

Bev is an inspiring writer and speaker and a champion for women's empowerment. Recently, she created her first ever Women's Empowerment event. Women who attended the event said their lives were forever changed. They felt more worthy, that they belonged, and that they **deserved** happiness and joy.

Bev spent decades in a corporate executive role, where she was known as a respected leader; mentoring, influencing and inspiring many people to be the best they could be.

At the age of 64, Bev made the decision to improve her physical health and strength and started to weight train as a power-lifter. A year later she entered her first competition and succeeded in setting provincial records.

At 67, Bev finally found the courage to leave her decades long abusive marriage. This allowed her to heal, find her true self, discover she was gay, and magically meet and marry the love of her life.

Bev presently lives in Edmonton, Alberta, Canada with her beautiful new bride.

DM to Bev Walkner or to BevWalkner5@gmail.com

Bonnie Senftner

Bonnie Senftner has always lived by MLK's motto *"Life's most persistent and urgent question is "What are you doing for others?"*

She is a retired RN whose specialty was in wound care, earned her Master Degree in addiction counseling, and is an entrepreneur who created many successful real estate-related businesses with her husband Michael. She has enjoyed writing since childhood and plans to create a travel blog where she can share helpful information about her worldwide travels. She is proud and beyond blessed to have her husband Michael (33 years) two sons, (Luke and Tyler) and four grandchildren in her life. She loves to read, write, work out, travel, and enjoy philosophical discussions while fine dining with friends. She supports local charities such as Boost A Foster Family, Crystal's Critter Haven, and Pearl at the Mailbox (charity that educates impressionable people about the internet danger with trafficking) as well as better known charities such as ASPCA and St. Jude's Hospital.

Bonnie resides in Mesa, AZ and can be reached at grthealth@yahoo.com

Carol Koppelman

Carol Koppelman is the best-selling author of "Do the Necessary, Let the Rest Go to Hell," and a multi-published international best-selling contributing author. She was a corporate and technical writer for nearly 40 years in the biomedical and nuclear industry. Carol owns CPK Solutions, LLC and is also a Branch Director for Park Lane Jewelry. She loves to cook, to sew, to write, and most importantly, she loves to share wonderful adventures with her husband, Ken, and their Maltese mix dog, Biscuit.

Catherine Schwark (Catherine From Minnesota)

Catherine is a Certified Master Integrative Life Coach and is the CEO and Founder of CAT Coaching *Conscious Action Transformations.* She is certified by the Instinctual Trauma Response Training Institute, is a Founding Member of the Recovery Church in St. Paul, MN and currently serves the recovery community in a multitude of ways.

She is committed to a Seven Ancestral Generation stewardship, living and working for the benefit of and to positively impact Seven Ancestral Generations into the future by establishing the Quinn-Schwark Foundation.

One thing still on her bucket list is to run off the side of a mountain and soar like an eagle (hang glide.)

She lives in Minnesota, USA and can be reached at MNCatherine11@gmail.com and followed at: http://www. facebook.com/MNCatherine

Cheryl McKenzie-Cook

I am a happiness coach. I had to learn how to be happy in the face of many challenges – three breast cancer adventures; heart failure; a diagnosis of auto immune disease; two failed marriages; financial disaster; two armed robberies; and many other things. I have known great heartbreak and great love. I only teach what I need to learn. My purpose is to help others to live a life of more ease, grace, and joy – no matter the external circumstances.

My superpower is Resilience.

I am 78 years and I still have many dreams left to fulfil!

My passions are facilitating retreats; music; dancing; hanging out with friends; good food and wine; laughing until my stomach hurts; reading; watching movies; being with my grandchildren.

Website: https://thinkittalkit.com

Email: cheryl@thinkittalkit.com Facebook: Think It Talk It

LinkedIn: linkedin.com/in/cheryl-mckenzie-cook-bS2S8S11

Cindy McKee

Hi - I'm Cindy McKee and I am a former professional in the Equestrian world. What I found through teaching hundreds of young girls to ride horses, was that as they strived for goals that often felt unattainable and overcame their fears, that I was witnessing growth on a major scale. I realized that their life transformations was what really lit me up.

For the past 2 decades I have immersed myself in the study of mindset, personal development and growth. Today, I facilitate transformation in my coaching programs for mature women just like you as you navigate this stage of life. Together, we tackle what might be holding you back and help you to create a life you love. We are all meant to grow, to connect, to love and to be excited about life at any age and I am delighted to help you do just that.

https://www.facebook.com/cindy.troymckee

https://www.instagram.com/cindyandbobmckee

www.linkedin.com/in/cindy-mckee

www.soaringaftersixty.com

Cis Ahearn

My name is Cis Ahearn. With over 47 years of nursing experience, I'm a seasoned healthcare professional turned life coach, artist, and author of two books. Having dedicated over seven years to volunteering and leadership in the Tony Robbins organization, I'm trained in NLP and the Coach Training Institute. As a semi-retired nurse, I now contribute to advocating women's rights and superpowers. Through coaching, workshops, and programs, I empower women and nurses to explore new possibilities, fostering mutual support, awareness and life tools on bringing out the best in women.. My goal is to help individuals recognize and own their superpowers, encouraging authenticity and thriving in both personal and professional realms. I am so excited to share in this amazing project to ageless awareness and the gifts in aging fun, fearless and fabulous!!

cis.ahearn@gmail.com

"Achievement doesn't come from what we do but from who we are." -**Marianne Williamson**

Debbie Prediger

I'm Debbie Prediger, celebrated for cultivating communities of Visionaries and changemakers. In my Empowering You community of 5000+ members, I lead as the catalyst and Empowerment Leader, guiding each individual's journey. Through my empowering Business Momentum and Strategy programs, I offer actions that ignite energy and fulfillment. With a background in nursing, holistic well-being, and Aroma Freedom Technique, my journey led me to found the Empowering YOU Community and co-found We Empower World. As a senior partner at The Wellness Universe, an international best-selling author, and JOYLEY Ambassador, I spread joy through a transformative process and engaging speeches. My dearest treasures are my children and grandchildren, reminding me daily to choose and embody JOY. As a 5th generation FarmHER, I hold a deep reverence for the land and the strength of community. I embrace the journey of crafting a life I LOVE, choosing JOY, Peace, and grace along the way. My mission is simple: to help others crave lives they truly love, embracing an ageless mindset where growth, joy, and transformation know no limits.

Thank you.

Debbie Prediger

Empowerment Leader & Strategist

Empowering heart-centered entrepreneurs to create awareness, impact, and transformation.

Let's Connect:

Www.askdebbie.club

Info.at.thh@gmail.com

Debi Lynn – Age 66

Debi captures the essence of life's incredible journey through the lens of service and compassion. Debi pursued her desire to make a difference in the lives of others by becoming a certified medical assistant. Her commitment to providing compassionate care and support to those in need became her mission. I started a group to heal after losing a child at 3 months while raising a sister. I am a Certified Grief Educator – committed to providing the highest level of grief support through education, experience, and insights into the often unacknowledged rocky terrain of grief. Learn the steps I took to overcome the feelings of grief, guilt, sadness and anger to reclaim and regain your life.

From a young age, Debi found solace in the beauty of nature, capturing its essence through her lens. Photography became a cherished pastime, allowing her to document the stunning landscapes she encountered during her travels. Debi currently resides in Plano, Texas, a mom of two grown children, six grandchildren and loves to take road trips in her miata taking pictures of architecture, flowers, rivers and streams. There is always beauty around us and to marvel at its majestic beauty. Connect with me:

igapstexas@yahoo.com

https://www.facebook.com/debitx/https://

www.facebook.com/debitx/

https://www.facebook.com/profile.php?id=100090126992591

https://www.facebook.com/profile.php?id=100090126992591

https://www.linkedin.com/in/debi-lynn-5b897b208/

Denise Yonkers

Denise Yonkers is a writer, co-author, and vocalist. She is from Chicago, Illinois. After being widowed, and retiring from her career in Social Services, Denise is ready to rediscover herself and explore new horizons, discovering the many new opportunities available to her. She is compassionate, enthusiastic, and genuine. Denise is a positive force and loves to work on various projects. Denise loves to support, encourage, and inspire others to become their best selves and live their best lives with an ageless mindset.

Denise is dedicated to practicing her song sets weekly, learning and practicing different voice techniques. She is living her dream of flying without fear. Denise is passionate about traveling and visiting new exciting places, making lasting friendships on her journey. She loves lifelong learning and is interested in keeping herself current on new technology and business strategies. She focuses on mind, body, spirit, and energy health, and stays physically active. She believes that having a good sense of humor and rolling with the changes is key.

yonkers942@att.net

https://DeniseYonkers.beekonnected.com

Diane Berg

Diane spent 40 successful years in the financial services industry, establishing her expertise in both direct sales and managing and training new recruits to success. Recognizing the value of sharing her knowledge Diane went on to create a revolutionary free online training course. Through this course she inspires and coaches individuals wanting to take their careers to a new level.

In this next chapter she is reigniting her passion for painting and delves into the world of art with a renewed vigor. In her leisure time Diane enjoys playing bridge and a round of golf.

She also cherishes the joys of gardening.

To stay active and fit she attends regular fitness training, aqua aerobics and yoga. Diane leads a full and fearless life, constantly seeking new experiences and personal growth.

Diane currently lives in Alberta Canada with her partner John and their big black lab, Hank. They spend most of the winter in Mexico to escape the cold Alberta weather. This getaway allows her to rejuvenate and enjoy the beauty of warmer climates and the beautiful Mexican culture.

For those interested in connecting with Diane she can be reached at dianebergfinancial@gmail.com or through her website at www.dianebergfinancial.com With her extensive experience and passion for helping others, she is ready to assist you in achieving your goals in the financial services industry.

Dolly Kennedy

Introducing Yvonne "Dolly" Kennedy, a remarkable individual whose journey began in Buffalo, NY, on March 2, 1926. Dolly embarked on a fulfilling career as a Registered Nurse, graduating from Meyer Memorial Hospital's School of Nursing in 1946. In 1948, she married Paul Kennedy, and together they welcomed seven children into their lives. A true matriarch, she raised five boys and two girls.

Dolly's legacy extends beyond her family. The Dolly Steamboat, originally, a 48-passenger steamboat replica, bears her name and history. Originally constructed in 1972 by her husband, Paul Kennedy, it later became a global attraction when acquired by the Grimh family in 1975 and reconstructed to accommodate 140 passengers! Dolly has found her niche in public relations, relishing the opportunity to connect with people from all walks of life. Her life's journey is a testament to strength, resilience, and the power of forging connections with people.

Elizabeth Lupacchino-Donohue, CHt, RMP

As a Certified Hypnotherapist, Master Reiki Practitioner, Life Coach and a Student of Shamanic Studies, I have helped hundreds of women achieve their mental, physical, emotional and spiritual goals on their journey called Life. Open the eyes of my heart, Lord. These are words that I have said to myself each and every morning for years. And when I listened to the answers, my life has been amazing.

Thirty years ago, when I quit my corporate job to do what I was being called to do, wellmeaning friends and family members told me that I was making a mistake; that I would not succeed. Well, I proved them wrong. And, again, when the pandemic hit in 2019 and I switched from seeing clients primarily in person to treating them virtually, I was told I wouldn't succeed. Again, listening to my heart, I proved them wrong. I am happy to say that not only am I seeing clients both in person and virtually, but I also continue to hold workshops, seminars and corporate training programs.

For more information please contact me at my website www.elizabethlupacchino.com, or at www.facebook.com/elizabeth.lupacchino

Jana Lee Gattung

L.Ac., M.Ac., NeuroEncoding Specialist, Herbal Forager / Wildcrafter, Author, Health/ Wellness/Lifestyle Educator.

I'm a mother to 3 successful men and one amazing grandson. For 32 years I've endeavored to find the secrets to health, longevity, and true joy, not only for myself, but to share this knowledge with others. I've been a US Nationally Credentialled Acupuncturist (NCCAOM) for 25 years with other certifications as well. I also teach online classes to spread my knowledge and teach people what, how and when to eat, in order to put a stop to the health crisis plaguing over 90% of the population, many people who aren't even aware they are ill, until it's too late. Please follow me on Facebook at Jana Lee Gattung to keep up to date on my Live Events, Courses, Life Magnificent Podcast, and other exciting offerings.

Jo Dibblee

Jo Dibblee is first and foremost a humanitarian. She is an adventure and storyteller of truth, the founder of Frock off Inc and Team Humanity Baja. Team Humanity Baja is a not-forprofit that serves those in deep need in Baja California Sur, Mexico. Jo Lives in Canada and Mexico.

She is the author of several award-winning books

Frock Off: Living Undisguised - True Crime and Inspiration

Bella's Dash: How our Rescue Pup Rescued Us - Inspiration and Healing

Best Kept Secret to Success: In Life, Love and Business - Business and Self Development

While I Can: Finding Purpose and Legacy in a Distant Land - Travel and Inspiration

My Baja Snapshot: Hidden Gems, Mishaps and Discoveries – Travel and Guides

Jo Dibblee Author Facebook : https://www.facebook.com/profile.php?id=61551099985736

Website www.jodibblee.com

Instagram Jo Dibblee

Team Humanity Baja – Hearts and Souls of change https://www.facebook.com/groups/teamhumanitybaja/

Joanne Salvador

Joanne Salvador is an accomplished Egyptologist, Ancient Art Historian, lecturer and exhibitor. A graduate of S.U.N.Y Stony Brook. She was accepted into the prestigious Egyptologists Forum Yale List. As an Alumni she was invited to curate her own show "Ancient Egyptian Evening" at the Stony Brook University Museum when she discovered an exquisite 3,300-year-old New Kingdom yellow limestone carved portrait head of the pharaoh Tutankhamun. After leaving the Egyptology field in 2020, she became an art appraiser and teacher of fine and decorative arts.

A Long Island native, her entire life , she returned to her childhood home where she lives with her dog Ciel , Russian Tortoise Cubby , and hundreds of house plants. Her haven is surrounded by antiquarian books, classical music ,and an eclectic mix of collectibles. She is currently working on two books "The Great Antiquities Game" detailing her experiences as an Egyptologist and "American Kitsch, The Imaginary World of Fantasy and Fairy Tale Art" a whimsical look into this surreal art form. She lives by the creed "Live a life full of adventure and discovery and if you have lived it you can write wonderful stories about it."

She can be contacted by email for programs, events, and appraisals. circe13@optonline.net

Joellyn Martin

Hello, I am Joellyn Renulfi Wlazlowski Martin. As a young mom, I was dedicated to my 3 sons. As an active volunteer from Cub Scout Den Mother to PTO President. I had not realized it, but I was in leadership training. Mary Kay Cosmetics, Hallmark, and my new career as a health and wealth advocate have all confirmed that. My proudest professional achievement thus far was, when as a Hallmark Store manager, my team surpassed the biggest sales goal for that store!

For years, I knew that I would have a business, do storytelling within book writing and be a part of something bigger than me; all have occurred during the last 2 years. I enjoy working with my husband, being at our lake house and restoring furniture. I love the continued family holiday traditions of the legacy tablecloth that began in 1986 and visits to Hallmark for ornaments with the grandchildren. I enjoy saving our memories with individual albums.

I look forward to my new role in the health industry to grow my business by leading other women to create the lifestyles they deserve while helping others.

I see God Wink's everywhere for the direction that I should go!

Live Your Life Ambitiously Now and Your Future Self Will Thank You - Joellyn Martin

https://Linktr.ee/JoellynEyeforDesign

JoyAnn Gold

I'm JoyAnn Gold and at 81 years young, I have founded the Ageless Star Project where we created our documentary film, AGELESS VOICES along with this collaborative book. Following over 30 years in the interior design world, I shifted my focus to helping women over 60 design and live beautiful lives filled with joy, passion and purpose. I consider it my mission and legacy to help shift society's story around aging! Instead of focusing on fear and decline, our story can be an empowered one of how to be FUN, FEARLESS & FABULOUS after 60! When we develop an ageless mindset, these can actually be our grandest years! To help spread the message, I intend to hold film screenings throughout the US and beyond. I invite you to join in our mission to reach one million lives through our book and film.

44joygold@gmail.com

www.agelessvoices.org

https://www.facebook.com/joyann.gold.44

Dr. Karen Mhina Entrantt

Dr. K. Mhina Entrantt, affectionately known as "Dr. K." Executive Director, I Found My Voice-The Movement! Conversational Spanish Academy, Co-Owner & Master Instructor, Transformational Speaker, Award-Winning, Author, and Poet. She is known for igniting her workshops with passion, humor, laughter, and intense practical tools. *"I love being an Instigator and Witness of my Workshop Participants' A-ha moments. I count it my purpose to incite positive change, resilience, and action steps!"*

Dr. K is a retired Mental Health Professional and Counselor, who created culturally sensitive mental health services for people experiencing chronic homeless, children & families experiencing domestic violence, bilingual children & families, and BIPOC. Dr. K's 2 favorite songs are *"Ain't no stopping us now"* by McFadden & Whitehead, *"Golden"* by Jill Scott and her favorite past-times are going to R&B, Jazz concerts, Word Search Puzzles, watching crime mysteries. She lives in North Carolina with her daughter and twin grandchildren, Will & Zel.

She is an author of 5 books. All books can be purchased at www.lulu.com. Click Bookstore. Type I Found My Voice.

Dr. K can be reached at drkworkshops@gmail.com and all Social Media Platforms-Karen Entrantt.

Katherine Merritt

A proud contributor to *Ageless Voices*, Katherine is not just a writer but a passionate advocate for living a vibrant and fulfilling life at every age. As Nana to her three beloved grandchildren—Tyler, Kayleigh, and Sophia—she finds daily inspiration in the joy and wonder they bring to her life. Katherine champions the philosophy of "ageless living," encouraging people to defy outdated stereotypes about aging and embrace a lifestyle full of vitality, purpose, and adventure. Her writing resonates with the belief that every chapter of life holds the potential for growth, discovery, and happiness. Being part of *Ageless Voices* is both a privilege and a joy for Katherine, as it allows her to share her heartfelt stories and insights with readers. She aspires to spark positivity, challenge perceptions, and inspire others to embrace the journey of aging with excitement and confidence.

Laura Taylor Cox

Laura Taylor Cox was born in Nashville, TN and raised in Lewisburg. She earned her BS degree from Vanderbilt University and holds a Master of Communications in Theater Arts from Regent University. While studying at Regent she met her husband, Bill. They have been married, over 40 years and have four children and 7 grandchildren.

Laura studied drama at the American Academy of Dramatic Arts in Los Angeles, then studied Shakespeare at the Royal Academy of Dramatic Art in London, England. She has had numerous roles in industrial films and videos. Laura has written, produced, directed and acted in many plays and sketches for her local churches over the years.

When Laura was in her mid-50's, she began renovating distressed properties and making them more beautiful than they were when they were new. She enjoys tearing out walls, building new walls, and has learned basic plumbing skills. Power tools are now her favorite toys!

Her first book, This Divine Mystery: Faith for Answered Prayer, was published when Laura was 66. She expects to publish her second book while she is 67, with more books to follow in the decades to come!

www.thisdivinemystery.com

IG @laurataylorcox

FB - LauraTaylorCox

TikTok - authorlaurataylorcox

Laura@thisdivinemystery.com

Lucie Rosa-Stagi

Lucie's life has been a tapestry of experiences, from her roots in French Canada to living in big cities like Montreal, New York, Madrid, 35+ years of teaching in San Francisco and living as an expat in Mexico since 2001. She's an avid sports enthusiast, a passionate traveler, and a dedicated pilgrim on transformative journeys to places like Egypt, Israel, India, and Bali.

As a Business Mentor for Seniors, she passionately empowers women aged 60+ to share their wisdom through online events, breaking down age-related stereotypes. Her commitment to a pro-aging mindset celebrates experience and defies age as a limitation. Lucie's journey extends to her role as the Community Builder for Launch Lab Academy, where her team, spanning generations and nationalities, has helped countless coaches and course creators launch and scale their businesses organically online. Her affiliation with Tony Robbins and Dean Graziosi's "Self-Education Is the New Norm" marked a pivotal moment in her career.

But Lucie is more than just a mentor and business strategist; she's also a storyteller. Her three incredible stories are set to captivate readers, leaving a lasting impression. Lucie Rosa-Stagi's tales will not only inspire but also remind you that age is just a number, and wisdom is timeless.

Connect with Lucie: https://LucieRosaStagi.beekonnected.com

Moriah Hudson

My name is Moriah Hudson. I have created Healing Your Broken Heart to share the things that I have learned to move through grief and the pain. And my life is unrecognizable now. And yes, I miss my wife every single day, but it no longer hurts to breathe. I've been able to accomplish things that I have wanted to do all of my life that I thought that I couldn't do. And as a grief coach I wanted to share with you what I've learned. There's so much more to life than just grief and pain.

I have created a webinar called Healing Your Broken Heart. Grief and loss play such a big part of all of our lives. And I am no exception. I did this because my wife of 35 years died in March of 2020. And I didn't want to go on. The only thing I wanted was to die. The first two years of grieving were the worst two years of my 70-year-old life. And after two years I decided that it was either going to destroy me or I had to change it. And Healing Your Broken Heart is the result of that change.

I have found that the hardest thing in my life was finding

someone I couldn't live without and then having to learn to live without them.

I have discovered 3 steps that as a senior lesbian widow that you need to help you move through the paralyzing grief process and begin to get out of the quicksand of pain. I would like you to friend me on Facebook or contact me by e-mail at moriahehudson@earthlink.net

Do you have a friend in your life you would like to give the gift of healing her broken heart? Please share this information. This club is not something any of us, wanted to ever have to join, but we are all in this together. Let me join you on this journey to an empowering new exciting life for you.

Nancy Johnson

Nancy Johnson is a dedicated Mindset & Wellness expert, specializing in empowering women 40 to 70 to overcome limiting beliefs, health concerns and mindset barriers that hinder them from the life they desire. With a deep passion for guiding women toward their true potential which can be achieved naturally, without side effects. Nancy inspires women to embrace their present moments and live life to the fullest, fostering a sense of well-being and balance in both body and mind. Nancy is an advocate for mental wellness causes, actively supporting initiatives that promote emotional well-being.

Her love for travel grants her the freedom to explore various places, allowing her to spend quality time with her children and granddaughter who reside in different states. Her personal passions include dancing, meditation, breathwork and walking in nature.

To connect with her:

Intentiontobalance@gmail.com

www.Intentiontobalance.com

http://instagram.com/intentiontobalance

http://www.linkedin.com/in/johnsonnancy

http://facebook.com/nancy.johnson3

Dr. Sally Cleland

Dr. Cleland has more than 45 years of business experience in both the corporate and private sectors. Her career has been diverse; it has spanned industry, academia, private practice, and since the mid 1980's she has operated her own consulting firm, EsTeam Consulting. Her business motto is ""Business Success is Merely an Extension of Personal Success." In all areas, she has proven expertise in facilitating interactive seminars and experiential workshops, clinical and administrative management, interaction with government and regulatory bodies and research collaboration. As well as being a professional educator, trainer, public speaker, author and self-esteem practitioner, her business interests focus on assisting her clients build and maintain healthy self-esteem. She regularly advises others that healthy self-esteem does not make life easier; it makes living fully possible. Whether referring to her staff or her students, she noted throughout her career that their level of performance and productivity, happiness, and contentment with both their professional and personal lives AND the successful reaching of their goals is directly related to their level of self-esteem.

Dr. Cleland received her Doctor of Veterinary Medicine (1975) from the Western College of Veterinary Medicine, University of

Saskatchewan, and her Bachelor of Arts, with distinction (1971) from the University of Regina. She has numerous post-graduate certificates in management, communication, negotiation, and various aspects of personal development (including self-esteem facilitation).

Dr. Cleland is the mother of one child, now an adult woman, and is grandmother to four the oldest of which has Cerebral Palsy (for whom she was instrumental in her care during her developmental years). Her family care-giving duties also extended to her paternal grandparents and her own parents. As far as recreational interests, she loves crafting, singing, and playing the guitar, family activities, travelling, aromatherapy and creative writing.

As a dedicated teacher, guide and mentor exceling in the classroom, teaching laboratory and the boardroom, she is passionate about encouraging people in their own journey of self discovery.

DrSallyCleland.com

scleland@sasktel.net

Shirley Turner

Shirley Turner 63yrs, wife to a wonderful husband, mother of three amazing children, and proud granny of 5 beautiful grandchildren. With a diverse background as a certified Life Coach, Personal Trainer/Pilates Instructor and Eckhart Tolle Teacher of Presence, Shirley has dedicated her life to helping ladies discover the beauty and potential that lies within.

Born, with an innate curiosity and passion for personal growth, Shirley has spent the last 4 decades immersed in researching, studying and experimenting in the field of Personal Education and Development. Through her unwavering determination, she transformed her own life into something she never thought possible.

Now Shirley focuses her expertise on guiding women 50 years and older to do the same, discovering their purpose, finding contentment and personal liberation. Bridging the gap between where they currently stand and where they aspire to be, physically, mentally, emotionally and spiritually. Creating a safe space for women to feel seen, heard, validated and supported is at the heart of her work. Shirley's transformative approach is based on her proven 5 step Program PRIME, which helps women uncover their hidden strengths and talents. Together they create a roadmap to success, ensuring that no matter what the circumstances, each woman can thrive and live life to the fullest.

You can contact Shirley on – turners@vodamail.co.za

Visit her Website – theprimelifemastery.com

Sunshine Deb

Certified Life Enrichment Wellness Coach (Since 2004).

Hi, my name is Sunshine Deb (aka Coach Deb), a nickname given to me during my youth, inspired by my deep passion for nature, especially sunrises, and my zest for life. With over 30 years of experience in the health, fitness, and wellness industry, and a passion for personal and spiritual growth, I became a certified life enrichment wellness coach dedicated to helping individuals break free from limitations, discover their unique potential, and cultivate a purposeful and healthy lifestyle. Through the six pillars of wellness, which align with N.A.T.U.R.E, I address the whole person—physically, mentally, emotionally, and spiritually—to inspire, empower, and enrich lives, promoting optimal energy, health, and well-being.

Connect with me at creativhealthcoaching@gmail.com, and let's embark on a journey of purpose, wellness, and youthful vitality.

Susan Farling 79

Susan Farling is delighted to be part of a growing cohort of passionate people of all ages who enthusiastically challenge the ageist myths that can block the rich potential of people over 60 to live purposeful, engaged, well-resourced, vital, and flourishing lives. Susan's formal education took her from an undergraduate arts degree to working in psychiatry as a registered nurse for a decade. In her late thirties, she obtained her master's degree in counselling and was a founding member of a thriving counselling center where she enjoyed decades of private practice.

Now in her late seventies, in her private practice and through her *Thrive Over Sixty-Five: Live with Purpose, Peace of Mind, and Vibrant Well-Being* programs, Susan supports people from sixty to one hundred plus to navigate their challenges with grace and compassion, and to develop their lives as a fulfilling time of connection, contribution, and growth, full of joyful moments, and with positive anticipation for their futures.

Susan brings a fascination with body-mind-spirit connection, her keen insight, grounded wisdom, and honed sense of humour to her work.

She is a besotted mother and grandmother, loves learning, nature, family, friendships, community, and camping with the CUPS (see the article *Camping With The Sisters*). She is the author of the book *One Choice at a Time: A Practical Guide to Peace of Mind and Well-Being*, a book that draws on her years as a counsellor and psychotherapist, her fascination with holistic healing, and her delight in good stories to weave together practical, results-oriented, body-mind practices with her own story and glimpses into counselling sessions.

You're welcome to connect with Susan through susanfarling.com and at susan@susanfarling.com.

Susan "SueZee" Finley

SueZee Finley, affectionately known as the Queen Bee of Happiness, is the creative force behind the Happiness Now Network, SueZee's Happiness Hive FunShops, and Acoustic Therapeutix. Her overarching mission is to guide others in discovering their inner joy.

SueZee's "FunShops" are an innovative blend of sound therapy, happiness mindset techniques, improv, and laughter yoga. These high-energy events create a transformative space where change isn't just possible—it's inevitable. Regardless of where you are on your journey, SueZee will meet you there, offering either a gentle whisper of encouragement or a loving push towards your true path.

Her core philosophy is beautifully simple: everything you seek is already within you, waiting to be awakened and expressed. The key, according to SueZee, is to tune in and listen. She brings this philosophy to life through her virtual sessions and in-person retreats, as well as at her sound therapy practice located in Babylon, NY.

SueZee resides in New York with her loving entourage of four fur babies: Taji, Dilbert, Nefer, and Cupcake, two bearded dragons, Nesse and Harford, and a lush jungle of houseplants.

https://www.facebook.com/groups/acoustictherapeutix

https://acoustictherapeutix.com

https://www.facebook.com/SueZ.Finley

https://www.linkedin.com/in/suezeefinley/

Terese Parkin

I am a wife, a mother and a grandmother. Family is my #1 priority.

I am the founder of Ageless Beauty Lifestyle. I believe that beauty is love, divinely given, and both are ageless.

I'm known as the Ageless Beauty Queen. Because, as someone who's won a beauty pageant at age 65, with grey hair and no pantyhose, I know how to bring out your natural beauty, no matter your age.

And I'm on a mission to help more women feel beautiful in their own skin again.

In this book you will read my story "Full Circle Beauty". My hope is that this story gives you the tools to change the way you look at yourself, so that you can bring out the ageless beauty in you!

Connect with me and other ageless beauties:

https://www.facebook.com/groups/agelessbeautylifestyle/

https://www.instagram.com/agelessbeautylifestyle_/

Tina Taylor

Meet Tina Taylor, an ageless living enthusiast and proud member of the Ageless Star Project. By day, she's your dental insurance expert, dedicated to a heartfelt mission: keeping seniors smiling without draining their savings.

Hailing from the vibrant city of Portland, Oregon, Tina shares her life with her beloved husband, Kevin. At the youthful age of 61, Tina defies the myth that age defines us. Her desire for living life with an ageless mindset was profoundly influenced by her grandmother, Anne, who is featured in her stories within this book as a heartfelt tribute.

Tina firmly believes that life becomes infinitely richer when you embrace being fun, fearless, and fabulously ageless, no matter how many trips around the sun you've taken. Join her mission to empower everyone to live their best life each day, because age is just a number, and the best is yet to come.

And if you're seeking a more affordable way to maintain your healthy smile, don't hesitate to reach out to Tina at healthbydesignforyou@gmail.com. She's here to help you radiate with confidence, because your smile is a reflection of the ageless spirit within you!

Victoria McRay

Meet our inspiring coach, Victoria McRay. As a former educator and fitness instructor, she's now on a mission to redefine aging, proving that life after 50 is an adventure to embrace. She has a passion for helping women recognize that it's never too late to embark on their own path of rediscovery and well-being.

In her online coaching program for post-menopausal women, "31 Sneaky Ways to Reduce Weight Sustainably Without a Diet", she shares an easy, doable method for reducing weight that simultaneously builds confidence and vitality.

Victoria's personal motto is:

Aging happens every day. We have the ability to either hinder its process or aid its progression. It is our habits that make the difference.

When not coaching, she enjoys urban hikes, social activities, family dinners, restorative meditations, and world travel.

Let's connect on Facebook at: https://www.facebook.com/groups/agewellwithintention/

Winnie Anderson-Brown

Winnie Anderson-Brown is a Jamaican educator and wellness coach. She is a writer, singer, a published author, Reiki Master, Laughter Yoga Teacher, mother, grandmother and wife. She has had over forty years' experience as an educator and over thirty years as a wellness coach. She brings together her wealth of experience in good times and bad, along with training in various wellness modalities to help others as she continues to learn and grow. Her love for linguistics has fueled her passion for Artificial Intelligence, especially Large Language Models such as ChatGPT, Google Bard and others. She has completed her ebook on CHATBOTS FOR EDUCATORS 50+ and is a chatbot coach.

She is deeply spiritual and relies on God for strength and guidance each day.

Connect with her at laughyesglobal@gmail.com

THANK YOU

Thank you to all of the incredible co-authors, whom I affectionately call my Ageless Stars. It is an immense honor to have earned your trust and to embark on this collaborative book project alongside you. I am profoundly proud of you for opening your hearts and courageously sharing your stories, filled with the challenges you've overcome along with the joy and wisdom that embody an ageless mindset. Your contributions shine brilliantly, lighting up a path of inspiration for everyone diving into these pages.

An extra special note of gratitude goes to three of our Ageless Stars! Thank you Dr K. Mhina Entrantt for your dedication and generous spirit in helping with the writing of our individual stories. And to Katherine Merritt for the multiple hours spent with editing. Special thanks to Debi Lynn for your creative talent in designing our amazing logo!

To every Star, please know my heart will forever be filled with gratitude for the tireless creative energy you've poured into this collaborative project!

JoyAnn Gold, Founder - Ageless Star Project

JOIN THE AGELESS VOICES MOVEMENT!

Discover the power of community and transformation with Ageless Voices. Together, we're rewriting the narrative of aging, embracing each chapter with a fun, fearless, and fabulous flair. We invite you to be a part of this inspiring journey—a movement driven by heart, courage, and shared wisdom.

Why settle for the sidelines when you can be at the forefront of this exciting stage of life? Whether you're looking to share your story, learn from others, or simply enjoy the company of like-minded individuals, there's a place for you here.

Don't wait—step into your future with Ageless Voices today!

www.agelessvoices.org